Visions of the Maid

Cultural Frames, Framing Culture   Robert Newman, Editor

Robin Blaetz

Visions of the Maid

Joan of Arc in American
Film and Culture

University Press of Virginia
Charlottesville and London

The University Press of Virginia
© 2001 by the Rector and Visitors of the University of Virginia
All rights reserved
Printed in the United States of America
First published 2001

♾ The paper used in this publication meets the minimum require-
ments of the American National Standard for Information Sciences—
Permanence of Paper for Printed Library Materials, ANSI Z39.48-
1984.

Library of Congress Cataloging-in-Publication Data

Blaetz, Robin, 1955–
    Visions of the maid : Joan of Arc in American film and culture / Robin Blaetz.
        p. cm. — (Cultural frames, framing culture)
Includes bibliographical references, filmography and index.
    ISBN 0-8139-2075-2 (cloth : alk. paper) — ISBN 0-8139-2076-0 (pbk. : alk. paper)
    1. Joan, of Arc, Saint, 1412–1431—In motion pictures.   I. Title.   II. Series.
    PN1995.9.J57 B59 2001
    791.43'651—dc21

                                                                            2001002172

To my mother and the memory of my father

Contents

Illustrations

Preface

The story of Joan of Arc has fascinated writers and visual artists from the moment of the heroine's death to this day. The medieval poet Christine de Pisan wrote her *Ditié de Jehanne d'Arc* in 1429, two years before Joan died, and 1999 saw two new English-language films about Joan, shown both in theaters and on television. The story is a spectacular one, full of glowing apparitions, bloody battles, and a fiery death. At the same time, the tale is perplexing and mysterious. Common sense cannot quite connect the story of the religious peasant with her remarkable historical accomplishment in precipitating the end of the Hundred Years' War. In addition, the story challenges many deeply held beliefs about gender and class. Yet despite the ever-sharper demise of the story's religious context, the romance of Joan of Arc continues to have considerable symbolic weight.

Looking at Joan of Arc in the twentieth century, one finds that the Maid,[1] as she called herself, has been envisioned in thousands of novels, plays, poems, songs, operas, and biographies, and in media ranging from popular women's magazines to three dramas by Bertolt Brecht. She is the subject of uncounted sculptures and paintings to be found in tourist shops and in the Louvre. She has been invoked by advertisers and politicians to sell everything from cigars to beans to political agendas. The most striking factor in this sequence of representations is the instability of her iconography. While all historical figures change over time, Joan of Arc, as opposed to Napoleon, for example, changes drastically from one century to the next as she is used to serve causes that span the ideological spectrum. The characteristic panache, the feathered headdress first seen in the sixteenth century, and the hint of armor may suggest her identity, but she remains an ambiguous figure. Historians have spent centuries attempting to find the real Joan of Arc. They have focused on the sculpted head of a wistful youth in the Musée d'Orléans (which now carries a disclaimer in fine print), on the drawing in the margin of Joan of Arc's trial records made by a medieval scribe (now known to have been sketched before the Maid's arrival), and on the trial records themselves, but to no avail. No authenticated image from life exists, and it may well be that this absence helps to drive the extraordinary body of material called Johannic studies.

This book examines the ways in which Joan of Arc was represented in film and popular culture in the United States in the twentieth century, specifically in relation to women's roles in wartime. As a female warrior, Joan was depicted in ways that became ever more complex over the course of the century. During the First World War, for example, Joan was ubiquitous. She appeared on a successful fund-raising poster aimed at women, in a song popular with American soldiers at the western front, and in Cecil B. DeMille's *Joan the Woman*. During the Second World War, films such as *Joan of Paris* and *Joan of Ozark*, both of 1942, used Joan of Arc as a subtext in stories about women's self-sacrifice and incompetence. The principal Joan of Arc film of the time, a major production in 1948 starring Ingrid Bergman, redefined female heroism as a retreat from battle and a return to conventional roles.

In examining the ways in which Joan of Arc has been represented, I assume that images of the heroine are always made with specific ideological intent. While at times I suggest these intentions in the text, the scope of this book does not allow for rigorous investigation of concrete ways in which the idea and icon of Joan of Arc shaped American culture.[2] Instead, I place movies within the discursive context surrounding them—posters, advertising, popular criticism, cartoons, songs, and literature—aiming to elucidate how and why Joan of Arc appears in American culture in a given time.[3] I take a functionalist approach to the widely interdisciplinary material. The method presupposes that fictional films about historical subjects are concerned largely with the cultural context in which they are produced. In order to achieve the popular and financial success necessary to film production, these Joan of Arc films are assumed to balance the events of the story and the social situations that provoked the making of the films.[4] From the rich and varied blend of possible issues raised by the Joan of Arc story in conjunction with contemporary history, I concentrate on the ways in which conceptions of androgyny, virginity, and sacrificial violence are represented in film.[5] My general methodological approach consists of textual and contextual analysis, in which the narrative is analyzed in relation to the romance plot and the iconography is studied in regard to the history of representations of Joan of Arc. When appropriate I examine the material in the light of feminist approaches to film, specific film genres, the Hollywood star system, issues of performance, national cinemas, and the film industry.

To investigate the iconographic and narrative history of representations of Joan of Arc, I turned to several institutions, including the Joan of Arc Collection of the Boston Public Library and the Centre Jeanne d'Arc in Orléans. The Boston Public Library's collection, assembled by Cardinal John Joseph Wright, was my most valuable resource, since Wright was a thorough scholar with wide-ranging interests. From 1920 through 1960 Wright was in continual contact with booksellers, galleries, and other collectors in the United States, searching for virtually anything to do with Joan of Arc. The eclectic archive was given to the library in 1975; it has been supplemented with other collections since then and today encompasses more than 4,500 volumes, consisting of biographies, novels, plays, musical scores, and popular journals of all persuasions. One-third of the printed material seems to have been produced in connection with a religious press or organization, and the remainder comes from secular groups of all kinds.

Unlike the printed and visual material, much of the ephemera is impossible to date precisely. The collection has approximately 2,000 items that can be assumed to have been made throughout the twentieth century for consumer venues ranging from tourist sites to jewelry stores. A partial list includes: posters, paintings, drawings, figurines, toys, medallions, pencil boxes, letter openers, prayer cards, jewelry, plaques, dolls, spoons, paperweights, a wine taster, a ball diptych, relics, plate sets, individual plates, tiles, bookends, coin purses, whistles, and cookie tins. Humorous as this list is, the ephemera and other mass culture manifestations of Joan of Arc cannot be dismissed. The familiar iconography, portrayed simply and often with affection, can be imagined to operate in our time in much the way bas-reliefs, stained glass, and mystery plays did in the Middle Ages and beyond. Here, rather than in the *Joan of Arc* by Peter Paul Rubens that resides in the North Carolina Museum of Art, for example, one finds evidence of Joan's pervasive cultural presence.[6]

My study ends with the years just before the Vietnam War, when the concrete relationship between representations of Joan of Arc, particularly in film, and the discourse of war all but disappear. At that point, Joan of Arc was reenvisioned in the shepherdess persona that dominated the nineteenth century, rather than the warrior mode of the first half of the twentieth century, mainly because the powerful cultural boundaries separating women and war had begun to dissolve with considerable tension by the 1960s. Joan of Arc was no longer purely a symbolic figure whose connection to war could be used to inspire whatever society needed from women, whether donating money or leaving jobs for the sake of returning soldiers. As women achieved the right to enter actual combat, Joan of Arc was increasingly represented as a meek herder of sheep. Yet the image of the girl Joan of Arc in armor is such a long-standing icon that Joan of Arc comes to mind whenever a woman appears in battle of any kind.[7] Indeed, I would argue that the warrior Joan of Arc continued to haunt the films of the Vietnam War every time a young Viet Cong woman took up arms against American soldiers.[8]

By the time *Courage Under Fire* (Edward Zwick) and *G.I. Jane* (Ridley Scott) appeared in 1996 and 1997, respectively, women had become combatants in the Persian Gulf War. *G.I. Jane* makes several fleeting references to Joan of Arc and the heroine of *Courage Under Fire* is engulfed in flames, but the ambiguity of Joan of Arc's persona no longer functions to investigate the relationship between women and war, since women were legally allowed to fight in war by the mid-1970s.[9] The most recent Joan of Arc films, including 1999's *The Messenger: The Story of Joan of Arc* by Luc Besson and the television movie *Joan of Arc* by Christian Duguay, contain plenty of spectacular war scenes but focus ultimately on the supernatural as a causal force in Joan of Arc's story. In the pages that follow, I return to the beginning of the twentieth century to explore the path of the Joan of Arc persona through the decade that followed the Second World War as a way to understand how a single icon operated in relation to women and war in the United States.

Investigating the presence of Joan of Arc in the United States, Marcelline Brun cites the American attachment to the heroine as second only to the French.[10] Brun concludes that Joan is not merely an object of interest in the United States but an exemplary figure, whose positive, dynamic, supernatural qualities, as well as her success, have accompanied the United States through its history. Joan's status as simultaneously an underdog and a divinely determined enemy of the English all but eliminated the potential problems caused by her political and religious conservatism.

The focus of Chapter 1 is the conjunction of Joan of Arc, the First World War, and the social transformations of the first decades of the twentieth century. This chapter sets forth the context for the appearance of Joan in the twentieth century by examining the rise of medievalism in relation to consumer culture in the United States. Chapter 2 analyzes the first major American film about Joan of Arc, Cecil B. DeMille's 1916 *Joan the Woman*, and the critical discourse surrounding it. The two versions of *Joan the Woman* (it was completely reedited for French audiences) clearly manifest the ways in which an American Joan of Arc differed from a Joan of Arc who would be recognizable to the French. Questions of cultural hegemony raised by this film, in which the American film industry reformulated Joan and attempted to sell her back to her native land, are echoed throughout the book.

Chapter 3 continues the investigation of women and the First World War through lesser films and a range of popular culture material. Chapter 4 charts the transition between the First and Second World Wars, in which Joan of Arc's cinematic presence was either oblique or perverse. Chapter 5 examines three films made in 1942 in which the Joan of Arc story is the definitive subtext. While most Joan of Arc films are concerned inherently with issues pertinent to feminism and the changing roles of women, the films discussed in Chapters 4 and 5 are exceptionally forthright in their efforts to remake the heroine in an American mold.

During the Second World War, in which women were indispensable in heavy industry at home and in every capacity but combatant abroad, no historical fiction films about Joan of Arc were made.[11] Only after the war did Joan again appear in popular culture, although she was transformed in film into a girl or woman who was beautiful, prone to tears, and often marked with a foreign accent to differentiate her from American women. This new Joan is discussed in Chapter 6. Chapter 7 approaches the era of the Vietnam War, in which Joan was reconfigured yet again in the light of changes in the postwar American family and of contemporaneous considerations of the feminine mystique, as formulated by Betty Friedan in the 1960s.[12] The conclusion of the book investigates briefly the figure of the woman warrior in relation to the Vietnam War and the Persian Gulf War.[13]

From my vantage point on the far side of the twentieth century, the connections between Joan of Arc, women, and war appear to have become tenuous during its last thirty years. As research on earlier decades suggests, however, the full extent of these interrelations will be discernible only in retrospect. Considering the complexity of Joan of Arc's connections to women's roles in relation to the First and Second World Wars, one can only speculate about all that future study of the Maid will reveal about the end of a century that saw such drastic changes in the status of women and the nature of war.

Acknowledgments

The following people, archives, and institutions made the research for my work possible: Marie-Véronique Clin and the Centre Jeanne d'Arc in Orléans; the Boston Public Library; Matt Severson and the Academy of Motion Picture Arts and Sciences in Los Angeles; the Cinémathèque Suisse; the British Film Institute; the George Eastman House in Rochester, New York; the Museum of Modern Art in New York; Maja Keech and the Library of Congress; Phyllis Sametz Cohen and the Municipal Art Society of New York; Jim Cheevers and the United States Naval Academy; the George C. Marshall Research Foundation; the Wisconsin Center for Film and Theater Research; the Museum of the City of New York; the Alliance Française in New York; the Metropolitan Museum of Art in New York; David Pichaske and the Spoon River Poetry Press; the Corcoran Gallery; the Syracuse University Film Study Center; and the Woodruff Library at Emory University.

I also thank Adrienne McLean, James Meyer, Suzanne Guerlac, David Pratt, Ramona Curry, Alan Nadel, Kevin Harty, Brent Plate, Eric Smoodin, Joan Marder, Gail O'Day, Leslie Taylor, Mary Noble Ours, John Dreyfuss, and Charles Spencer for their intellectual and research support. I continue to be especially grateful for the scholarship of Nadia Margolis and Marina Warner; for the inestimable assistance of Mark Bauerlein, Cosmas Demetriou, and David, Peter, and Pierson Blaetz; and for the commitment and enthusiasm of Cathie Brettschneider and Ellie Goodman of the University Press of Virginia, and of Barbara Salazar, who copyedited the electronic manuscript. Finally, I thank Gordon and Meredith Spencer-Blaetz for making it all worthwhile.

Visions of the Maid

Introduction

The crux of the story of Joan of Arc is embodied in her allegiance to her visions of Saints Catherine, Margaret, and Michael. Joan claimed that she visualized and communicated with her saints for five years before she persuaded the dauphin of France to give her control over his army in 1429. While Joan called the presence of the saints her "voices," the Roman Catholic Church considered her claim of direct access to the divine to be heresy. Although Joan recovered Orléans and defeated the English, ending the Hundred Years' War and creating France as a nation, she allowed herself to be burned at the stake rather than deny these visions. It is not surprising, then, that Joan of Arc appears to the twentieth century to be a figment of historical legend who is closer to an Amazonian Arthur than to Napoleon. Yet records show that a peasant girl named Jehanne Romée, daughter of Jacques D'Arc and his wife, Isabelle Romée, was born in war-torn France in 1412 and died before she could turn twenty. In the late Middle Ages, when she lived, the boundaries between heaven and earth and between the spirit and the body were blurred, and her visions of the saints, beginning at age thirteen, were accepted as real. Her success in ending the year-long siege of Orléans in eight days, however, and in having the dauphin (a title used for the eldest son of a king of France) crowned Charles VII in the English-controlled city of Rheims did not fit into any common expectations of female peasant behavior. Consequently, by the end of May 1431, the figure known as Joan of Arc had been condemned by the Inquisition as a heretic and sorceress and burned at the stake by the civil authorities in Burgundy.

If nothing else is known about Joan of Arc, most people are aware that she went up in flames. In one of history's most notable backfires, the attempt to obliterate the young woman who had defeated and shamed the English army had the opposite effect. Burning Joan of Arc and any potential relics and throwing her apparently indestructible heart into the Seine River were done in vain. In their attempt to erase this anomalous female, Joan's executioners inadvertently determined that her corporeal presence would continue to fascinate storytellers and image makers for generations to come.

Who Is Joan of Arc?

Although the pertinent incidents of her life were extensively recorded by the scribes at her trial,[1] Joan of Arc has come to be known largely through a series of familiar archetypal motifs that often have little correspondence to any historical record. She is the Amazon warrior of classical lore whose sexual ambiguity and disdain for conventional female roles are balanced by her death. She is the epitome of female virtue and the abstract personification of faith and courage, the contradictions and mysteries of her life sublimated by a celebration of virginity and martyrdom. Since the mid–nineteenth century, the shepherdess Joan of Arc has come to embody the purity of the natural world, in which naiveté and poverty provide access to divine forces. In sum, she is an amalgam of religious, political, and folk myths, each reflecting its own time and adding to the ever-changing persona.[2]

The events of Joan's life, which are known through trial records, letters, and eyewitness accounts, have been memorialized through five centuries into a legend. Fredric Jameson has described the form through which a story of this sort is known as a "strategy of containment."[3] This frame organizes the events in a manner acceptable to a given culture and at the same time represses insights that might come from examining the evidence in chronicle form. Although there are variations in the telling of this narrative, representations of Joan of Arc's life tend to cohere into the outlines of the romance plot. The romance, or quest narrative, envisions heroic action in terms of innocence regained through sacrifice. The hero's progression from an extraordinary birth to an initiation into experience through a quest, followed by a reversal, reintegration, and epiphany, remains on the human side of myth to function as a model for behavior.[4] The historic Joan of Arc serves the cultures in which she appears to the degree that her story can mask or resolve social conflict.

Joan of Arc was both a historic personage of great accomplishment in medieval France and a martyr of mythic proportions. This unlikely blend has given her story considerable symbolic weight. Although the original sacred significance of Joan's story may have lessened over the centuries, the fact that she existed as an embodiment of the romance narrative has kept Joan alive. The essential optimism of the romance, which envisions the birth of the new from situations that appear to be immune to change, almost guarantees Joan's continual popularity. Jameson describes the nostalgic value of this genre as an expression of authentic needs and desires, which provides a "symbolic meditation on the destiny of community."[5] The fact that Joan of Arc actually lived only adds to the authority of the romance, an authority that empowers each new construction of her life and, in turn, the ideological position that motivates the new representation.

Joan of Arc's romance has developed over the centuries through the chronicles, literature, visual art, and biographies in which the story has been transmitted.[6] In order to be recognized as being about Joan of Arc, each version must contain a number of iconographic and narrative markers. The kinds and degrees of alterations carried out in relation to the romance plot suggest the cultural reasons for each new representation of the heroine. My brief version of Joan of Arc's life contains information that is included in countless biographies and is invariably disputed in others.[7] This portion of my study is concerned not with attempting to establish any factual chronology of the life of Joan of Arc but with providing both a sense of the romance elements from which narratives are constructed and a broad overview of her story as it is popularly perceived.

Joan of Arc's birth is often said to have fulfilled prophecies. Both the Celtic wizard Merlin and the Venerable Bede predicted that a girl from Bois Chenu, near Joan's birthplace of Domrémy in Lorraine, would work wonders. A nun called Marie d'Avignon warned that France would be desolated by a woman and saved by a virgin. In actuality, Joan of Arc's deeds undid the actions of Isabelle de Bavière, Charles VII's mother, who had married her daughter to Henry V of England so that Henry VI would permanently end the patriarchal line of French kings. In addition to the prophecies, Joan of

Arc was frequently rumored to be a daughter of Lois, duke of Orléans, in the romantic tradition of the foundling. Evidence has continually arisen to support this royal birth: Joan was often referred to as "princess," she wore the colors and herald of Orléans, and she was apparently indifferent to her family in Domrémy.[8]

Over the past two centuries the enigmatic aspects of Joan of Arc's birth have been deemphasized as her story has been increasingly told as a peasant romance. Joan is now most often portrayed as an average hardworking French farm girl, not as a mysterious descendant of royalty.[9] She tended sheep in the pastoral town of Domrémy in Lorraine, in what is now northeastern France. The trial records note that she sewed, spun, and gardened and that she favored both a "fairy tree" and the woodland shrine of Notre Dame de Bermot. In this milieu, in which natural and magical worlds merged, Joan began at the age of thirteen and for a period of five years to hear the voices of saints accompanied by brilliant illuminations and chiming bells. She claimed to have been hailed by Saints Margaret, Catherine, and Michael as the "daughter of God" and told to put on men's clothing, bear arms, and lead the army to drive the English from French soil. Later, after succeeding in her assigned quest, Joan remained so faithful to the voices of her saints that she died by fire rather than deny them.

A brief review of the iconography of Joan's saints provides clues to the origins of many aspects of her legend.[10] For example, Saint Margaret of Antioch (third century) was said to have entered a monastery disguised as a man. Her martyrdom occurred when a prefect, seeing her tending sheep, asked her to marry him and she refused. She was tortured in prison, but the force of her resistance was so great that five thousand bystanders were converted before she was beheaded. Other aspects of her legend include a leap from a tower at the age of fifteen in order to preserve her chastity, and a confrontation with the devil. In the latter instance, Margaret was swallowed by a dragon even though she held a cross before his eyes. Yet the cross grew so big that the dragon split open and Margaret escaped unharmed. Saint Margaret is pictured trampling a dragon, holding a cross and a sword; she is the patron of women in childbirth. In the same period, Saint Catherine of Alexandria, supposedly of royal blood, became the "celestial spouse" of Christ in a dream and woke up wearing a ring. She was called to defend her faith before the emperor Maxentius and fifty learned men, who were put to death when they could not defeat her. When Catherine refused to marry the emperor, on the grounds that she was the virgin bride of Christ, she was sentenced to be killed on a four-wheeled torture device. When the device miraculously exploded before it could be used, she was beheaded. She is pictured with a book, a sword, and a broken wheel and is the patron of philosophers, students, and virgin girls. Finally, Saint Michael, an archangel, is known as the protector of the church militant, the captain general of the hosts of heaven, the guardian of the redeemed, and the conqueror of satanic dragons. He is an emblem of resistance, painted on standards throughout the Christian world. He appears as a young, beautiful man in resplendent armor, carrying a sword, a spear, and a shield, and bearing large wings.

Gathering about herself the iconography of her saints, Joan of Arc received her orders in 1429, when France had been all but occupied by the English; the population had been decimated by the plague; the church was in the midst of the Great Schism with its multiple popes, corruption, and heresies; and the Hundred Years' War (1337–1453) had lasted more than ninety years, with twenty-four yet to go. The notoriously weak dauphin was unable to get to Rheims, where French kings are crowned. In addition, the prince's own mother labeled him a bastard in an effort to make her daughter's son the king of a united England and France. Joan of Arc began her mission to recover France in mid-1428 by seeking the assistance of a local official in the fortified town of Vaucouleurs, near Domrémy. After several attempts, she gained his trust by predicting future events: she revealed that a battle had been lost days before it was reported as such and then foretold the imminent death of a man who apparently had insulted her. In the spring of 1429, Joan arrived at the court in Chinon, where she passed the first of many tests of her authenticity by recognizing that an impostor had been dressed as the dauphin. After finding the real Charles in a crowd of three hundred courtiers, she purportedly assured the future king that he was the legitimate heir to the throne. Joan apparently impressed the dauphin and inspired his confidence in her by knowing of his concern about his legitimacy.[11]

Once the church had confirmed her background and technical virginity in Poitiers, Joan was given a brilliant suit of armor and a sword. The only sword that Joan would accept was said to have appeared to her in a vision before it was unearthed behind the altar at St. Catherine's Chapel in Fierbois. When polished, the rusty sword was found to be engraved with five crosses. In evidence given at the retrial of Joan in 1456, one of Joan's soldiers claimed that she had broken this sword over the back of a camp follower, and when the weapon was gone, so apparently was her power over the French king. The object most associated with Joan of Arc was the standard that she herself designed, in a period in which banners were conventionally the provenance of victorious male military saints. With a central image of Christ surrounded by an aureole, two kneeling angels, the words "Jesus Maria," and an even scattering of gold fleurs-de-lys, the banner proclaimed the blend of religion and nationalism that is integral to the Joan of Arc story.[12]

In early May 1429, Joan of Arc achieved the principal goal of her quest. In only eight days she raised the eighteen-month siege of Orléans, which had symbolized France's submission to the English. This success was preceded by Joan's insistence that the French army purify itself by giving confession and driving all prostitutes from its camps. Joan's victory was facilitated by a shift in wind direction over the Loire River, which was attributed to Joan's prayers and which allowed the army to sail directly into the town. In this series of semimiraculous events, Joan apparently recovered almost instantly after being shot in the chest with an arrow. Immediately after this success, Joan's apotheosis as a hero occurred in Orléans when she was glorified by the city she had saved. In July 1429, Joan traveled to the English-occupied city of Rheims, where all French kings were crowned. Surrounded by the full majesty of the French court, Joan participated in the coronation of the king, wearing full armor with her standard in hand.[13]

Joan of Arc spent the year after the victory at Orléans at the court in Chinon, while King Charles VII negotiated with the English over the fate of French land. Purportedly opposed to compromise and bored by inactivity, in May 1430 Joan made a brief military foray to Compiègne, where she was captured by the Burgundians. In a political system in which the ransom of captured nobility was the rule, Joan was abandoned by her financially and politically weak king, who had begun to make treaties instead of going to war. During her confinement in Burgundy, Joan was sold to the English by her compatriots, who were allied with the British. After this betrayal, Joan was imprisoned at the top of the seventy-foot tower of Beaurevoir, from which she attempted to escape by leaping from a window. Taken to Rouen in early 1431, Joan faced the hatred of the populace, rapacious guards, and a full Inquisition trial.[14] She endured five months of constant harassment in both the courtroom and her cell, without knowing the indictments against her and having neither lawyers nor witnesses in her favor. Near the end of her trial, Joan recanted briefly before reasserting once and for all that she had heard and continued to hear her voices.

Joan of Arc was condemned as a heretic and a sorceress on 28 May 1431 and burned at the stake two days later.[15] Legends about the death scene abound. Although Joan claimed that her fear of fire had caused her temporary recantation, she was reported to have walked peacefully to the pyre and prayed to the cross held before her by sympathetic priests. Some accounts of Joan's death claim that the fire was temporarily extinguished immediately after she died of smoke inhalation so that the spectators could see her naked body and be certain that she was indeed a woman.[16] One bystander claimed to discern the name of Jesus in the inferno and another to see a white dove emerge from the blaze in Burgundian Rouen and fly toward France. In the end, Joan of Arc's heart is said to have resisted the flames of destruction and to have been thrown into the Seine River.[17]

Joan was burned for a variety of heretical acts, chiefly her assertion that she had direct access to the divine through the voices of saints and her defiance of the biblical injunction against the abomination of women wearing male dress (Deut. 22:5). If Joan had given in to her fear of fire and "become female" by accepting the dress that she was offered, she would not have died but would have spent the rest of her life in prison. In this scenario, Joan would have been forgotten instead of martyred and France would have lost its most potent and tenacious symbol of divine right and redemption. Instead, Joan's life and death came to herald the birth of France as a nation. Joan's death also atoned for the disruptive and arrogant assumption of the role of victorious warrior on the part of a female commoner. The ambiguities of Joan of Arc's life created by her gender have continually inspired new representations of her. Here I am particularly concerned with the ways in which Joan's androgyny, virginity, and sacrificial victimization gain pertinence when she is called upon during wartime.

The Androgynous Heroine

One consistent aspect of the Joan of Arc iconography is the suit of armor, which can range from the full metal costume to simply a helmet-like haircut or a severe line in the cut of a dress. Generally speaking, a female in armor is so rare in Western culture that any woman so attired is assumed to be Joan of Arc. Yet as anomalous as the woman warrior may seem in light of contemporary concepts of women's roles in the Middle Ages, Joan of Arc was actually part of a tradition of female fighters and mystics.[18] A woman known as Matilda of Tuscany rode with her parents at the age of fifteen against Norman invaders, Eleanora de Arborea of Sardinia defeated the attacking king of Aragon, and numerous revolutionary women visionaries completed extraordinary tasks with no more authority than a self-proclaimed access to the divine.[19] Another contradiction to modern perceptions that women in male dress challenge gender distinction is the argument proposed by Natalie Zemon Davis that transvestism operates as a safety valve within a hierarchical culture rather than as a sign of change.[20] Cross-dressing merely provides each gender with a sense of the other in a carnivalesque moment but finally reasserts the fact of sexual difference. In addition to its historical and sociological functions, the motif of the woman warrior has had practical purposes as well. Before the professionalization of war in the late Middle Ages, constant combat was a part of feudal life, and children of both sexes were trained for it as a matter of survival. Not until certain classes of women were relegated to the private sphere of the home did the female warrior come to be envisioned as either an unnatural woman or a witch with satanic powers.[21] At this point, the *image* of the woman warrior remained as a necessary antidote to the growing notion that women were inherently peaceful and against war. Since the Middle Ages, Joan of Arc has been a symbolic point of identification for women, whose actual roles include both the practical facilitation of warfare and the embodiment of all that is under attack by the enemy in war.[22]

The possibility that a woman might fight, or rather that she could fill in to save the day, has always been part of the Joan of Arc narrative. Yet it is a matter of record that Joan was burned as a witch partly for the heresy of refusing to take off the apparel of a male soldier. In the end, Joan's blasphemy was not her transvestism as such, since plenty of churchwomen dressed as men within ecclesiastical confines. Joan erred in not disguising that she was a female dressed in male clothes while in the public sphere. Furthermore, Joan failed to conform to the acceptable model of the martial maid introduced in the Renaissance, who is fierce and strong in battle but attractive and passive afterward.[23] Joan of Arc crossed and blurred the boundaries between male and female behavior and thus revealed the artificiality and permeability of the lines delineating sexual difference. After Joan's death, France's grand inquisitor, Jean Graverent, gave a sermon leaving no doubt that the assumption of male dress was Joan's greatest sin and the sure sign that she had listened to the Devil.[24]

The Virgin Warrior

While Joan of Arc's conduct on the battlefield broke through the lines separating gender roles, her behavior had the opposite effect in relation to her own strictly virginal body.[25] Joan's virgin status was a complex and powerful factor in her life and legend, in a manner that is easy to misunderstand today. As soon as Joan gained the approval of the dauphin in Chinon, she was examined and certified to be a virgin. This test was repeated several times by both her supporters and her enemies before her death, since Joan's visionary status depended on her physical integrity.[26] In the Middle Ages, virginity still bore signs of its significance in the pre-Christian era, when a virgin was defined as one who is "not tied by any bonds to a male who must be acknowledged as master."[27] In order to discipline this threatening figure, Christian dogma sought to make the autonomous and self-determined virgin less attractive by associating her behavior with dread and shame. As a result, female rejection of males eventually came to be read as prudery rather than choice.[28] Although the church had come to define virginity as the intactness of the maidenhead by Joan of Arc's day, the aura of virginity as a magical state that conferred strength and ritual purity had not entirely disappeared. As a virgin, Caroline Bynum notes, Joan of Arc still "scintillated with fertility and power."[29] However, just at the moment when Joan of Arc might have been empowered by association with the charismatic virgins of the early fifteenth century, whose connections to the divine raised them above earthly authority and allowed them to speak, the Roman Catholic Church began to consolidate its power in an effort to squash the multiple heresies that had culminated in the Great Schism of 1378 to 1417. The female visionary, once an esteemed figure in chapel and court alike, had become disruptive and threatening. Joan of Arc's fate can be understood to a degree as a stage in the gradual elimination of the virgin mystic.[30]

Joan's abstemious behavior in regard to her own body also manifested it-self in fasting. Surviving on a diet of bread and wine, Joan found the strength to reject the dictums of the church. In the tradition of her mysti-cal sisters who would recognize sinners or vomit unconsecrated host, Joan of Arc was thought to have performed one of several miracles when she identified the dauphin in a crowd of courtiers at their first meeting. As is now understood, one of the results of prolonged fasting is the cessation of menstruation, which is a condition cited fairly often in relation to Joan of Arc. Amenorrhea hyperbolizes the image of the body as an intact, even in-human vessel that is capable of superhuman strength of both body and will. This holy wholeness was imagined to allow the medieval virgin to pass un-marked through fire before reappearing in heaven.[31] Within the xenopho-bic arena of war, it is little wonder that the virgin warrior, who remains in-tact despite the onslaught of the outsider, has stood as icon and ideal.

Much of Joan of Arc's appeal has come from her unnatural demise while still a young, virgin female. At the end of her life, however, Joan's enemies continually struggled to get her to wear a dress, to signify that she was not male and that her allegiance to her voices had weakened. Most versions of Joan's story imply that Joan was either raped or threatened with violation when she temporarily wore a dress in exchange for receiving Communion in prison. This subtext to the generally heroic story implies a repudiation of the virgin warrior. To rape Joan of Arc was to overpower and even im-pregnate her, thus gaining the upper hand on the potential for maternity that is inherent in the virgin state.[32] Surely a Joan of Arc forced into child rearing and old age rather than virgin martyrdom would have been erased from history. For the most part, Joan's battles with her jailers have been for-gotten. What is remembered is that she died young, radiating the power of the virgin warrior, never manifesting the bloody or drooping female flesh that is disdained and feared for its connection to natural birth and death.

The Sacrificial Victim

Joan of Arc is most easily recognized and adored when she is chained and tied to the stake as a sacrificial victim. This image of acquiescent suffering encapsulates the reasons for Joan's omnipresence, particularly in time of war. As a female peasant warrior, Joan was both part of her community and an outsider, so that her death could satisfy the violent impulses that engulfed her world without evoking fear of reprisal. The immolation of Joan of Arc as a human offering guaranteed that she would absorb the tensions that threatened social order and thus become sacred. Once dead as a surrogate victim, Joan played a key role in the structure of her culture and had to be continually invoked in rites and festivals to keep violence at bay.[33] Hence the increased presence of Joan of Arc during wartime.

Joan entered the twentieth century as a carefully preserved scapegoat, since she could be both a meek shepherdess helpless in the face of violence (as popularized by the French historian Jules Michelet in the mid–nineteenth century) and a revered cult figure surging forward in bronze on her horse. As she is remembered, parading in her white sheath through the streets of Rouen, she absorbs the impurities of her community in preparation for death. Yet at the same time, Joan manifests the victorious, good violence that was evidenced in retrospect by her burning at the stake, since the death of Joan of Arc is understood to be the mythic cause of the end of the Hundred Years' War and the birth of France as a nation. As an evanescent physical presence who sees and hears angels, is unharmed by arrows, and passes through fire, Joan of Arc is the ideal monstrous double who hovers at the fringes of the community. The abuse that she suffers causes the veneration she receives. Just as the sacrificial ceremony demands the collective participation of the group, the full-scale symbolic evocation of Joan during war acknowledges and appeases the fear of violence.

I have concluded that the pervasive appearance or marked disappearance of Joan of Arc during war, whether in film, song, posters, or even cigar wrappers, indicates unease in the relations of women, war, and violence. In the secular twentieth century, the historical Joan of Arc in her scapegoat role became a talisman who was represented in the community to reaffirm the belief that violence could be controlled. In addition, Joan of Arc's conservative Catholic and monarchist ties were paradoxically significant in this period of transition in American religious life. Although Joan was an outsider as a cross-dressing female, her strong convictions permitted her to stand for the maintenance of social order in its most rigid form. Concomitantly, Joan's outsider status and her unquestionable character and efficacy made her attractive at various times to women's rights advocates, who found her a potential source of identification.

⊶⇒ 1   Joan of Arc in America, 1911–1920

In the earliest years of the twentieth century, the widespread tendency to find advantage by associating one's agenda with Joan of Arc coincided with both the First World War and the birth of the mass-produced image. The years before and during the First World War were marked by the rise of consumerism, in which religious and other traditional iconography was appropriated by advertising. This disorienting transformation, in which cultural authority seemed to dissipate with each ephemeral image, was facilitated by the technical refinement of photography and various printing methods during the late nineteenth century. Not coincidentally, the advent of this mechanically generated visual culture coincided with the defining event of this era, the Great War of 1914–18. As in the culture at large, this first modern world war was marked by the large-scale dominance of technology. However, the war was celebrated in art and in life as if it were a glorious endeavor in the chivalric mode, despite overwhelming evidence to the contrary. This contradiction between the presence of technology and the refusal to acknowledge it underlies the medievalist antimodernism that characterizes the early part of the century, which helps to explain the presence of Joan of Arc in the United States.

In the context of World War I, references to the Middle Ages facilitated a slippage between the contemporaneous negative situation and a highly desirable and idealized sense of national identity. This period was particularly hospitable to medievalism because it suffered the widespread breakdown of traditional political and social powers at the hands of new and unfamiliar enemies.[1] These enemies were not just the conventional opponents of war but also the lack of domestic consensus about the war, as well as disagreement over immigration and gender roles. The myriad conflicts and the signs of unwelcome change were assuaged to a degree by a return to medieval geocentricism. While a revival of the Middle Ages provided general reassurance that the immutable laws of civilization would hold, Joan of Arc's presence was of particular use in debates over the proper place for women. Joan may well have come to mind with the appearance of the flapper, who echoed the heroine's androgynous appearance and rebellious behavior. At the same time, although Joan stands for transition in gender roles and the violence inherent in innovation, her fate offers a reactionary symbol of the ultimate stability of gender difference.

The pure spectacle of Joan of Arc as a warrior appealed to the filmmakers and advertisers of the era as a pretext for extravagance. Yet any use of a military personage or situation during wartime is also an attempt to link the current conflagration with a mythic war tradition. In the American context, which lacked the richly allusive war literature of Europe, Joan of Arc's frequent presence provided the sense of romance that made the war seem to be part of a meaningful continuum of experience. The return to a specifically medieval tradition was particularly opportune. In the Middle Ages, writing about the military was a genre in itself, which was characterized by extraordinary detail involving equipment, clothing, rations, and strategy. As these details have been generally absorbed, they not only are firmly tied to ideological values such as organization, discipline, responsibility, and expertise but provide a powerful sense that past glories can be reproduced by exacting attention to these very particulars.[2] In addition, the medieval Joan of Arc carried a hard-won Christian justification along with the concept that war is a virile, character-building enterprise, in which self-sacrifice is the highest goal available to females.

The woman warrior Joan of Arc was also implicated in the era's crisis in representation, in which the female body was increasingly idealized in consumer culture in types such as the American Girl and the Protecting Angel. The disequilibrium in social roles and religious life was often imagined to be the result of a gender problem that might be controlled on the level of the sign. In this regard, study of images of Joan in film and in other areas of popular culture helps to elucidate the social expectations of women during the war. Joan of Arc serves as a particularly useful lens through which to see the often submerged story of female experience in relation to war.

The American Joan of Arc of the late nineteenth century is epitomized by the sweet, pathetic child, little more than a minor example of chastity to religious women, found in Mark Twain's *Personal Recollections of Joan of Arc by the Sieur Louis de Comte (Her Page and Secretary)* of 1896. Thus it comes as something of a shock to find Joan looking out boldly from the phenomenally successful fund-raising poster for war stamps designed by Haskell Coffin in 1917. Moreover, one wonders how this peripheral French Catholic girl came to be enshrined in 1915 by a monumental statue on Riverside Drive in New York City as the focal point of American patriotism in the form of multi-gun salutes throughout the war. Martha Banta's comprehensive book about this period, *Imaging American Women,* suggests some answers. Banta considers the turn of the twentieth century to be a period in which the impasse between artist and audience that was endemic in the United States reached an extreme state. On the one hand, artists influenced by European experiments with form were playing with images as mere signs, but on the other, a flood of imagery overwhelmed the everyday lives of the American people. In response to the confusing onslaught, the public increasingly insisted upon receiving images of known and already significant phenomena, such as Joan of Arc, which would reinforce commonsense perceptions about the external world. Imagery that had once been grounded in sacred or patriotic systems, however, inevitably became currency in the field of marketing because of its very recognizability. Angels, for example, were used to sell corsets (one was a "godsend") and the Statue of Liberty sold beer and thread.[3] In a similar way, the clichéd but simple poses and gestures of melodramatic performance that were used in theater and film and on posters in this period were valued for expressing familiar if idealized emotions.

The Revival of Medievalism

Images of Joan of Arc in this era circulated in popular usage in multivalent ways. On the simplest level, Joan was a figure of the medievalist movement, in which stories and legends that had been polished by centuries of repetition were revived for the reassurance they imparted. Jackson Lears quotes

Joan of Arc featured in a Ringling Bros. Circus spectacle. Strobridge Litho. Co. (1912). (Library of Congress)

a mid-nineteenth-century observer who expresses the complexity of this desire in yearning "for one look of the blue sky, as it looked when we called it heaven!" In this period, the plethora of heterogeneous images led to a vague but profound desire to see the world once more as magical. The superficially liberating cornucopia of images that had been loosed from the moors of religion and history in fact only masked the actual limitations of a consumer culture driven by efficiency and productivity. Whereas a figure like Joan of Arc once evoked an authentic sense of piety or patriotism within a specific context, she was ever more being *used* to do so as a free-floating marketing device. The attempt to simplify and reduce Joan was of a piece with a society that was itself beginning to be experienced as melodrama. In a period characterized by a sense of dislocation, social behavior was ever more the self-conscious presentation of the signs of emotion rather than a reaction to actual feeling. Joan's life, with its otherworldly voices, monumental courage, and agonizing immolation, easily provided the much-desired authenticity that melodrama translated into clear, popular terms. Contemplating Joan of

Arc allowed participation in a passion-filled set of experiences distant from life as it had come to be lived in the early twentieth century.[4] Furthermore, Joan's powerful and mystical being was democratized as all classes were hailed by the same poster and film images.

Yet Joan's presence was not free of tension. In this period of social transition, the control of traditional authorities wavered in reaction to technological change, the weakening of religious influence, and shifts in social roles.[5] The visionary and occult aspects of Joan and her status as a transitional figure between the medieval and the modern came to the fore in this regard. The turn to a figure like Joan of Arc illustrates that the roots of modernism were not necessarily in the disillusionment that followed the First World War, but were the result of an older, more complex yearning toward what Lears calls a "therapeutic culture."[6] Joan of Arc's appeal stems from her familiarity. Having been continually reenvisioned for 500 years, she seems perfectly knowable. Yet, more specifically, she offers an endless replay of the cycle whereby a disruptive female is destroyed to reestablish the solid dichotomies that structure culture. Joan simultaneously evokes the wavering of coherence and the loss of cultural authority felt at the time, as well as the eventual reparation of these very ruptures.

In *The Great War and Modern Memory* Paul Fussell reveals the degree to which the First World War was steeped in mythic and medieval rhetoric, in spite of and in reaction to the pervasive presence of modern industry and technology. Fussell describes the tone of the period as an inverse skepticism in which "anything might be true, except what was written."[7] In the milieu of the war, in which amulets and charms were rampant and everything was seen as a sign, Joan of Arc was a natural part of the landscape. On one hand, the cyclical nature of any romance, including Joan's quest story, helped to shape the experience of the war, in which horror resulted not just from the excessive blood and gore of trench warfare but equally from the modern emphasis on efficiency that facilitated the decimation. In an era in which time had become something to be saved or spent, the rebirth cycle of Joan of Arc's life became redemptive. Yet images of Joan also masked the technological aspect of the war. While Joan's armor made her a pertinent warrior figure, the female martyr aspect of her persona prevented contemporary consciousness from acknowledging the realities of modern warfare. The contradictions between the idea of the Great War and the actual war are clear in the selection of the metaphor used in 1916 by an opponent of military pre-paredness, who declared it useless to stand in fear before the "specter of a dragon."[8]

The use of medievalism in the early twentieth century was connected to a more general demise of cultural authority. Johannic iconography in par-ticular was part of a cultural eclecticism that saw Egyptian gateways in Protestant cemeteries and Greek gods holding up ashtrays. While this ten-dency has been celebrated as indicative of American energy and spontane-ity, Lears interprets the heedless return to the past as an indication of cul-tural confusion resulting from the lack of a shared symbolic system. As traditional icons were used without context to signify legitimacy, the icons themselves evolved into mere commodities. Lears extends this critique of images to condemn the secularization of Protestant religions, in which mere solace replaced the emotional weight and moral force of a lived faith. Not coincidentally, the characteristic illness of this age was neurasthenia, which was marked by a paralysis of will in paradoxical reaction to the increasing ease and lessening demands of physical, intellectual, and moral existence.[9]

The Cult of the Strenuous Life

One reaction to this fragmented and overcivilized culture was a powerful hunger for intensity and authenticity, which could transcend banal pleasure and utilitarian morality. While anything medieval was useful in this quest, Joan of Arc exemplified a life that was lived according to moral stakes so high that only flames could extinguish it. Joan's fate suits the era's fascina-tion with what Lears calls a "pornography of pain," in which newspapers chronicled accidents and bloodshed in detail for people who seemed to have lost connection with what was physically and psychologically real.[10] The at-traction of war during this period is easy to understand. War offered the pos-sibility of purification and the sense that wholeness might be gained through a willingness to suffer and die for a cause. What has always been alluring in chivalric warfare in particular is the romantic aura that it lends to violent death and the "lost cause" of an individual life.[11] Joan of Arc is a brilliant persona in this regard since she died by fire with her quest appar-ently lost, yet succeeded in saving her country. In addition, Joan was best known at this time as a young girl with flowing hair, struggling against ropes

Joan of Arc gracefully struggling against her fate. One of many representations of Joan popular in the nineteenth and early twentieth centuries. Lith. de G. Engelmann, after Fragonard, 1822. (Courtesy of the Centre Jeanne d'Arc, Orléans)

and chains. This eroticization of bodily pain, combined with Joan's unquenchable dedication to her mission, could only have helped to create enthusiasm for the war. Both men and women could respond to the blend of the sacred and the profane found in the virgin warrior.

Late nineteenth-century culture celebrated the autonomous individual whose moral strength derived from willpower. The discipline to choose and carry out one's duty was an end in itself, which could lead to self-legitimating prosperity.[12] Joan of Arc served well as a model of control because her story is based on absolute allegiance to a strict inner voice. Marina Warner describes Joan as part of an old iconographic tradition in which strength is represented as an armed woman. The figure is female to suggest that this particular virtue is desirable and attractive. Furthermore, there was no greater example of fortitude than the woman who managed to fight her sensuous nature to remain chaste.[13] Joan's control over base instincts made her particularly appealing in a competitive, public-oriented economy that depended on self-discipline. Yet what made Joan most valuable was the fact that she had weakened, by briefly denying the existence of her voices, and that she had ended up dead after rejecting the authority of both church and state.

The Victorian striving for individual autonomy and moral discipline surely masked intense personal conflict. Lears describes the central dilemma of the era as the need to reconcile the inner-directed self, which was based in traditional morality and religion, with the outer-directed self, which had adapted to the increasingly competitive marketplace. The public persona had become a collection of social masks used to deal with various aspects of bureaucratic society. Furthermore, the sexes were ever more split in their roles, particularly in relation to one another. While women often assumed the role of invalid in response to the pressures of playing the parts of household angel and selfless mother, men tended to be ever more haunted by a sense of sterility, impotence, and what Lears describes as a feeling of "unreality."[14] As an antidote, Joan of Arc encapsulated the era's most desirable qualities, including a genuine sense of self characterized by child-like directness and simplicity. At the same time, Joan represented the irrational and the mystical, which were actively sought at the turn of the century through explorations of hypnosis and the unconscious. With the hope that the self was more complex than it was beginning to look in the marketplace, Joan of Arc embodied a vision that was fabulous at its core.

Joan of Arc fights the evils of liquor. Currier & Ives (1874). (Library of Congress)

The cultural return to the Middle Ages came from the same impetus that drove the angst-ridden protests of the avant-garde. While the latter overtly expressed fury at the social and personal fragmentation caused by war and technology, medievalism masked the present and any sense of rage with images from an idealized past. The same repression and confusion that allowed accommodation and protest to coincide in medievalism saw no contradiction between nostalgia and the desire for material progress. These conflicting sentiments integrated themselves into the American psyche by way of what was widely known as the cult of the strenuous life. Sports and other vigorous outdoor activities were seen in this period as conducive to the discipline and self-reliance necessary in the marketplace.[15] The return to and reconfiguration of chivalric ideals helped to balance this juxtaposition of contrary positions. For example, groups such as the Boy Scouts and Woodcraft Indians, which were increasingly popular in the United States in the years before World War I, redefined nobility as the product of moral character rather than high birth or inherited wealth. A book called *Twentieth Century Knighthood: A Series of Addresses to Young Men* claimed that "chivalry during its golden days made the world a much pleasanter place in which to live. It did away with low suspicions and jealousies and filled the land with an atmosphere of noble hospitality and courtesy." In fact, few medieval personages except the boyish Joan of Arc could manifest the "upright thinking, pure conduct, self-denying devotion, [and] courage" to which the Scouts aspired.[16] Although the public and children in particular were inundated with medievalist books and films intended to increase the value attributed to discipline in a secular era, the only commitment evoked was to being committed.[17]

Although there were few organizations for girls in the early days of the scouting phenomenon, the use of the anomalously female knight figure, Joan of Arc, offered intriguing possibilities for women. (An organization known as the Queens of Avalon started in 1902, led by the Lady of the Lake, and the Girl Scouts began in 1912.) Not only did Joan answer the need for spontaneity and intensity felt by both sexes but she called into question the social structures that valued passivity and invalidism in women. Images of Joan of Arc both evoked the medieval and suggested a critique of the aristocratic, patriarchal authority that had opposed her. In addition, while chivalry called for men to restrain their sexuality in polite adoration of a distant lady, the mere representation of Joan of Arc could unleash repressed female sexuality. A woman inspired by one of the medieval tales of the era wrote: "Fight hard and drink hard and ride hard. . . . Our clothes grow straight. Oh, for a horse between the knees, my blood boils, I want to fight, strain, wrestle, strike. . . . To be brave and have it all known, to surpass and be proud, oh the splendor of it!"[18]

Representations of Joan of Arc

An understanding of the reasons underlying Joan of Arc's pervasive presence in the United States before and during the First World War begs the question as to how the heroine was actually represented at this time. For the most part, the image of the heroine as a sentimental child perpetrated by Mark Twain at the end of the nineteenth century remained unchanged. A case in point is the illustrations for Louis-Maurice Boutet de Monvel's *Jeanne d'Arc*, written in French in 1896 and translated into English in 1897. The images were bought by Senator William Andrews Clark of New York in 1911 in the form of six framed murals and given to the Corcoran Gallery in Washington, D.C., in 1925. These panels exemplify the Joan of the turn of the century with their delicate, tapestry-like rendering and heavily gilded, single-plane surfaces. Often lost in the pageantry of the images, this Jeanne is a waif with pale hair and elegant, elongated limbs. In three of the panels she kneels with thin fingers extended. Although she is on horseback in two of these images, she is led by a phalanx of monks in one and is all but invisible as a tiny blurred form far in the background of the battle scene. Only in the final trial mural does she stand, dressed in the della Robbia blue of the Madonna, and confront a roomful of judges. Overall, the panels display the period's taste for childishly feminine qualities. This touching, fragile Joan is an elevated, sensuous child with roots in Romanticism. Moreover, the ethereal quality of the images recalls to the viewer that Joan died young and undefiled in the Victorian mode, so that her innocence and integrity are eternally unassailable. In this time of rapid technological innovation in the United States, these images of Joan of Arc may well have been simultaneously soothing in their lack of sophistication, giving the illusion that the United States was grounded in history, albeit the temporally distant Middle Ages.

The representation of figures from the past found an ideal material form during what has been described as the Age of Bronze. From the last quarter of the nineteenth century through the beginning of the First World War, as the United States shifted from an agricultural nation to an industrial one, public spaces were filled with male heroes and personifications of moral qualities in metallic female form. These frequently colossal statues represented the nation, largely with the Statue of Liberty's hard drapery, torch, and wreathed head.[19] Countless bronze statues of Joan of Arc appeared during this era, typified by the small figure of Joan at the United States Naval Academy made in 1913, as well as by the large equestrian statue by Anna Vaughn Hyatt that overlooks the Hudson River in New York City.[20] The

Louis-Maurice Boutet de Monvel, *The Crowning at Reims of the Dauphin* (1907). Oil and gold leaf, 29¾ in. × 70¼ in. (In the Collection of The Corcoran Gallery of Art, Washington, D.C., William A. Clark Collection, 26.145)

Naval Academy bronze, by the French sculptor Antonin Mercié, who had already sculpted several Civil War heroes in the United States, is reminiscent of the Boutet de Monvel Jeanne d'Arc. Mercié's Joan is a young girl, crowned with laurel, who stands in armor with her helmet and sword laid at her side. The most striking aspects of the figure are the excessive roundness of the encased body, with its tiny waist and ankles, and the ecstatic expression of Joan's upturned face as she appears to be communing with the divine with her eyes closed. The viewer's relation to this simultaneously childlike and sensual Joan is inescapably voyeuristic.[21] The attitude of Mercié's Joan recalls Bram Dijkstra's observation that the nineteenth-century male tended to equate "virtuous passivity, sacrificial ecstasy, and erotic death." In painting, the dominant mode of representing the "transcendent spiritual value of passive feminine sacrifice" was the beautifully posed dead woman.[22]

Mercié's divinely and erotically passive Joan is in marked contrast to the monumental Hyatt statue that was installed during the First World War. Hyatt won the commission for the bronze and did all the labor single-handed in an age in which women were generally thought fit to do only artisan consumer handiwork.[23] Hyatt entered the competition for the commission of the Joan of Arc sculpture and started working on the statue in Paris, using a delivery horse and a nude model to get the proper proportions and musculature. Hyatt's idea was accepted by a committee of prominent New Yorkers in 1909 after they saw her work in a salon show. The group selected to commission the sculpture previously had spent time in France studying representations of Joan of Arc, attending the many pageants in the heroine's honor, and, in the words of one reviewer, "finding out what not to do."[24] The committee apparently liked Hyatt's rejection of the popular dumb peasant and the pious angel, which were popular in France at the time, in favor of the healthy, impassioned young girl in historically accurate armor, whose face expresses courage and spirituality.

The New York version of the sculpture at 93rd Street and Riverside Drive was unveiled on 6 December 1915 with military bands and speeches.[25] Copies of the sculpture also appear in San Francisco and Gloucester, Massachusetts, and in the French city of Blois. Without exception, the work was heralded as a masterpiece. A typical reviewer wrote that it is "one of the few really monumental, impressive, and expressive equestrian statues of modern times."[26] Sitting so high in the saddle that she seems to continue going up and forward even while the horse remains posed, Joan thrusts her sword to the sky while her composed and determined face looks out from a full suit of armor. The statue itself looms above the park from a base designed by the architect John Van Pelt and made with stones taken from both the cathedral of Rheims and the recently destroyed dungeon in Rouen where Joan had been imprisoned.

The sculpture was also an unqualified success with the public and the press, who appreciated its magnificence as well as the fact that a woman had designed and built it. Hyatt was admired for her tenacity and skill. The reviewer for *The Century Magazine* attributed the statue's success both to Hyatt's background as a descendant of highly disciplined New England

Marius-Jean-Antonin Mercié, *Joan of Arc* (1913). (Courtesy of the U.S. Naval Academy Museum)

Anna Vaughn Hyatt's *Joan of Arc* (1915) at the center of a wartime gathering. (Courtesy of the Alliance Française)

Puritans and to her female intuition into the Maid's spiritual rapture.[27] The latter is thought to be evident in the fact that the sword is not brandished as a weapon but held aloft to reveal the five crosses engraved on it. The coverage of Hyatt's statue and the many celebrations and pageants around it leave no doubt that Joan was a contemporaneous figure. The reviewer for *St. Nicholas* magazine refers blithely to Domrémy in relation to the current war and in describing Joan's death writes confidently, "You remember the story. . . ."[28] This essay, which states as fact that the Germans had not destroyed Joan's village because she promised to watch over it eternally, is evidence of the talismanic appeal of Joan's story and the new statue during the First World War.

The Image of Woman

The use of the female form in early twentieth-century culture offers one of the keys to interpreting antimodernism. On one level, the idealized representation of the female body, particularly one known for its virginity, offered the illusion of wholeness. In addition, the evocation of traditional female inspirational icons permitted temporary retreat from the flux of modernity, with its shifting social roles. The female form represented Eternal Form in a world in which masculinity had come to be associated with change and expediency, and in which consumer culture had severed the connection between surface and substance. As Martha Banta has written, "the woman as image of a type [became] the dominant cultural tic" of the era between 1876 and 1918. She suggests further that "to enclose the historical past, the contemporary moment, and the time-free universal within one visual design which made the world of the actual reverberate with allegory and the realm of the allegorical seem realistic" averted the era's increasing sense of dislocation in time.[29] Investigation of a figure like Joan of Arc, however, reveals the degree to which old signs like the virgin warrior not only evoked conventional meanings but heralded the formation of new, less comforting ones. The armored or hard body, short hair, and social freedom of the warrior had a certain affinity with the Jazz Age flapper. Looking further ahead, one might also see the virgin's refusal of food and amenorrhea, which allowed the taut, thin body to represent strength of will and wholeness, as a harbinger of anorexia, a condition associated with a desire for control.[30]

The particular types with which Joan of Arc is aligned should be seen in the light of the ways in which the rapid social transformations of the modern era particularly affected the United States, with its lack of historical patterns and its cultural, ethnic, and religious heterogeneity. By 1900 personal appearance and the awareness of types had become a social obsession based on the desire to belong to a larger community.[31] The search for the American type was affected by democratic notions of equality that pertained even to the sexes. Until the end of the nineteenth century, the genre most suited to an exploration of these particularly American issues of identity was melodrama, with its empathy for the underdog and conviction that everyone has a chance to win in an egalitarian world. David Belasco's 1905 melodrama, *The Girl of the Golden West,* delineates the role of women in relation to the persona of The Girl, who in turn helped to pave the way for the presence of Joan of Arc during the First World War. Traditionally, women in myths of the American West were static characters who were either good at home or bad in the saloon. The former were ruled by the "cult of true womanhood," which was bolstered by books, manuals, and magazines that instilled the feminine virtues of "piety, purity, submissiveness, and domesticity."[32] In contrast, the reality of life in the West demanded energy and independence, which Belasco sought to integrate into the ideal by way of The Girl. Like Joan of Arc, The Girl is a child-woman. She is happiest among men's men who gamble, swear, and fight, but who express their humanity under her influence. The Girl was embodied in early American cinema and culture by Mary Pickford, whose aggressiveness was acceptable because it was tempered by childish spontaneity, good humor, and innocence. The Girl's freedom ends, however, at the moment she falls in love and leaves The World for The Home. Since the independence of The Girl, like that of the Virgin Warrior, is unavailable to the sexualized, potentially maternal woman, melodrama ends with a wedding. Joan of Arc's story is not unlike The Girl's. Joan has obeyed her own voice and desire, revealing female strength and potential, but she pays with her life when she refuses to go home. Like The Girl, Joan generally appeals to men as an erotic challenge who can be subdued and to women as an outlet for repressed fantasy and frustration.

Whether envisioned as The Girl, the personification of freedom, or Joan of Arc herself, the female who stands for male ideals during war is a complicated figure. A powerfully portrayed female icon can be more effective than words in evoking the visceral reaction that drives men to risk their lives in battle. The reference to the historical Joan of Arc, in particular, adds the sense of shame, since she was a mere girl. In addition, any depiction of the female body in a moment of peril has a potential pornographic quality.[33] In the tradition of representations of persecution that feature bound naked women, which are praised under the guise of criticizing the depicted intolerance, the danger to the United States during the war often was envisioned as a vulnerable nubile female. In addition, the image of Joan of Arc tied to the stake derives from the Amazonamachie tradition, in which hard-fought military victory over a powerful woman is infused with eroticism. While the many images of this type used in the 1910s successfully recruited men into the Army, they may have done so by inspiring more than the desire to protect the helpless women and innocent children. The Spanish-American War poster by Howard Chandler Christy, "The Soldier's Dream," featured the drawing of a homesick infantryman exhaling the shape of his ideal woman in the smoke from his pipe. The illusion that the man creates the woman for whom he goes to war eroticizes patriotism and calls to mind that Joan of Arc was the original girl in smoke who was repeatedly reproduced during war.[34]

A contemporaneous cartoon illustrates how various representations of Joan of Arc were used in relation to actual women. In the drawing, which appeared in an early version of *Life* magazine in 1913, "militant" feminists are shown "as they are," "as they think they are," and "as they appear to the police and shopkeepers." The first row, "as they are," shows four sour old women; the second row, "as they think they are," exhibits four versions of a radiant Joan of Arc (with helmet, halo, sparks, and laurel wreath); and the third row, "as they appear to the police and shopkeepers," pictures the women as devils and demons. The image suggests the complexity of the Joan of Arc persona as it is used both within and against patriarchal culture. The appeal in the cartoon to supposed female vanity was employed regularly to restrain the aspiring and successful women of the day. A more concrete example of this tendency is found in a *Good Housekeeping* article of 1912 titled "The Feminine Charms of the Woman Militant: The Personal Attractiveness and Housewifely Attainments of the Leaders of the Equal Suffrage Movement, Illustrated with Portraits." Descriptions follow of Elizabeth Cady Stanton's "beautifully ordered home," Susan B. Anthony's skill with her needle, and Carrie Chapman Catt's homemade pumpkin pies.[35] This discourse of domesticity can be traced back to the trial of Joan, where records reveal

Militants

AS THEY ARE

AS THEY THINK THEY ARE

Rodney Thomson
with apologies to
Orson Lowell

AS THEY APPEAR TO THE POLICE AND SHOPKEEPERS

Militants. Rodney Thompson, *Life*, 27 March 1913.

repeated allusions to Joan's largely irrelevant spinning, sewing, and gardening skills.

The most pervasive representation of Joan of Arc during World War I was most likely a successful fund-raising poster of 1917 by Haskell Coffin. This image persuaded Americans to purchase savings stamps with the words "Joan of Arc Saved France, Women of America Save Your Country!" A fully armored Joan confronts the audience in a pose that is reminiscent of Uncle Sam's as he thrusts his finger at the viewer. Despite the symbols of power in the image, Joan is first and foremost beautiful and erotically appealing. The feminine body is cut off just at the point where the flare of the hips begins and the top of the armor reflects light where it protrudes over the breasts. With her long hair, darkened lips, and wide eyes that look up and out, Joan is presented as an object of voyeuristic desire. Joan's open arms and raised sword create a sense of erotic vulnerability, yet Joan is equally an active and strong figure who is comfortably feminized. Unlike Christy's girl in smoke or the many representations based on Liberty, the Mother, and the Protecting Angel, Joan of Arc has concrete ties to the historical past that lend a unique moral weight to the causes that employed her.

Gender Play and Performance

As evidenced in public sculpture, war posters, and commercial imagery, Joan of Arc and related female types were increasingly present in everyday life in the early years of the century. Banta writes about a revival of cross-dressing, masquerade balls, and theatrical gender play, noting that the first three figures on a contemporaneous list of popular costumes were Joan of Arc, Miss Liberty, and Columbia. Speculating on the appeal of these figures, she writes, "Dressing as Joan of Arc on Main Street at high noon might not be wise; doing it at a masked ball [lets one] be woman, warrior, martyr, and saint to general acclaim and with no harm done."[36] On one hand, this temporary assumption of a powerful persona is a mere venting of pressure that is part of a process as old as civilization itself. The choice of costumes, however, may have been related to an exploration of female role models and a growing sense that femininity itself was a masquerade.[37]

The popularity of masquerade at this time was also evident in vaudeville, where play with the signs of gender was prevalent. Female impersonators dominated the stage, but there were also male impersonators such as Florence Tempest, who appeared in the Ziegfeld Follies between 1910 and 1914 as "Our American Boy." While these women dressed as men, their gestures remained feminine and the star discourse around them emphasized marriage and the difference between real life and the theater. A woman could perform masculinity on stage, but she *was* a woman. The careers of the singer-dancers Hetty King and Della Fox are a case in point. Rather than challenging gender roles in any way, over the course of their careers the women shifted their performances in soldier dress toward burlesque: their jackets became ever shorter and finally unbuttoned; the caps moved off center until they threatened to fall off altogether; and the pants became tights.[38] This carnivalesque play with gender roles was paralleled in other venues by a new questioning of performance styles in melodrama and in the Delsarte technique of acting. Both of these methods made a direct correlation between the specific emotions called for in a script and precise facial and body positions that could be diagrammed. François Delsarte was uncritically aware that he was attributing unquestioned aspects of identity, such as femininity, to analyzable poses and attitudes.[39]

In contrast to this controlled and conservative gender play on stage were the experiences of woman suffragists who were attacked for dressing as Liberty or Joan of Arc in protest parades. Located in the real world rather than on stage or at a masquerade ball, these women were punished for seizing the idea of real freedom for actual women through the symbolism of iconic female figures.[40] Thus, when the young socialist activist Elizabeth Gurley Flynn was dubbed the "East Side Joan of Arc" by Theodore Dreiser for her work with the International Workers of the World from 1906 to 1916 and with the Workers Defense Union from 1918 to 1924, the message was two-sided. "Gurley" Flynn was an effective, tireless activist who was frequently arrested. However, she was described as inspiring strikers with her lovely, dynamic appearance as "the very *picture* of a youthful revolutionary girl leader."[41] As women in ordinary life, as opposed to the vaudeville stage, began to gain power on their own, the Joan of Arc persona that previously had evoked only abstract qualities possessed by men had to be qualified. The tempering and continual renegotiation of the meaning of Joan of Arc's image begins in the First World War and escalates through the century in response to women's increasing social power.

Joan of Arc sells war savings stamps in World War I (1917). Haskell Coffin for the U.S. Treasury Department. (The George C. Marshall Research Foundation)

"Joan of Arc, They Are Calling You":
Propaganda and the First World War

The impulse that drove American culture toward medievalism and Joan of Arc as a way to escape an increasing sense of impotence in the face of consumerism, technology, and the demise of cultural authority also prevented the recognition that the United States' armed forces were unprepared for the twentieth century. Consequently, when the United States realized that it needed a coherent military policy in the years before World War I, it devised one that was defensive, isolationist, and inadequate. When war actually broke out in Europe in July 1914, the United States reacted with calls for pacifist neutrality. Woodrow Wilson took the small step of forming the bipartisan National Security League in late 1914, which did not stop the *New York Times* from referring to the United States as a "great, helpless, unprepared nation" as late as January 1915.[42] When the United States understood that the stockpiling of the machinery of war did not prevent war, then on 7 May 1915 faced the sinking of the *Lusitania*, which killed one hundred American civilians, the declaration of war became inevitable. With its approval by Congress in April 1917, the First World War became a battle between good and evil in the American mind. As Marc Ferro has written, "Americans judged superficially and sentimentally, and propaganda concerning 'the martyrdom of gallant little Belgium' affected them more than any account of violations of neutrals' rights in international law."[43] Propaganda aimed at the people of the United States succeeded best when it avoided portraying the horror of what had become an interminable war in the trenches.

The image of Joan of Arc was an ideal propaganda tool because the heroine embodied the principles of justice and noble sacrifice and she had fought victoriously in a great European war. At this moment in the larger culture, references to Joan of Arc exploded in popular literature, children's books, statues, songs, films, and slogans.[44] As Paul Fussell has observed, unlike the literary British, the soldiers of the United States had neither a store of redemptive illusions nor any skill at writing them. Yet the Americans could grasp the familiar and readily available Joan of Arc. With the heroine, the soldiers could participate in the discourse of a war that assumed the diction of the Middle Ages and saw itself as part of a continuum with the Hundred Years' War. In conceptualizing the soldiers of this conflict as "radiant, gallant warriors," propaganda for the war attracted over a million volunteers.[45] A typical popular poem from 1909 by Henry van Dyke initiates the role that Joan of Arc came to play. "Come Back Again, Jeanne d'Arc" elegiacally connects the present, when "doubtful leaders miss the mark" and "people lack the single faith and will," to Joan's time, when she "brought the courage equal to the fight" and "gave a heart to France!"[46]

The speech given by the French ambassador to the United States in 1915 at the dedication of the Anna Vaughn Hyatt statue of Joan of Arc in New York makes the connection between past and present even stronger:

> The saints who have watched over France in all these centuries are still with her. The nation has become one in a single purpose. She can fight, and will win the fight. Ste Geneviève, patroness of Paris at the time of the greatest danger, when the city was so near falling a prey to the enemy, prophesied that Attila would never reach it, but would turn toward the plains of the Marne, there to be defeated. And so it was—so it has been.[47]

The final, liturgical-sounding phrase figurally connects Saint Geneviève, Saint Joan, and France in World War I. The figure of Joan of Arc allows the speaker to feminize France while still protecting its military reputation. Joan alone can simultaneously stand for the threatened body of the nation and serve as its savior.

One of the more overt examples of its kind, with the late date of January 1920, is an essay by A. Evelyn Newman in the *Ladies Home Journal* that begins with the lyrics of one of the most popular songs of the First World War, "Joan of Arc, They Are Calling You," which had been published in 1917. Newman observes that American soldiers had two supreme "symbolic figures of femininity in their imaginations—the Statue of Liberty . . . and Joan of Arc." The essay ends with a series of connections: between the soldiers and their "medieval sister"; between the "Christianity" for which Joan died and "the New Democracy—justice, and right and freedom and love of God"; and between Joan's death at nineteen and the deaths of so many young Americans. The article is structured as a sentimental journey through a picturesque France, filled with descriptions of statues of Joan of Arc that have survived destruction. The location of the trenches in Joan of Arc's native country in eastern France apparently gives Joan an almost indexical presence during the war. Most notable is the degree to which Joan is made a contemporary as both a

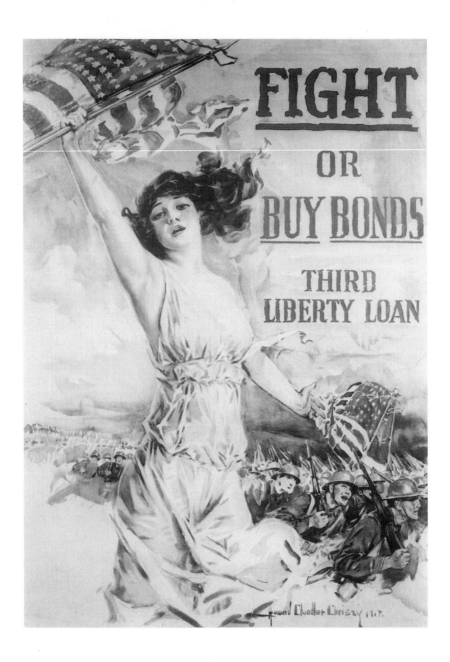

Howard Chandler Christy's eroticized Liberty (1917) encapsulates both the threat to the nation and hope for the future. (The George C. Marshall Research Foundation)

sister and a love object. The soldiers are described as being largely ignorant of Joan's history but fully susceptible to her "greatness" in the form of her chastity, which appealed to the "masculine" in them. Describing the presence of books about the Maid in reading rooms and the numerous staged pageants across France, Newman observes that "the Education Department of the Y.M.C.A. was not slow to perceive the romantic interest of our men in the Maid of France." The final line of the article points to Joan's importance as a tool of propaganda. Future generations making pilgrimages to Joan's shrines, "having grown up in the newness of that Democracy for which their fathers labored so zealously, may join in her triumphant cry and say [as she did on the stake]: 'No! No! Our voices did not deceive us. They were from God. Jesus! Jesus!' "[48] In response to sentiments of the type expressed in Newman's essay, and to the use of Johannic iconography in general, Vachel Lindsey wrote the following poem just after the war, which hints at the backlash of the 1920s.

Mark Twain and Joan of Arc

When Yankee soldiers reach the barricade
Then Joan of Arc gives each the accolade.

For she is there in armor clad, today,
All the young poets of the wide world say.

Which of our freemen did she greet the first,
Seeing him come against the fires accurst?

Mark Twain, our Chief with neither smile nor jest,
Leading to war our youngest and our best.

The Yankee to King Arthur's court returns.
The sacred flag of Joan above him burns.

For she had called his soul from out the tomb.
And where she stands, there he will stand till doom.

. . . .
But I, I can but mourn, and mourn again
At bloodshed caused by angels, saints, and men.[49]

Despite this later pessimism, Joan was essential during and after the war as a figural connection that linked the deaths of millions of young warriors to an abstract notion of eternal greatness.

Joan of Arc haunts the imagination of a soldier in the First World War. John C. Conacher in *Life* (c. 1918). (Library of Congress)

The *New York Herald-Tribune* observed just after the war that "it was an outstanding fact of our campaign in the Great War that Joan of Arc was almost as much the heroine of the doughboys as the *poilu*."[50] The sculptures and images that were created for broad public spaces are obvious signs of this regard. Yet the smaller manifestations of interest in Joan are equally indicative of her influence. Although many of these Joan of Arcs remain hidden because they were not made for large-scale consumption, one can derive a general sense of the attention paid to the heroine from what has been uncovered. Aside from the many monumental and small bronze statues of the equestrian Joan noted earlier, there were few visual images outside of book illustrations. Only ten paintings are on record as having been made in the United States from the turn of the century through the start of the war.[51]

Joan has turned up more often in public places, as she does in Edwin

Blackfield's mural *Ideals* in the Drexel Library in Philadelphia, than in museums. In 1913 the American Numismatic Society had a "Joan of Arc Exhibition" where presumably medals, engravings, and stamps were displayed.[52] This society and the Joan of Arc Statue Committee both issued medals in 1919, the latter's featuring the Hyatt sculpture seen from across the river, in a line directly between two battleships with their searchlights crossing just above the monument. The ephemera of this period collected by the Boston Public Library consists of numerous small images on paper or worked in metal, as well as a number of containers. A functional painted milk-glass statuette of Joan is topped by a cork; a round candy tin has a contemporaneous-looking Joan on the lid; and plate sets display the high points of her life. In each case, Joan serves in a particularly mundane and familiar way not often associated with the memorializing of saints and martyrs.

It is far easier to quantify the amount of written information concerning Joan. The New York Public Library published a booklet in 1915 to inform patrons about the twenty-two titles relating to Joan of Arc that it owned. Approximately thirty such books were written at the time, seventeen of them covering several heroes, of whom Joan was one. Many magazine articles appeared, fifteen of which are listed in the Joan of Arc Collection at the Boston Public Library. Three serialized plays were staged between 1910 and 1918, four professional plays and a vaudeville act in 1914. Appearing a bit earlier, the Joan of Arc pageant at Harvard University in 1901 set the stage for the era with its star turn by the Irish actress Maude Adams and 1,300 actors, 100 horses, 15,000 spectators, and Beethoven's *Eroica* Symphony.[53] Many of the books of the era were aimed at adolescents but virtually all had a similar mission, conception of Joan, and notion of Joan in relation to history. *The Wonderful Story of Joan of Arc and the Meaning of Her Life for Americans* by Charles McClellan Stevens, published in 1918, is a characteristic and vivid example. The dedication to the book reads:

From the
Inspiration AND FAITH of the
WONDERFUL WOMAN
to
MY DAUGHTER
and to
ALL THE DAUGHTERS OF MAN AND GOD.

In the book's description, Stevens declares his mission to be the telling of the "historical truth" about Joan of Arc, to whom so many references have been made during the war but whom many people think of as a "French legend or a Church superstition." By the end of his convoluted mélange of chronological fact and abstract deification, Joan has been neutralized as one of the "immortal few" whose lives are too great for history or biography and who stands for nothing offensive but only the "lowliest simplicity" and "human motherhood in action." She was, as Stevens tells all Americans, a "Goddess of Liberty" who engaged in war to restore order.[54]

In one of the more important propaganda tasks in the United States during what was often called the "European War," Joan of Arc was used as a unifying figure in the recruitment and control of immigrants. Many of these new residents had been born in Catholic countries, and their differences made them easy scapegoats for the decline of the country and the loss of cultural authority. The dilemma facing the war propaganda agencies was to persuade massive numbers of people of all classes who felt allegiance to other nations to fight as a unified group for a country that treated them negligently. The marginal status of Joan of Arc made her an effective tool. Although Joan was a European female, her life was free of the sensual indulgence that encumbered Europeans in American eyes. Joan partook of neither food nor sex and eventually defied both the monarchy and the Catholic Church. In addition, conventional representations of Joan gave her the Gaelic physiognomy that had been privileged in American medievalism for its proximity to WASP features. Thus Joan was a peasant outsider who originated the concept of France as a nation exclusively for the French in the popular mind, but who had been accepted and even valued in the United States for many years. As an ultranationalist commoner with a crusader mentality, Joan appealed to the inherently patriotic and conservative immigrants, who came to the aid of their new country when it offered even the least hope of acceptance.[55]

Propaganda and the Cinema

The recruitment of immigrants was one of the chief goals of the Hollywood propaganda offices of George Creel, who headed the Committee on Public Information (CPI). Creel was particularly effective in the use of Hollywood stars, many of whom were immigrants themselves. People were made to feel American, many for the first time, in doing their civic duty with all other immigrants by fighting for and thus joining a traditional America. The role of the movies in idealizing the United States, by way of recognizable images, concepts, and historical figures with which immigrants could identify, cannot be overestimated.[56] In the early years of the century, the cinema was largely an inexpensive vaudeville amusement that was associated with the lower and urban immigrant classes.[57] During the Progressive Era, from 1908 through 1914, the film industry began to ingratiate itself with other levels of culture by assuming the high moral tone of the time and successfully entering uptown theaters to align itself with the legitimate stage. By 1914, most government departments had a film section, and most major companies advertised with film and used educational films internally. Growing numbers of film journals indicated increasing critical acceptance of the medium, which had daily audiences of over 10 million people, 900 theaters in New York City alone, and 20 film studios in the Los Angeles area.[58]

Between 1912 and the end of the war, the film industry established a powerful position in American society and an adversarial stance in regard to the dominant culture. Until 1914, films were able to blend social critique and exploitation by portraying the evils of drink and drugs, political corruption, and the dangers encountered by women seeking independence. The ability of film to have it both ways, by vividly showing while ostensibly criticizing, led quickly to attempts at censorship at every level of distribution. State boards existed by 1914, and by 1916 the National Association of the Motion Picture Industry (NAMPI) was formed with William Brady at its head in an attempt at self-regulation. In addition, several cities started agencies such as New York's Clean Picture and Play League of America, Inc.[59] By 1918, all exported films except those going to Canada were censored.

The film industry continually fought both censorship and taxation by arguing that film was educational, like the press, rather than merely entertaining. In early 1915, D. W. Griffith's *Birth of a Nation* was shown in the White House for President Wilson and his family in what was an important step in asserting both film's legitimacy as a means of relating history and the cinema's status as a middle- and upper-class diversion. Late in the same year, Wilson was asked to speak at a Motion Picture Board of Trade dinner with an invitation that boldly described the cinema: "As a propaganda medium, it is unexcelled. It speaks a universal language. It speaks convincingly." During the years of neutrality, the film public clamored for cinematic images of the war transmitted with the photographic immediacy that was unavailable in any other medium. The government propaganda agencies recognized the power of the cinema and by September 1914 they had begun to insert title cards bearing Wilson's signature into film screenings that warned audiences: "Don't Take Sides," "Be American First," and "Forget the Horrors of War."[60] Concurrently, Hollywood sold its product by associating its preparedness films with the government in order to create a sense that its films were serious and educational. In 1916 the first book of film theory appeared, suggesting a growing recognition of the influence of the cinema in American culture. *The Photoplay: A Psychological Study,* by the Harvard psychologist Hugo Munsterberg, asserted that film can uniquely reproduce the workings of the human mind (for example, a close-up signals concentration and a flashback evokes memory) and thus is capable of profoundly affecting the emotions and then the actions of the spectator.[61]

As the First World War encroached on the United States, it became apparent that a shift from pacifism to militarism would have to be made on all levels of the film industry. By April 1917, George Creel's Committee on Public Information was at work advocating publicity over censorship. Creel carried out an effective campaign that involved film, photographs, posters, press releases, billboards, newspapers, cartoons, speeches, pamphlets, books, and exhibitions, all of which were supported by William Brady (NAMPI), who was the liaison between the industry and the government.[62] During the First World War, "propaganda" did not imply coercion, since there was no real debate as to whether the war was good or bad. The reinforcement of the culture's dominant values was the sole intent. Consequently, the industry did not make many war films as such; five war films were made per month in 1917 and ten per month by July 1918. Under the "work or fight" rule, however, film workers were considered essential to the war effort, and theaters were centers of patriotism, offering decorations, slide shows, food drives, speeches, and recruiting desks.[63] Not coincidentally, Hollywood stars, including Mary Pickford, Douglas Fairbanks, and Charlie Chaplin, were the war's most effective fund-raisers.

The most popular and effective films of the war effort were not those that provided rational explanations of the world's problems or those that turned the horror of battle into entertainment. Successful films fulfilled the desire to be part of the thrill of wartime by engaging vicariously in the conflict within the communal and energized space of the theater. The historical warrior Joan of Arc was a perfect subject in this regard, since she was separate from the present conflagration but representative of the wartime values of courage, freedom, democracy, nationalism, and conformity. Not unlike the lives of the stars who spoke on behalf of the war, the heroic, intensely lived life of Joan represented an idealized, highly desirable existence beyond conventional moral distinctions. In her investigation of Mary Pickford's war work, Leslie Midkiff DeBauche describes war films as occupying an "alternate and elevated position" in the industry and claims that war-related content is not always obvious and can be understood only in relation to a film's context and function.[64] Regardless of its method, when the United States entered World War I in April 1917, the cinema had helped to prepare the country emotionally and psychologically, if not militarily.

Women, Propaganda, and the Cinema

The shift from pacifism to war in the mid-1910s was part of the larger Progressive Movement, in which the urge to ameliorate the military was part of a larger effort to reform society in general—to humanize the cities, curb the monopolies, improve the functioning of government. In what Finnegan describes as having become "a popular fad and a craze, [the progressive current included a call to] national efficiency and individual duty." The Preparedness Movement became a Trojan horse of sorts that worked to unify an increasingly diverse and rebellious country under a New Nationalism. Women were the targeted audience in the effort to discourage pacifism and to encourage universal conscription as a morally invigorating act. At the same time, increasing female freedom was decried as "too much personal liberty," which was the "ever-increasing grist of the divorce mills."[65] The girlish Joan of Arc in armor appealed to these mixed emotions by suggesting simultaneously the besieged female and the frighteningly independent one, both effective in shaming men into action. All of J. Stuart Blackton's preparedness films of 1915, including the elaborate *Battle Cry of Peace*, *Wake Up America!*, and *Womanhood, the Glory of a Nation* (as well as D. W. Griffith's *Birth of A Nation* of the same year) implied that terrible things awaited the women of men who were too cowardly to fight.

The variety of roles available to women in wartime listed in Larry Lang-man and Ed Borg's *Encyclopedia of American War Films* is fairly predictable. Although women served as allegorical representations of peace, civilization, and justice in *The Four Horsemen of the Apocalypse* of 1921, they were usually cast as mothers, spies, or endangered young girls. Blackton's 1915 *Battle Cry of Peace,* for example, is a preparedness film about a mother who shoots her two daughters rather than let them fall into enemy hands; the plot illustrates both the symbolic value of female chastity in war and the degree to which violent behavior is an unquestioned norm. The program for *The Battle Cry of Peace* includes the lines: "Through the country sweeps a wave of patriot-ism. In every home men pledge their lives; women pledge their sons and husbands to the campaign for peace."[66] The difference between what the two sexes have to sacrifice—that is, lives versus male relatives—clarifies the passive role expected of women during the war. The *Encyclopedia of Ameri-can War Films* lists numerous films about self-sacrifice that feature in their titles nouns for women that indicate dependency: a woman named Joan in *War Brides* of 1916 shoots herself in front of a king in protest over having to produce sons for war. *Arms and the Girl* of 1917, *Daughter Angele* of 1918, and *Daughters of Destiny* of 1918 feature unsung heroines. In behavior that inevitably involves the sacrifice of the female body either literally or sexually, the woman in each film acts in relation to a man who gains recognition. In a pattern that continued through the Second World War, literal or icono-graphic references to Joan of Arc served to palliate the fact that women's war efforts generally went unacknowledged.

In retrospect, the use of images of Joan of Arc for propaganda purposes during the heightened years of the First World War indicates some uncer-tainty over the roles of the sexes in previously gender-specific arenas. Yet during the war, the freedom with which Joan of Arc was used (in compari-son with her absence during the Second World War) suggests that the issue had yet to be recognized as a problem. Joan of Arc served in the early part of the century as a reassuring figure whose medieval roots provided a sense of tradition and moral stability. The fact that she had won a war despite a ter-rible death by fire gave her a talismanic power in this bewildering period, in which the very definition of war was changing in light of technological de-velopment and deep questioning of traditional cultural authority.

⊸≫⇒ 2 "Joan of Arc Saved France, Women of America Save Your Country"

Cecil B. DeMille's *Joan the Woman*, 1916

The decade that began just before the First World War and ended with the events surrounding Joan's canonization in 1920 was filled with images of Joan of Arc. Out of the numerous texts and images that appeared in the United States in particular, two essays in magazines that were popular in 1911 suggest the nature of Joan's significance in the prewar era. In *Harper's Weekly,* an article titled "A Jeanne d'Arc Pilgrimage by Automobile" offers a sentimental version of the American author's journey through France and a survey of Joan's life story. As the author, Charles Johnston, drives through the countryside, he is astonished to find Joan of Arc "everywhere," whether in murals, in statues, or on medallions around the necks of Parisians.[1] He surmises that Joan symbolizes a blend of national fervor and adoration of God. All who supported Joan receive his praises while those who opposed her are painted as buffoons. The precious tone of this essay, along with novel observations about, for example, the "smiling courtesy" of the French, create a folkloric Joan of Arc who supports the author's vision of a distant, medievalized France.

With a very different attitude but no less admiration for Joan, a reviewer for *The Dial* approaches his subject with a humorously dismissive style and tone. Allen Wilson Porterfield begins his essay by referring to the heroine's birthplace as "the Mason and Dixon line, as it were, between Teuton and Gaul" and to Joan as "the *victime glorieuse* [who] breathed out her last on a

stack of burning wood."[2] In his generally sympathetic review of two contemporaneous biographies (by Mary Rogers Bangs and Grace James), the
author observes that "one of the most remarkable things in connection with
the Maid is the amazing amount of art and history and poetry that owes its
most remote inspiration to her baffling life. . . . Poetically, any thesis can be
proved or disproved by her case." Porterfield notes that the two simultaneous Joan of Arc biographies, as well as the multitude of previous versions
and images of Joan, reveal that history can be shaped to support any "truth."
The ingenuousness of the traveling writer for *Harper's*, however, is most
characteristic of responses to Joan in the early years of the century.

Joan of Arc in Early American Cinema

Most of the films that evoke Joan of Arc before and during the war use Joan
freely with little sophistication or care for historical detail, starting with the
intriguingly titled *The Mexican Joan of Arc* of 1911. Joan's cinematic presence
is felt in myriad ways: through advertising featuring Pearl White, the queen
of the serials, as "A Modern Joan of Arc," a description of the lead character
in *Liberty: Daughter of the USA;* plot lines such as the story of Joan of Arc
inspiring a child in *The Little Patriot;* or, more distantly, the use of the name,
as in *Joan of the Woods* and *Joan of Rainbow Springs*.[3] In addition, until the
French film industry was destroyed by the war, European films specifically
about Joan of Arc were imported for American audiences. A film titled *Joan
of Arc* by F. Wolff, for example, was distributed in the United States in 1914
by the Eclectic Film Company, whose motto was "The Cream of the European Market Selected for America." Known as *Jeanne* in Europe, this attempt
to tell the life in its historical context (as is suggested by the flyer about the
film printed by the distributor) is part of a tradition of European versions
of Joan's story, including *Jeanne d'Arc,* released by Georges Méliès in 1900.[4]
However fantastical in imagery and sentiment these films may have been,
the European films appear to differ from their American counterparts in the
attempt to envision Joan of Arc in some connection to her historical and national context.

The American films in which Joan of Arc is evoked are ultimately serious in intent despite the levity that was inherent in cinema at this time,
owing to the relative novelty of the institution and its practices. While many

of the films have fatuous titles or highly melodramatic plot lines, they clearly were made in the context of preparation for war. One genre of Joan of Arc film is typified by *The Little Patriot* of 1917, in which a small child is inspired to be a patriot after her teacher reads her a story about Joan. An innocent, she not only persuades her father to enlist but also prevents a mysterious German from blowing up a local munitions factory. In addition, the little girl plays at being a soldier in a general's uniform and is even wounded during her escapades. In a serendipitous and charming way she is a catalyst in the war effort, and in the end she is adopted by a wealthy warmonger who is discovered to be her grandfather. Numerous films in which "daughter," "girl," or some diminutive of the name Joan appear in the title echo the theme in which the persona of Joan of Arc is called up and then diluted. *Miss Jackie of the Army* of 1917 depicts a young girl who helps her father, a colonel in the army, catch spies. *Battling Jane* of 1918 features Dorothy Gish as a spunky heroine who aids the war effort by winning a baby contest with an abandoned infant, whom she then keeps. *How Could You, Jean* of the same year is a Mary Pickford vehicle that, although not about the war, had a press book that featured articles about Pickford's war work.[5] The prevalence of this story line, in which women are positioned as heroic girl-helpmates in discreet relation to the war, with more or less reference to Joan of Arc, is also suggested by the names of government documentaries such as *Women Become Democracy's Valiant Helpers* and the oddly titled *A Girl's a Man for A' That and A' That*, in the "Says Uncle Sam" series.[6]

Another evocation of Joan of Arc occurs in popular tales that feature a girl, often a Red Cross nurse or a Salvation Army volunteer, who ends up sacrificing her body for her country while spying. *Salvation Joan* of 1916 relates the story of a wealthy, bored young woman who assumes the disguise of a gangster's moll to help her country. The suggestively titled *The Road through the Dark* of 1918 tells of a young French patriot who saves her village and her people by becoming the mistress of a German aristocrat in order to spy for the Allies. The sexualization of female war work is equally implied in the earlier *Mexican Joan of Arc*, which was apparently based on a true story about "the Widow Talamantes." Joan of Arc is invoked as a generic heroic female in the Mexican story, but an older tradition of the woman warrior is used to send a more subtle message. The film suggests that the heroine's widowhood, a state of sexual inactivity and immunity to pregnancy, makes her eligible for warrior status. Yet when the widow uses the tactic of sleeping with the enemy to capture him, she paradoxically disqualifies herself for participation in war.[7] This conflation of Joan of Arc and Mata Hari is a subtext that continues throughout the century.

The particular reasons for Joan of Arc's popularity as a cinematic subject are obvious. In addition to the riveting narrative and the potential for visual spectacle, the female lead is both successful in her war work and punished for blurring the boundaries between gender roles. Some of the broader reasons for Joan's consistent appearance are suggested in George Custen's study of Hollywood biographies.[8] Generally, the subject of a successful film biography must be so well known that the events of the life can be reorganized, often in quick montage sequences, flashback, and flash forward, without losing the sense of the character's story. In addition, Hollywood biographies had to support anachronistic but familiarizing elements when necessary. Joan's rural childhood, for example, allowed Cecil B. DeMille to extrapolate to such a degree that a contemporaneous reviewer of *Joan the Woman* described his Joan as a "girl as you might meet in the smaller farming communities of our country."[9] The Joan of Arc story accommodates several narrative events that Custen considers crucial for an effective film biography. Starting in medias res as it does with the voices of saints, Joan's story has the benefit of divine inspiration. Moreover, Joan appears to be a self-made individualist of a particularly American bent. Her story also contains a trial, which allows complex events to be reduced to an easily understood causal structure that ends with a verdict. Most important, Joan's story features a powerful death scene that allows for a final encapsulation of the film's message. The potentially iconoclastic aspects of Joan's story can be stressed or diminished, and Joan's enemies can be painted as either innocent tools of a manipulative king or anomalous forces of evil in an otherwise benign system.

Cecil B. DeMille's *Joan the Woman*

The variety of ways in which Joan of Arc's story can be used is illustrated in the history of the international distribution of DeMille's *Joan the Woman*. The version of the film that has always been shown in France is very different from the one that premiered in New York City on Christmas Day in

1916. On one level, the reediting of the film done before exportation means little, since in the years preceding the entry of the United States into the First World War the Committee of Public Information's Foreign Film Service censored most of the films distributed in Europe. Minor reediting was common practice, since title cards in the appropriate language had to be inserted in any case. In addition, when 30 percent of a film's profits came from overseas distribution, the industry did whatever was necessary to suit its foreign audience.[10] However, the excessive reconfiguring to which *Joan the Woman* was subjected before being seen by the French implies an awareness that DeMille's Joan of Arc was a quintessentially American figure who would not have been welcomed or perhaps even recognized as the French national heroine. A comparison of the two versions of the film suggests that the version of *Joan the Woman* intended for American audiences had more to do with the changing roles of women in the war years than with the patriotism that underlies the French version. For this reason, of all the World War I–era films made about Joan of Arc, DeMille's film and the discourse surrounding it offer the fullest picture of Joan's place in American culture.

In mid-December 1916, just before the American premiere of *Joan the Woman,* an eight-page publication called *The Joan of Arc Journal* appeared as part of the film's elaborate publicity campaign. Formatted as a mock newspaper, the *Journal* contains reviews, articles, photographs, and drawings concerning the film and its star, the opera diva Geraldine Farrar. Issues raised in the *Journal* include the film in relation to the status of the cinema, Joan of Arc's place in American culture, the role of women, and the connections between the United States and the war in Europe. As a supplement to the film, the material offers insight into the perceived meaning of Joan of Arc in late 1916.

A review of the film in the *New York Times* claimed that *Joan the Woman* was one of the six best films ever made.[11] The *New York Sun* responded more specifically in describing the film as "altogether different and superior to the average cinema . . . [with] less of a bad taste and banality and the appeal to the lower standards of enjoyment common to nearly all of these pictures." It characterized the film as a masterpiece in a league with the films of D. W. Griffith.[12] Another review suddenly recognized cinema as the universal language and as "visualized thought," stating that the film took "the sting of childishness from a great art and [clothed] it with respectability and power."[13]

All the positive reviews stress the authenticity and magnitude of the sets and props, all of which had been heavily publicized in order to impress the critics. *The Joan of Arc Journal* included a letter to the editor that tried to take the notion of authenticity one step further by asserting that Farrar was, "if such a thing were possible, the living reincarnation of Joan of Arc."[14] Farrar's fame and the gender issues raised by her powerful performance, however, caused her to be the focus of the critical attack on the film. One negative reaction to *Joan the Woman,* which was generally respected and liked, seemed to stem from resentment that the lowly cinema would adapt a high-culture figure like Joan of Arc, who rightly belonged to Shakespeare, Voltaire, and Schiller. The reaction of Heywood Broun, writing for the *New York Tribune,* was that all was not quite "as it should be."[15]

The reviews of the film leave no doubt that the story of Joan of Arc was current. On the first page of the *Journal,* the *New York American* wrote that "the ordinarily accepted story of Joan of Arc is a household word [*sic*] and needs no retelling here." *Moving Picture World* quoted DeMille as saying, perhaps in reference to his choice of the film's title, that "no woman of history in all time is better known to the public of all nations than Joan of Arc, or the Maid of Orleans, as she is called, but the thought we were particularly eager to convey was the humanness of this remarkable woman."[16] However, a second strain that ran through the rhetoric of the familiarity of Joan of Arc was marked by references to her story as one of the most beautiful in all of "literature" (in a review that praised DeMille for his self-denial in refraining from a happy ending).[17] Likewise, reference was made to the "legend" in which the love story that DeMille added to the narrative was permissible, since "little definite or authentic in the history of Joan is known anyway."[18] *Exhibitor's Trade Review* referred euphemistically to the love story by saying that this Joan "dreamed dreams as she herded her sheep." The same review also claimed that the film had nothing to do with propaganda, but that "there will be something of the modern movement of feminism."[19] In sum, *The Joan of Arc Journal* is full of contradictions. Various articles state that Joan of Arc is real and famous but no details of her life are known; that the film is meant to inspire Americans during the war but films about women cannot be serious enough to be propaganda; and that the film is feminist but the virgin warrior dies for love rather than principle.

Largely because of Geraldine Farrar's outsized presence and performance, the film seems to foreground issues of gender. The film's style ranges from broad historical spectacle to intimate melodrama and the press reaction to Farrar ran a similar gamut. Carrying with her the cachet of the Metropolitan Opera, where she sang, Farrar was cast to elevate the status of the film. On the surface, this tactic backfired. Alexander Woollcott, writing about what he called "Joan the Prima Donna" for the *New York Times,* was his characteristically malicious self. In an attack that was aimed as much at the aspirations of the cinema as at the star, he wrote of the "rampageous Geraldine Farrar," whose notion of Joan was "not sufficiently different from her notion of Carmen." He "shudders to think what impression of Jeanne d'Arc is thus being imparted to this generation. . . . Thousands will come to think of her as a buxom and somewhat amatory lady with an extraordinarily knowing eye." What he wanted was "something of the valiant frailty of the idealized, canonized Joan, something of the spiritual beauty, something of the ecstasy of the maid . . . all this we might have had if someone else, Mae Marsh, perhaps, had been chosen for Joan of the screen."[20] The combination of Farrar herself, who was a society figure and an independent working woman who publicly expressed ambivalence about marriage, and her intimidating rendition of Joan of Arc apparently overwhelmed some of the critics.[21]

The pointed attack on Farrar was a pervasive aspect of the response to the film. The *Photoplay* review of the film by the critic Julian Johnson praised *Joan the Woman* as second only to *Birth of a Nation* and one of the few to use "the psychic force of active photography [as described by] Hugo Munsterberg." Johnson's tone changed considerably, however, when he discussed Farrar, whom he characterized variously as "a steak at a stake," "Arc's fanatic virgin," "a farmer's daughter," and "a girl David." More sharply, he described Farrar as being of "battle-cruiser weight [with one of her eyes reflecting] Riverside Drive, the other Fifth Avenue, and her mouth [seeming] to say 'Broadway.'"[22] As the founder of *Photoplay,* an early fan magazine, Johnson was clearly knowledgeable about the cinema and would have been familiar with the tension between star and character that is inevitable in a photographic medium. The apparent discomfort caused by one powerful woman playing another elicited other reactions as well, one of which is evident on the first page of *The Joan of Arc Journal,* where an almost unrecognizable photograph of Farrar was made to resemble a saint on a religious card. On the same page, the *New York Herald* used such phrases as "star merges into maid" and "her own personality disappears" to try to diminish this tension between contemporary star and legendary saint.

Discussing his work in later years, DeMille expressed regret that *Joan the Woman* was remembered as a spectacle. He wrote that he had wanted "to tell an absorbing personal story against a background of great historical events" and that he had seen Joan of Arc as "a strong peasant girl, with a sense of humor and human sympathy, ever faithful to her Voices, but tempted and fearful too—a woman of flesh and blood, whose heroism was as much a victory over herself as a victory over the English."[23] The implication that female heroism manifested itself in sexual restraint was evident in many reviews of the film. The headline of an article in the *New York Evening Journal* enigmatically claimed that Joan of Arc's life was "shaped by her womanhood."[24] The insistence on this vague state of being was found even in the most sympathetic reviews. The *New York American,* for example, wrote that the film showed "the quivering heart of all womankind," "the everyday quality of her womanliness . . . pleased by compliments, responding to the first approaches of love, fondling a babe . . . even as you and I," and "a glowing type of womanhood."[25] This desire to normalize the strong female was also present in a review in the same paper by a sympathetic minister. The "noted clergyman" wondered whether women could maintain their "goodness, beauty, divine reserve of soul, purity of heart" while entering the war and the world. He appeared to support the liberation of women but feared that the qualities generally assigned to women would be lost in the process. Joan of Arc's death, the ultimate removal from the world, was honored as a sacrifice for this ideal of "womanhood."[26] The message that the logical end of femininity was self-obliteration was conveyed in the photograph of Farrar in chains with the caption "They Killed the Woman, but not the Spirit."[27] The degree to which the agony of actual death was subsumed is evident in the *Journal's* reproduction of the murals that had been painted in the lobby of the theater where the film premiered. One image in particular improbably depicts a peacefully deceased Joan of Arc "lying in state," in her gown and armor, holding her sword.[28]

Although Farrar tried to appear woebegone in publicity photographs, with a pensive, downward gaze when appropriate, her Joan was a strong, vital woman who could not help but make everyone else in the film appear to be insubstantial in both body and spirit. One photograph of Farrar, which was distributed with a map showing the way to the theater in New York, depicts her kneeling with raised sword, dressed in armor, with the words "The Girl" written above.[29] Clearly, Farrar's Joan of Arc is an attempt to resemble the melodramatic figure of The Girl, who is characterized by masculine abilities and asexuality. The *New York Evening Journal* evoked these very traits with its description: "Tain't enough that she can act; she can ride a horse like a veteran, fight like a bull-dog, love like a queen and die like a martyr." The paper adored Farrar: "'Gerry' on horseback, 'Gerry' leading her army . . . 'Gerry' in the midst of the fight . . . 'Gerry' everywhere." This enthusiastic tone reached yet another level in two decidedly feminist reviews. The "Screen Girl" in the *New York Evening Journal* derided the misuse of power by church and state shown in the film and described Joan as "not the Saint popularly visualized in our minds, but Joan the Woman, a living, suffering person struggling for the freedom of her country." Another essay claimed that the film taught "respect for the power and hearts of womankind who can rise to the highest pinnacle of success without the aid of men" and that the film "will take the conceit out of the male mind."[30]

Joan the Woman happened to open just after the closing of Griffith's anti-war film, *Intolerance,* which also focuses on a central female figure. The films are further connected by the suggestion in both of the crucial place of women in the economy of war. The nature of this role was evident in Farrar's appearance during the Boston run of the film, in which she wrapped herself in the American flag to sing the National Anthem.[31] *The Joan of Arc Journal* is filled with captioned drawings and photographs that associate the film with the war, and more particularly connect Joan of Arc's actions with those of American women. Around a close-up of a pious Farrar looking like an advertisement for facial soap are drawings of Farrar as Joan in a dungeon and of an anonymous woman exiting a chauffeur-driven car. Another image of a praying Farrar as Joan is accompanied by the line "Would Joan of Arc Be Burned Today?" Most pointedly, a drawing of Joan at her spinning wheel is placed next to one of a modern woman working in a factory with the direct appeal: "Who in the world has not heard 'voices'? Imagination is nature's greatest gift to man. . . . Not every poor girl may crown a King—there are not enough kings. . . . 'Joan the Woman' is an inspiration to every girl today. You, who are ambitious, should see it. You, who are sliping [*sic*] in life's battles, will find help in its human lessons."[32]

Looking at DeMille's *Joan the Woman* from a midcentury vantage point, the French critic Luc Moullet captured what is recognized to be problematic in the director's films. DeMille, he wrote, "incarnates the contemporary American culture . . . that which negates problems, mysteries and resolves everything into evidence."[33] In portraying Joan of Arc, DeMille abandoned the heroine's potential for significant ambiguity out of a need to mold a Joan of Arc who could prepare America for war. The French version of the film is a straightforward romance quest, in which Joan is a lightning rod for ecstatic dedication to country. Joan's mystical attraction is only strengthened by the film's strict adherence to the conventional romance plot. On the contrary, variations in the American version attenuate Joan because of the need to use her in relation to the specific social problems related to women during war.

Although DeMille's spectacular film is largely unknown today, it was highly publicized and moderately popular in its time. Within this particular Joan of Arc vogue in the early years of the century, at least nine films about the heroine had been made internationally by 1916. Moreover, the cinema had discovered that it had an affinity for medieval subject matter generally. As the art of space and time manipulation, film showed itself to its greatest advantage in its early days by presenting distant but easily recognizable periods and places as if they existed here and now. The reality effect manifested through photography begged for events as spectacular as a burning at the stake.

For many of the same reasons that film and medievalism were compatible, however, they were also at odds. DeMille's *Joan the Woman* manifests the reason for this ill fit. On one hand, the film is about the life of a saint of the Roman Catholic Church who has been written about, painted, and sculpted for five centuries by some of the world's most gifted artists. On the other hand, the woman representing this figure in a photographic medium characterized by the close-up on a large screen was a famous diva who was a pop icon of her day and known chiefly through fan magazines and the gossip of star discourse. The combination of film's impression of immediacy and photography's reality effect, along with the sense of distance in space, time, and culture, creates a dissonance that Roland Barthes has aptly characterized as that of "an excellent music-hall gag."[34] Citing the later Joan of Arc films by Denmark's Carl Theodor Dreyer (*La Passion de Jeanne d'Arc*, 1928) and France's Robert Bresson (*Le Procès de Jeanne d'Arc*, 1961), Peter Williams rightly notes that the Europeans do better than their American

Geraldine Farrar in Cecil B. DeMille's *Joan the Woman* (1916). (Author's collection)

counterparts with medieval subjects.[35] The reason is found precisely in the deliberate demedievalization cultivated by the Europeans. Both Dreyer's and Bresson's films neutralize sets, costumes, and performance style in order to transmit most clearly the matter of the trial records on which they are scrupulously based. The vulgarity of the American *Joan the Woman*, particularly in regard to its interpolated love story, in relation to the reedited French version exemplifies this difference, and finds its rationale in the particular national contexts and concerns of the First World War.

In the original *Joan the Woman*, Joan of Arc's tale is bracketed by a frame story, in which a World War I soldier, played by the same actor who later plays Joan's lover, pulls a sword from the wall of his bunker, which in turn conjures the ghost of Joan. The hovering heroine tells the contemporary soldier that he must expiate his betrayal of her (committed during his earlier incarnation as her paramour) by accepting a suicide mission. After telling its version of Joan of Arc's life, the film returns to the contemporary frame story with a title declaring that the enemy trench has been destroyed. Joan's ghost then floats over the dead soldier as the film ends. Suggested in this brief description are just a few of the ways DeMille uses cinematic technique to depart from conventional linear storytelling. DeMille superimposes the medieval Joan and the modern French countryside, the split screen showing the battlefield and the interior of the trench, the panoramas of bombs and flying bodies. With these abrupt temporal leaps between centuries, the film simultaneously transports the viewer into the past and brings the medieval into the present with a startling immediacy.

Within the narrative, the frame story adheres more to the romance plot that conventionally establishes heroism than does the body of the film relating Joan's life. The soldier's birth is magical—he is a reincarnation of Joan's lover—and his youth is marked by the miraculous act of pulling a sword from a stone. He is given his quest by a saint, he heroically carries out his mission, and he dies for his country. While Joan compromises France and becomes a victim of her own emotion, irresolution, and bad luck, the soldier embodies the simplicity at the heart of the romance. In addition, Joan's demand for the expiation of her death indicates that her demise was not part of a divine plan but the result of human error. Although Joan of Arc is inspirational, the male soldier is the actual role model for men during the war. The comparison of Joan of Arc's deeds with those of the soldier underlines the film's message that women and war do not mix. Women are welcome to sacrifice themselves for the crusade but the deeds of war itself and the attendant glory are reserved for men, and in particular for men who have not married.

The French version of *Joan the Woman* eliminates the frame story almost entirely. The film begins with Joan's youth rather than that of the young man, and the character of Joan's lover, who is supposedly reincarnated as the young man in the trenches, is identified as an English general. From the start, the absence of the frame excludes the notion that Joan's death was the result of a mortal error that had to be expiated, and it elevates Joan to full heroic status. The French film ends with a brief, decontextualized shot from the excised frame section, which shows an armed Joan of Arc floating over the battlefield. Rather than existing as a specific historical individual, she is an abstract moral quality in female form.

The original film announces its position from the start with a title describing Joan of Arc as "the Girl Patriot, Who Fought with Men, Was Loved by Men, and Killed by Men—Yet Withal Retained the Heart of a Woman." While the traditional quest narrative with its male hero could include a minor love story, *Joan the Woman* evokes the tribulations of Romeo and Juliet far more than those of Saint George and the dragon. DeMille turns the romance into a full-fledged adventure/love story. Joan not only carries out the heroic actions of her mission but also assumes the role of the conventional princess of the romance, whose hand is won by the successful hero. To muddle the issue even further, the male love interest is played by the enemy who is threatening the princess figure in the first place. This chaos, in what conventionally would be a series of clear-cut roles, suggests that a traditionally passive heroine was more desirable than a female hero. The combination of the quest and the love story serve to lower Joan's status to the merely human. She is flawed and her identity and what Lesley Brill calls her "legitimate place in the world" can be established only with a mate.[36] In the same way, Joan's miraculous actions are explained to the degree that they are associated with the illogical and spontaneous world of love.

The importance of the love story in the original film is exemplified by the way Joan's quest is assigned. Saint Michael (rather than the more familiar Saints Margaret and Catherine) gives Joan her directive immediately after her first encounter with the enemy who becomes her lover. During this initial tryst, Joan is infused with erotic power when she slips her hand into the glove of her enemy/lover, Eric Trent. Thus, when the armed Saint Michael appears, one is unsure whether Joan's inspiration comes from the divine force or from her infatuation with a mortal man. This compromise of purity, in terms of both Joan's virginity and her relationship with the enemy, is ultimately attributed to what the film has called Joan's "heart of a woman." This female flaw leaves her incapable of moral absolutes, and her betrayals provide a justification for blaming her for her own death. In addition, the authority that Joan continually confronts is atypically sexual. In the script written by Jeannie MacPherson, the encounter in which Joan meets Saint Michael and Eric Trent is described as follows: "The Radiant Sword . . . begins to glow directly *between* Eric and herself. Joan pulls back, awe-stricken." When Joan touches Trent's gauntlet, her "expression suddenly changes . . . she looks with wide, wondering eyes at the gauntlet. Where, when and how is she to feel that strange touch of steel again?"[37] DeMille's creative interpretation of Joan was rejected by the French, who eliminated Joan's encounter with the enemy entirely and included little of the heroine's innocent youth. Rather than painting Joan of Arc as a naive girl whose success was miraculous, the film takes full advantage of Farrar's mature physical presence to suggest that Joan of Arc was the very embodiment of liberty and strength from the start. The weakness toward the enemy exhibited during Joan's love scene in the original film might have suggested an unacceptable human failure on the part of the French.

The narrative complexity of DeMille's original film is matched by an editing pattern that presents short, dynamic scenes on the battlefield and in the castle so rapidly that any sense of events leading logically from one to another over time is eliminated. The hectic pace and the accumulation of somewhat unrelated story fragments facilitate the introduction of the unconventional additions to the story. The quest itself, with the depiction of the battle of Orléans, the coronation, and the capture, is interspersed with sequences involving Joan's lover. These appendages transform the penultimate stage of the romance, including the time suffered in jail and the march to the stake, into the climax of a love story in which Joan gives up her boyfriend for her country. Although Joan still acts nobly by sacrificing herself, her virtue is strictly personal. The restoration of the traditional gender hierarchy that comes with her death is her ultimate act of patriotism.

The climax of the quest, in which Joan defeats the English at Orléans, contains the most marked example of the reformation of the romance in terms usually reserved for the love story. In a victory that conventionally would be portrayed as the simple triumph of good over evil, the conquest is bathed in dramatic irony. Not knowing that Joan is leading the French, Trent mocks and threatens his opposite number while Joan marches forward to defeat her unrecognized enemy. The scene depicts not the hero's apotheosis but the minor tragedy of a world that pits lovers against each other. The gist of the romance, which is the creation of moral absolutes, is irrelevant here, since both sides represent thwarted virtue.

Joan the Woman's depiction of the victory at Orléans is followed by a scene in which Joan gazes at a cross given to her by Trent, torn over whether to bestow her allegiance on him or on France. Although Joan chooses her country, she frees Trent in a maudlin gesture for which she pays with her life. At a crucial moment, the assertion that had characterized this Joan gives way to indecision and passivity. Joan's enemies make the most of her emotional weakness and lack of military cunning by using Trent to capture and finally kill her. Too sentimental to imprison her lover/enemy, Joan sacrifices herself for her man. As the film's introduction says, she may have entered the male realm temporarily but her female heart brings her back to her social place in the end. Joan not only chooses her own death over his but sacrifices her public task for her private life, thus demonstrating woman's essential unsuitability for the male job of war.

In contrast to the American Joan, whose quest is tangled with erotic longing, the French Joan challenges the English invaders even before her mission is divinely instigated. This Joan is introduced as she strides down the street of her deserted village, ready to defend her native soil, already holding a baby that she has rescued from its fear-stricken parents. The message she later receives from above is a mere formality. Whether through intuition or simple faith in her virtue, Joan is confident of victory. This initial encounter between good (the French) and evil (the English) is as clear-cut as in any Western. In fact, the English general, identified as Joan's nemesis, Talbot,[38] confronts the "pious and modest" young woman with a gang of men on horseback in the middle of the town's main street.

The physical excision of large portions of the original film for the French version has other repercussions as well. On one level, the scenes that follow

Saint Michael's initiation of the mission are compressed so that the events of the quest, such as the visit to the dauphin, become a juggernaut unaffected by historical complexity. In addition, the dynamic battle scenes, which are balanced in the original by the many segments involving Joan's mundane affairs, dominate the French film. The relative length and number of fighting sequences seem to glorify war and idealize the soldiers. The elimination of both the more human aspects of the romance and the stabilizing historical context of the original film's frame story serves a similar purpose. The *Joan the Woman* seen in France made Joan's story more familiar and thus more plausible, modeling aggression and valor for the soldiers of the First World War.

In eliminating the debilitating effects of Joan's love for a mortal man, the editors made the French version of *Joan the Woman* a purer romance. The original film demythologizes Joan so that the quest is constantly in danger of failure and never appears to be absolutely virtuous and right. Although the French version also humanizes the story by making military success the result of native strength rather than divine intervention, it schematically opposes good and evil. The French audience is given none of the mixed messages of the original. War is not the tragedy of divided loyalties but an unambiguous crusade for the integrity of the French nation. The revised film's attempt to make Joan a romantic hero at times overcompensates for DeMille's creative excess and elevates Joan's story at least temporarily to myth. For example, rather than enduring the symbolic nine-month wait to convince her superiors of the merit of her quest, when the French Joan cuts her general's sword in half she magically transforms him into a believer. In her peasant strength and directness, this Joan represents an all-powerful France taking its rightful position once and for all.

DeMille's original film includes very little of Joan's imprisonment and trial. The minimization of these events attributes Joan's death not to her challenge to the institutions of her day but to the demented actions of a few personally motivated individuals who fear her as a witch. Substituted for these segments is a sequence in which Joan's lover/enemy attempts a cowboy-style rescue. Although the rescue fails, the gesture gives Joan the strength to stand up for what she has done. Joan's romance is a melodramatic love affair in which the heroine faces a particularly nasty punishment at the end, rather than the traditional journey from innocence through ex-

Geraldine Farrar in *Joan the Woman* (1916). (Author's collection)

perience to a higher innocence. The romance hero and role model in *Joan the Woman* is the soldier of the frame story, whose noble death ends the film.

The French version of the film eliminates the most obviously Western-style sequences and manages to attribute Joan's demise to the machinations of evil advisers, rather than to the good if ineffectual King Charles VII. Yet, much as in the original version, Joan barely suffers, and rather than showing the traditional fear or doubt, she displays only resignation and ennui. The film departs from the romance by excluding the temporary fall and the test inherent in the quest. As the personification of France during a difficult historical period, she is indefatigable. Joan dies in the French film as a passive and maternal figure whose immolation is meant to inspire or shame men into action. DeMille makes Joan of Arc the very sign of the inviolable nation by placing wings on his heroine and superimposing her image over the battlefields of World War I in the frame story that concludes *Joan the Woman*. The viewer is reminded that Joan may have existed and succeeded in history but that she disappeared in smoke as an appropriately self-sacrificing female. DeMille visualizes this concept in the often reproduced still from his film in which Farrar stands with arms extended in the light formed by a giant fleur-de-lys.

Finally, *Joan the Woman* was a commercial product that softened its propaganda so as neither to insult European allies nor to offend the American public. The original film offered a role model for women during a war for which a strong Joan of Arc would have been inappropriate. France, on the contrary, was desperately in need of a hero when it received DeMille's ersatz version of Joan of Arc's life. In addition, since Joan had been beatified in 1909 and her early canonization was anticipated, France was more interested than usual in magnifying the image of its progenitor and national heroine. By rearranging DeMille's film to adhere more closely to the romance plot, the French transformed it from a dramatization of gender roles to a plea for national pride and self-sacrifice. The comparison between the two versions of the film manifests particularly well the degree to which the historical film is concerned chiefly with its own place and time.

Sumiko Higashi notes that *Joan the Woman* did not attract its anticipated crowds, despite the huge amount of publicity, discussion, and praise the film received.[39] Higashi argues that the film failed because it did not create a sense of community across class and ethnic lines, but rather used the pageant model of historical display and summary to create an idealized notion of the past in accordance with the dominant culture. What is at stake in this study is not the film's financial or popular success but the fact that investors were willing to risk unusually large sums of money during a war on a Joan of Arc vehicle. The publicity surrounding the film and the way Joan of Arc was represented reveal much about popular notions of female heroism during the First World War.

⊸⊷⟾ 3 The Demise of Joan of Arc

One of the more unusual Joan of Arc documents born of the First World War is a short, quirky book that was apparently self-published in 1926 by one William Paul Yancey titled *The Soldier Virgin of France: A Message of World Peace by a Soldier of the A.E.F.* Yancey's conclusion that Joan of Arc's highest accomplishment was to become a "sacred torch," as opposed to winning battles, is characteristic of a narrowing of the heroine's significance in relation to war in the United States after World War I. With the disillusionment that followed the end of the war, the virgin warrior had lost her appeal as a subject around whom to create a work of art. Instead, Joan was more often a device through which to speak about more general issues, such as the preparedness movement, as evidenced in the George Loane Tucker film *Joan of Plattsburg* of 1918. Representations of a strong Joan of Arc had served their purpose when women's resources had to be appropriately directed, but as soldiers began to return home to the shifting gender roles of the period, the independent Joan epitomized by Geraldine Farrar in DeMille's *Joan the Woman* was ever less attractive.

Yancey's conflicted adulation of Joan of Arc is simultaneously a call for peace, an antipacifist tract, and a book of advice for women. The text praises the mystical Joan of Arc and admits to making up some of her story, yet is loaded with appeals to logic, proof, and truth in a narrative that weaves George Washington and Theodore Roosevelt into the medieval tale. Although the writer's anxiety is evident in lines such as "We have reason to believe that somewhere in the vast universe there is a central place where an eternal commander directs . . . like a wise executive," the book captures the period's ambivalence toward Joan. Yancey envisions Joan as a little sister to the Virgin Mary, who is likewise an example rather than an agent. For example, Joan "was commanded," Joan "was given," "it was decided," and Joan "did not attempt to command the expedition. She only expressed desires and wishes, leaving all decisions to her knights." The very idea of Joan's physical presence causes the author consternation. Joan is a "tall, vigorous girl as God intended" with a "boyish form," yet she is a seductress on the battlefield, as "the opposite side simply gazed spellbound at the sight of a beautiful girl in dazzling armor, holding a sacred pennon aloft while she gracefully rode a magnificent black horse at the head of an advancing column." The description of her as "beautiful yet so manly" suggests that Joan moved disturbingly between the categories that defined the functions of women and men during war.[1]

As a book of advice for women, the book continues this slippage between roles. Yancey writes that women now

> must go out into the world to do the work of men; when they are often forced to do coarse work and be surrounded by coarse men amid the dangers of the world, they very much need a model of faith, of chastity, of purity of body and mind, of devotion to line of duty and of willingness to abstain from such gratifications as may mar their ability for success. [In addition] the world needs a model to teach men respect for the rights of woman. Man needs to be taught that the Creator does not intend woman to be his slave or toy, but to do her part of the world's work.[2]

Later Yancey abruptly inquires: "Ye twentieth century girls: What would you do? . . . You have a valid excuse for failure to fulfill your mission . . . take the hand of the knight whose heart you have won, and leave the unworthy king his fate. But you would, like Jeanne, rise above your difficulties and tell the temptor where to go."[3] The goal of this mission finally is represented in an image found often in the poetry of the time, in which Joan is likened to a sacred torch. In this free play with history, legend, and expediency Yancey encapsulates many of the reasons Joan was so useful in the war years. She inspired and shamed men to act and eventually disappeared.

More specifically, Joan of Arc entered the discourse of the preparedness movement through *Joan of Plattsburg*, directed by George Loan Tucker. While the title may sound humorous today, it in fact refers to a well-known officer's training camp in Plattsburg, New York, which has been described as "a conversion experience of patriotism, individual responsibility, and collective action" that changed the moral direction of a generation of upper-class young American men, whose convictions then became law for the rest of the country.[4] The first camp was held in the summer of 1915; by 1916 a junior Plattsburg had been started for boys from the age of twelve and a Women's Preparedness Camp was established outside Washington. The movement became a craze: individuals used private funds for volunteer corps, people drilled during their lunch hours, a thirteen-year-old girl raised $20,000 through the donation of 10-cent stamps, and a Boston auxiliary registered cars "for the purpose of carrying the virgins inland in case of invasion."[5] The inspiration for these measures came from the mythic imagery that had been called forth through the use of figures like Joan of Arc. For example, the 1919 book *The Maid of Orleans: The Story of Joan of Arc for Girls,* by M. S. C. Smith, figurally aligns Joan's peasant hovel with Lincoln's log cabin and her leaving of it with the departure of American boys for the front. Likewise, when finally forced to advocate the war, President Wilson spoke of Joan and Orléans in tandem with Grant and Appomattox to imply the cyclical necessity of the Great War.[6]

Joan of Plattsburg was released in mid-1918 with much fanfare and press coverage. The reference to Joan of Arc seems to have been widely understood: several reviews of the film casually compared its heroine with "Joan of old." The noted eccentricity of this film may be attributable to its star, the slapstick comedian Mabel Normand, who was known for her bawdy performances in Max Sennett films, and the context in which the film was shown. In this ostensibly serious film, Normand was described as being "the funniest ever."[7] The *Exhibitor's Trade Review* of May 18, 1918, suggested that the film be presented in theaters as part of a theme night. The French flag was to cover the stage and the "Marseillaise" played. In the issue of May 25, 1918, the Rivoli Theatre in New York is described as presenting the impressive musical offering "'Jeanne d'Arc Speaks': Original Nocturnal Fantasy." Surrounded by the Rialto Male Quartet, a woman apparently costumed as Joan sat posed on a pedestal and sang. While this practice of framing a film in extra-cinematic events was not unique, the juxtaposition of the Normand persona with the serious apparatus of French patriotism was probably somewhat jarring.

The film itself, which was provided with a musical setting, tells the story of an orphan girl in Plattsburg who is given a biography of Joan of Arc by one of the officers at the camp. One reviewer described the film as follows: "Somehow or other she got dreaming of Joan of Arc and strange as it may seem she was able to save her country from a band of enemy spies. The amusing story of this little girl's life is amusingly told." This article was accompanied by a full-page advertisement for the film featuring a photograph of Normand in skirted armor that is several sizes too big for her, with the visor of the upturned helmet lifted to show her face peeking out with a hint of a smile on her lips.[8] The film is driven by a series of accidents through which Normand's character discovers German spies and has them caught before marrying one of the soldiers at the camp. One article about the film, which described "the new Mabel Normand" as having moved from "hoydenish comedy to inspired patriotism and beautiful self-sacrifice," saw the film's message as "calculated to teach the truth that no matter how humble a person may be, she may do her part in service of her country."[9] The reduction of war to romance and melodrama may have helped to overcome the disillusionment at the end of the war by linking it to the battles of a storybook Joan of Arc.

At the same time, the film was repeatedly praised for *not* being a war film. The *Exhibitor's Herald* of 4 May 1918 assured the reader that there were not "any of the depressing features usually found in a photodrama dealing with the great conflict." Instead the film would "arouse intense zeal and fire latent patriotism" and would answer the question "What can I do for my country?" The use of the sexy, modern Normand to play Joan of Arc took advantage of one of the chief characteristics of the historical film. As noted earlier, the sense of anachronism created by costumes from the past in the inescapably present and contemporary medium of the cinema is often ludicrous. Yet in this case the usually contradictory forces of sexual energy, moral imperative, and altruism are united. One reviewer of the film found fault with Normand for being overwhelmingly physical and incapable of showing spiritual transformation.[10] *Wid's Daily* wrote that "Mabel's too darned plump and easy to gaze upon to be considered one of those ethereal spiritual gooks who imagine things."[11] In sum, the film reflects the dichotomy between the virgin and the whore; the spirit of Joan of Arc provides men with the rationale for fighting, while the body of Mabel Normand makes it all worthwhile.

Joan of Plattsburg's message to the women of the United States is similarly bifurcated. The film suggests that women are to provide potential soldiers with the intensity of a Mabel Normand to show that the home fires will continue to burn. This display, however, must be seen as a form of self-sacrifice, which is to say that women are also to possess the spiritual purity and, however impossibly, the chastity of Joan of Arc. Normand herself seems to have acted out the effects of the film's contradictions. Told by the film's producer, Samuel Goldwyn, to appear onstage at the film's Washington, D.C., premiere with Mrs. Woodrow Wilson, Normand purportedly arrived late and inebriated. Her feeling toward the role had been in evidence throughout the shooting of the film, during which she apparently was fond of mocking the earnest portrayal of Joan by Geraldine Farrar in DeMille's film by striking melodramatic attitudes.[12] Norman's theatrical behavior brought attention to DeMille's use of the formal logic of the nineteenth-century tableau, in which women were posed so as to make historical subjects seem mythic.[13] It is impossible to know whether Normand found Joan of Arc to be the silly figure she apparently enacted in the film or whether she recognized that the juxtaposition of the conventional meaning of Joan and her own comic persona was inherently absurd.

The contradictions born of Mabel Normand in the role of Joan of Arc suggest some of the diversity in women's roles and attitudes toward them during the war. Ranging from numerous forms of engagement to pacifism, these roles were not easily encompassed by Western concepts of armed civic virtue. As Jean Bethke Elshtain has noted in this regard, women have traditionally behaved in war as private mirrors held up to male deeds or willing sacrificers of sons.[14] The film producer Jesse Lasky best captured the conflict over the roles of women in a letter on the subject of Mary Pickford written in March 1917 to DeMille and Jeannie MacPherson, the scriptwriter of *Joan the Woman*. Lasky wrote: "I wonder if you and Jeannie couldn't write something typically American and something that would portray a girl in the sort of role that the feminists in the country are now interested in—the kind of girl who jumps in and does a man's work when men are at the front."[15] Lasky's ideal was an amalgamation of American types, including Woman as natural pacifist and The Girl from melodrama with the gumption to fill in as needed.

The popularity of *Joan of Plattsburg* demonstrates the degree to which the

World War I poster for the United War Work campaign. Adolphe Treidler, colored lithograph (c. 1918). (Museum of the City of New York, 43.40.630)

particularly American girl had become a new and influential version of the woman warrior. Posters showing spunky, attractive women in work clothes with captions such as "For Every Fighter a Woman Worker" created a discourse of equality between men and women. In April 1917 the *New York Times* advertised what it called a "military preparedness suit" for women, with a photograph of women in a self-defense league charging with bayonets. This fashion-based advertising and the use of terms such as "Yeomenettes" for the Navy and "Marinettes" for the Marines indicate an awareness that the successful recruitment of women for war work had the potential to backfire.[16] Once women had abandoned corsets for trousers, gained skills and a sense of competence, and felt free to smoke and drink in public, it would be difficult to go backward. In literature, in advertising, and especially in film, women were seen flying, driving, and spying. Michael Isenberg in fact concludes that the disparity between film and reality was greatest in regard to women's roles.[17] The considerable rift between what women did in movies and what they could expect to do in actual life probably made it more likely that women would remain in their traditional places. Until about 1920, the idea of women fighters was so unlikely as to be safely showable. Yet as women appeared to begin to enjoy their new roles, Joan of Arc all but disappeared as a military figure until her transformation after the Second World War.

The Dissipation of Joan of Arc after World War I

One of the best-selling books of the First World War, with eight editions by 1919, was *The Love of an Unknown Soldier,* which was ostensibly based on letters found in a tin box in an empty trench on the western front. These romantic epistles were purportedly from a shy English soldier to an American Red Cross nurse. He compares her to a modern Joan of Arc, whose "charger is a Ford car."[18] While the book converts the female warrior into a romantic figure, the story's elevation of people whose lives have been lost indicates a more profound use of Joan. In a war in which technology had all but erased individuality, Joan's distinctness and the general sense of her purity and ascension through pain made her an icon of the lost. Each death in the war therefore could be seen as unique through her. As a ritual figure who had already died, Joan of Arc could be invoked to extend the hope of those who were threatened and to purge the guilt of the survivors.

For the most part, Joan of Arc's value declined as the war progressed. Early in the century, Grover Cleveland spoke of the nature of the female role in war in a way that complicated the status of the woman warrior. Cleveland described women as constituting "an army of . . . constancy and love, whose yearning hearts make men brave and patriotic. They . . . transmit through mysterious agencies, to soldiers in the field the spirit of endurance and devotion. Soldiers . . . never forget to accord to woman the noble service of inspiration she has thus wrought with womanly weapons wielded in her appointed place."[19] While these "womanly weapons" may well have been love and faith, they also could be interpreted to refer to the techniques of irregular warfare, including "concealment of wireless sets, sexual infiltration, terror and sabotage" carried out by "disorganizers . . . teachers, [and] spreaders of propaganda."[20] However necessary these roles were during the war, they ultimately suggested that women are inherently deceitful and devoid of conviction. By this logic, women are doomed even when they succeed at their tasks. The part of the Joan of Arc story in which Joan recants before finally reasserting the reality of her voices was particularly useful in implying that women can help in war but are not fully trustworthy.

A series of three films made during the United States' involvement in the war illustrates the ways in which Joan of Arc was construed as irregular and progressively defused as an inspirational image for women. *Susan Rocks the Boat,* made by Paul Powell and produced by D. W. Griffith in 1916, stars Dorothy Gish as a bored society girl who decides to use her energy and money to help the poor by founding the Joan of Arc Mission. According to the description of the film in a contemporaneous *Moving Picture World,* the protagonist has done "much reading of the story of Joan of Arc, [and] is inspired to become a modern Joan."[21] This act apparently makes men want to "take advantage of the young girl's innocence," and particular note is taken of a man with "a trace of resentment for her interference." A later review in the same issue connects Gish more closely with Joan of Arc by featuring a photograph of her wearing a hat that strongly resembles a helmet, while *Variety* appreciates the film for Gish's funny walk after she spends too much time on a horse.[22] Finally, the same *Moving Picture World* review notes that, although "her honest little venture is an interesting one," Susan's only success lies in nursing the male lead back to health after he is injured while saving her, then transforming him through love. The film's reviews stress that the active woman who "rocks the boat" under Joan of Arc's inspiration both physically and ideologically endangers the world around her.

Womanhood, the Glory of a Nation was made by J. Stuart Blackton for Vitagraph in 1917, apparently with suggestions by "ex-President Roosevelt," and with an appearance by Woodrow Wilson. In this action-oriented preparedness film, Mary Ward falls in love with a foreigner whose country has attacked New York City. Mary, whose mother and sister were killed in the battle, is rescued from her error by Paul Strong, the "Minister of Energies." Mary seduces the foreign enemy/ex-lover in order to extract secrets that help to lead the United States to victory. Meanwhile, Paul's unnamed sister is killed while impersonating Joan of Arc during a preparedness rally. The film implies that women should use sex and love as they are told, since their own instincts are faulty, and that playing the woman warrior is not only ineffective but deadly. A contemporaneous source, which uses language that ignores the very existence of women, states that "if [the film] does not wake every spark of manhood in a person, that person is not much of a man."[23]

In late 1918, Joseph De Grasse's *The Wildcat of Paris* was released by Universal Studios. Set in Paris, the film relates the story of Collette, known as Wildcat (but called Joan of the Apaches in the *Exhibitor's Trade Review*), who is caught by a painter named Jean as she attempts to rob his studio.Later, while painting her, Jean "teaches [Collette] to pose, and her soul is awakened by hearing the story of Joan of Arc." The Wildcat's notorious temper and untamed sexuality are subdued by Jean's presence. In the course of the film Collette emulates Joan of Arc under Jean's orders, and her rousing speech leads the Apaches to the battle front, where her single act is to save a young girl from German brutality.[24] Jean, bearing the masculine version of Joan of Arc's name, reveals that the outlaw female is incompetent, then tames her by telling her Joan's story and integrates her into patriarchal law through marriage.

By the end of World War I, the discourse of the modern role of women in war had solidified in a way that made the active warrior Joan unusable. Whether women drove ambulances, acted as couriers, or nursed the wounded, they were said to be "behind the lines." The film *Woman*, however, directed by Maurice Tourneur in late 1918, indicates that the boundary demarcating the sexual division of labor in war had slipped. In the film, a man whose wife has left him looks in the encyclopedia for a definition of "woman" and finds that "woman has been the cause of trouble in various ways throughout the ages and never really found her place until the opportunity of war work was presented to her."[25] In the First World War, women's work was defined as being behind the lines, since the experience of death in battle belonged to men and differentiated them from women.[26] However, the boundaries that had divided masculine and feminine and life and death in previous wars had not held in World War I. In this first modern technological war there was little difference between being at the front and being behind the lines. In *Good-bye to All That* of 1930, Robert Graves reflected on his experience in World War I: "Patriotism. There was no patriotism in the trenches. It was too remote a sentiment, and rejected as fit only for civilians."[27] Clearly, anyone who had been near the front knew the brutality and wastefulness of the war. Yet the attempt was made to keep women from the trenches so that they could serve in their traditional role as an audience for stories that might redeem the experience of the war for the teller.

By the end of the 1920s war had become an unpopular subject in the cinema. *Motion Picture* magazine wrote, "The 'war stuff' thrills us no more. . . . Now we have become blasé and bored with warfare."[28] Yet Joan of Arc, cloaked in the mythic and distant past, continued to function to a degree as a distracting tool for dealing with postwar trauma. On one hand, it may have been satisfying to those who had suffered in the war, for the sake of women who had then seized their independence, to witness the archetypal woman warrior burning at the stake. Yet women's antiwar groups such as the Women's Peace Party, started by Jane Addams and Carrie Chapman Catt early in 1915 with the slogan "War against war," had rejected all warriors, including female ones, throughout the war. In 1916 the poet Amy Lowell described war as a "social disease" that was alien to femininity. She expressed horror at being conceptualized as the stake of war, for which she knew she must be resented. The disgust and sense of impotence at being simultaneously reduced to doing trivial tasks such as knitting and "elevated" to the symbolic cause of war are expressed in her poem "In the Stadium." There is nothing glorious or redemptive in war, which she describes as

The white bodies of young men
Heaped like sandbags
Against the German guns.

This is war:
Boys flung into a breach
Like shovelled earth.[29]

When Lowell refers to a medieval woman in a later poem called "Patterns," it is not to a gloriously armored Joan of Arc but to a grieving woman in an ornamental garden, who is imprisoned in the stiff material of an elaborate dress.[30]

Male combatants, who had been recruited through the discourse of myth and chivalry, would have expected to return from World War I to civilian life and to the women they had left behind. Yet the war had led to major social shifts that found women in jobs formerly held by men and either remarried to younger men or happily independent. With the bobbed hair and free dress of the flapper as the very signs of these new women, the original short-haired woman-of-the-world began to lose popularity. In addition, the extremity of Joan of Arc's experience, which previously had been so attractive to what Lears calls this weightless era, had become too concrete. The war was over and the drive for self-fulfillment was now more easily placated through consumption as opposed to action. Medievalism did not disappear, however, but had been absorbed by the WASP ruling class as a symbol of vitality and integrity in architecture and social organizations.[31] Even more than other icons of the Middle Ages, Joan of Arc began to appear on consumer goods, and the juxtaposition so undermined her image that she was eventually thought to be but a legend, despite her canonization by the Catholic Church in 1920.

Indeed, Joan of Arc was declared a saint 500 years after she died for very practical reasons. After the French lost Alsace and Lorraine in the Franco-Prussian War of 1870, the Alliance Française was born in a spirit of revenge and anger. This right-wing, xenophobic organization took Joan as its symbol because she had been born in Lorraine and stood for the concept of France for the French. During the First World War, the pro-Austrian pope was disturbed by the growth of the group, and when he condemned the organization, many French left the church and he had little choice but to sanctify Joan to placate them. Yet this common explanation of political expediency ignores the fact that the sanctification of Joan as a virgin martyr rather than as a militant one disarmed Joan as a model for female independence. A sympathetic writer in the *Literary Digest* in 1920 regretted Joan's canonization because "it seems to carry her further back into the mystic region of legend in which she is too deep already."[32] The two photographs that accompany these words show, first, the often-reproduced wartime image of crowds of people around the Hyatt statue of Joan of Arc in New York, but also an increasingly familiar scene from a pageant with a white-gowned, praying Joan tied to the stake. This new trend was to be found in poetry as well, with Joan no longer an agent but "a votive taper between us and God!" or "a sword—in Hand divine!"[33]

Not insignificantly, the 1879 painting of Joan of Arc by Jules Bastien-Lepage owned by the Metropolitan Museum of Art in New York found new favor in the early 1920s. The canvas shows a matronly peasant Joan at home with saints, who are seen as ghostly figures behind her. In 1924 *The Mentor* claimed that the painting had been criticized because "it had been the custom to portray the girl warrior in armor with gleaming shield and banner."[34] The Catholic *Living Age* of 1919 supported the painting, which it described in an extended essay that was dismissive of Joan except when "she knew her place." The reviewer directly commented on cultural uses of Joan and expressed the backlash against the new, active woman who had been inspired by the woman warrior.

> Although sculpture and painting have been pressed into the service of the Maid, there has been a certain dissatisfying unreality in most of these achievements. One of the countrymen of the Maid of Lorraine, impatient at the fancy of idealized statues and pictures of the peasant girl, boasted that he would paint a true Jeanne. . . . It somehow explains Jeanne. She is essentially a peasant, strong-boned, awkward perhaps; the wrists are thick, and there is a hint of thick ankles under the heavy homespun skirt. . . . [This] simple child of the soil looks quite out of herself into the region of things spiritual, unworldly and eternal. On her innocent soul the divine inspiration falls unimpeded by mists of self and sin.[35]

This combination of a mundane peasant and a suffering martyr found its way into many of the postwar biographies with revealing titles such as *St.*

Jules Bastien-Lepage, *Joan of Arc* (1879). (The Metropolitan Museum of Art)

Jeanne d'Arc: The Mystical Story of a Girl and the People (Minna Caroline Smith, 1922) and *My Jeanne d'Arc* (Michael Monahan, 1928).

This familiarization of Joan was accompanied by numerous attempts to appropriate the heroine's life as a legitimate area of study. The medical community was concerned with the anomalous physical manifestation of Joan's voices and explained her as a hysteric, a schizophrenic, and a paranoiac. In a similar way, the occult community focused on her connection to the otherworldly, dismissing what she actually did, with articles such as

"The Clairvoyance of Jeanne d'Arc."[36] Anthropological approaches such as that of Margaret Murray imagined Joan as a late Druid.[37] An extremely enthusiastic essay about Joan called "St. Jeanne d'Arc as a Soldier" appeared in *The National Review* in 1920. Claiming that it had yet to be done in English, E. W. Sheppard discussed Joan at length from "the purely military point of view," to find that her strategy, her intuition, and her knowledge were flawless and equal to Napoleon's. By the end of the essay, however, after descriptions of her faith, glamour, and idealism, Joan was overidealized as "more than human" and "a bright particular star that flashes for one brief moment across the heavens and finds its death in a blaze of fire."[38]

In the difficult postwar period, when relationships between men and women and new roles for women were in transition in the United States, the combination of woman and warrior was an uneasy one. From his position in a more stable and repressed society, Bernard Shaw was able to write the play *Saint Joan,* which straightforwardly portrays Joan as an annoying embarrassment to the social and political order of her time. The play premiered in New York in December 1923 and opened in London the following March. Carolyn Heilbrun has described Shaw's Joan as the prototype of the female hero because she is preposterous. Coming from left field, she is scarcely human, much less heroic, as she chooses to die in order to become a "functioning moral being."[39] The shift in Joan's significance from the wholesome, passively sexy girl epitomized in Haskell Coffin's World War I fund-raising poster to something less appealing is evident in the references to Joan in popular music of the 1920s and later. Songs such as "Joan of Arc, They Are Calling You" of 1917 were replaced by "Joan of Arkansas," which begins "I went down to Arkansas and met a girl named Joan," and a song by Jerome Kern with two titles: "Joan of Arc Was on Her Own When She Was Quite a Child" and the official title, "You Can't Keep a Good Girl Down."

In 1921, the last of the silent films with a Joan of Arc subtext appeared. *Sheltered Daughters,* directed by Edward Dillon, considers how women were to be controlled once they had embarked on the path to equal rights and economic freedom. With a motherless daughter named Jenny Dark under the care of a powerful policeman father, the film invokes the archetypal fairy-tale family. Probably unintentionally, the film characterizes the overly protective father, who would rather see his daughter dead than "immoral," with a detail from the original Joan of Arc narrative, in which Joan's father misinterpreted her mission and threatened to kill her as a camp follower. The heroine, called a "reincarnated Jeanne d'Arc" by *Variety*, is kept by her father in a world of books, where she dreams that she is a descendant of Joan of Arc.[40] Jenny inadvertently helps a group of crooks impersonate French soldiers who are supposedly collecting money for war orphans. Jenny is saved by her father, who continues to shelter her by marrying her to the man who helped to rescue her.

More interesting than *Sheltered Daughters* itself is the metatext recommended to theater owners by the film's distributors.[41] In a scenario to be enacted before the film was begun, a light was to reveal a girl in horn-rimmed glasses sitting on the stage, reading a book. With the "Marseillaise" playing, an armored Joan of Arc was to appear and advise the girl that every "sheltered daughter" has a duty to help in the world. At this point a local charity, such as an organization offering aid to war orphans, was to be advertised. This prologue suggests that the intellectual woman was less than helpful in the war effort and that women's volunteer work should be child-oriented. Moreover, Joan of Arc is portrayed as a mere figment of the dreamer's imagination. In a second recommendation, film exhibitors were advised to supplement the film with a fashion show to reflect a similar event that takes place in the film. This article and others stress that the film's strength lay in the beauty of its star, Justine Johnstone, and in her modeling of morally correct behavior for women. The purpose of these extrafilmic events was clear during the war—they were ways to create excitement and increase recruitment. After the war, this need to reinforce the film's message seems overly anxious.

Ten years after the appearance of *Joan the Woman*, William Wellman made *Wings*, which won the first Academy Award for best picture (1927–28). Starring Clara Bow, the film focuses on the relationship between two American boys, played by Charles "Buddy" Rogers and Richard Arlen, as they experience the thrills and horrors of the First World War. A subplot concerns the girl back home, who independently goes to France as a driver, dresses in military uniform, and is highly competent in her job. The significance of her role in the film increases when she attempts to save the man she loves from drunken humiliation and subsequent court-martial. To carry out this quest, the heroine changes from her uniform into a risqué sequined dress to seduce the wayward soldier out of a bar, so that she can take him to his

room and put him to bed. Before she can leave the soldier's quarters, however, she is caught by the military, half in the dress and half in her uniform.
Without question, this woman warrior is identified as a camp follower and
punished by being sent home and given no credit for her war work. The
men soar on to glory and one survives to return home and marry the girl.
The film celebrates male exploits and masculine affection, yet the control of
female sexuality and the maintenance of traditional women's roles are an
important subtext. Not many years after the heroine of *Wings* was sent home
from the war in shame, World War II again demanded the full participation
of women. For reasons to be explored in the next chapter, the vigorous Joan
of Arc of the First World War was no longer considered to be an appropriate
role model.

⤳⟹ 4 Joan of Arc between the Wars

The propaganda images of strong, competent women that had been used for recruitment during the First World War had largely disappeared by 1920. The freedom of the New Woman, embodied by Clara Bow, known as the "It" girl, who starred in *Wings,* or by Joan of Arc herself, had been more a media phenomenon than a reality. Although women had won the right to vote in 1920, the modern woman of the next decade did not effect a great deal of political change. The old upper-class model of femininity prevailed as women aspired to be intelligent, educated, and progressive, as well as beautiful, well-dressed, fun, and unoccupied outside the home.[1] A "Credo of the Newest New Woman" that appeared in the *Ladies Home Journal* in mid-1920 expressed the contradictions of the time:

> I believe in woman's rights; but I believe in woman's sacrifices also.
>
> I believe in woman's freedom; but I believe it should be within the restrictions of the Ten Commandments.
>
> I believe in woman suffrage; but I believe many other things are vastly more important.
>
> I believe in woman's brains; but I believe still more in her emotions.
>
> I believe in woman's assertion of self; but I believe also in her obligation of service to her family, her neighbors, her nation and her God.
>
> Following that faith we have the most modern expression of feminism. The newest new woman deifies not herself, but through her new freedom elects to serve others.[2]

Before 1920, the representation of the simultaneously militant and pious Joan of Arc linked the two poles of each of these oppositions imaginatively.

After the war, which had allowed women to experience or envision real independence, a life lived according to both sides of the equations had become unfeasible.

The period between the two world wars was rife with contradictions for American women, chiefly as a result of the rise of consumer culture. Women were to remain at home to run the family, but at the same time they had to work to pay for the rising standard of living. Women who worked outside the home after the war were portrayed as selfish unless the task was conceptualized as what the Department of Labor called "a stop-gap between whatever girlhood lay behind . . . and marriage."[3] The invention of Mother's Day in 1914 implies that the institution of motherhood had lost some of its natural status. As a means of solidifying the maternal role and its concomitant housekeeping duties, these tasks were ever more conceptualized to include the wider community. A well-known World War I poster called "The Greatest Mother in the World," by Alonso Earl Forringer, exemplifies the campaign to elevate the role of motherhood. The poster features a huge Red Cross nurse looming over a tiny soldier who rests on a stretcher cradled in her arms. This was also the era in which the care of the home and children was first professionalized in women's colleges, which officially started to train women as homemakers. In the first decades of the century, the serious university woman could be assimilated comfortably as an eccentric militant figure. Once large numbers of women aspired to higher education and the independence it allowed, the woman warrior motif largely disappeared from popular culture.

The American woman's social and economic situation in this transitional era was complicated by her shifting role in the culture of consumption. The rise of women's magazines, which were financed by manufacturers of household and grooming products, depended on the image of the happy homemaker. A *Life* magazine article of 1941 indicates that the domestication project initiated in the 1920s had succeeded. In a photo spread headed "Occupation: Housewife," the text informed the reader that "in the movies, in fiction and advertising in women's magazines, the modern U.S. housewife is portrayed as the sort of woman who keeps her figure, her husband, her makeup and her humor no matter how tough the going. One effect of this constant propaganda is that millions of U.S. women are doing just that."[4] In her study of Hollywood's depiction of "working girls" in the 1920s,

World War I poster for the Red Cross by Alonso Earl Foringer (c. 1917). (The George C. Marshall Research Foundation)

Sumiko Higashi discusses a standard narrative in which the young heroine achieves this middle-class ideal by first earning money to help her family and also gaining the chic veneer of independence.[5] Yet the nature of the heroine's labor is telling. The film *Manhandled,* for example, features a salesgirl; the main character in *Stage Struck* is a waitress; Mary Pickford is a stock clerk in *My Best Girl.* In all of these films the job that places the woman low in the hierarchy of consumption is a way station on the road to the ever-desired goals of marriage and motherhood. The central plot line in which the working girl's unaffected spontaneity captivates the affluent boss's son provides a lesson in patience and humility and implicitly validates consumer culture. Even a figure as unrelated to consumerism and marriage as Joan of Arc came to fit this model in a 1928 book by Theda Kenyon, *Jeanne: The Love-Story of the Maid of France.* One reviewer of the book described Joan as the "dupe of conniving priests and necromancers" and "the hysteric sweetheart of a wealthy youth," who is actually saved from burning at the stake.[6]

While this homemaking model for female behavior was ever more effective in contributing to the rise of American economic strength through the 1920s, women's roles became less stable in the Depression years. By 1933, with 30 percent of the population unemployed and American incomes at half what they were in 1929, women were both eliminated from the workforce in favor of jobless men and forced to work harder domestically to make up for reduced income.[7] The military buildup in response to the war in Europe eventually brought the Depression to a close in the United States. The nature of women's public roles in this period remained amorphous. Most certainly, the independent, willfully poor, and self-sufficient Joan of Arc was irrelevant during the interwar years, when the culture of consumption was consolidated. Indeed, one of the most popular films about World War I, *Sergeant York* of 1941, eliminates women from the scene of war altogether. Joyce Baker suggests that when women claimed real political and social rights after the First World War, not only did chivalry come to an end but any celebration of female heroism disappeared from representation. With few public role models on the screen, most women's concepts of their own roles in public life dwindled to the vanishing point.[8]

Joan of Arc's absence from popular film, literature, and culture in the United States between 1920 and 1942 indicates a shift in her cultural weight. While during World War I Joan had provided harmless inspiration for some viewers and an additional vaguely erotic charge for others, her presence declined in proportion to her perceived viability as a role model for women as the Second World War approached. A review of the 1924 premiere of Bernard Shaw's *Saint Joan* suggests a turning point in the American conception of the heroine. While the Irish Shaw and later European playwrights such as Bertolt Brecht continued to find Joan a powerful and challenging figure, the American critic George Jean Nathan responded to *Saint Joan* with the following:

> The story of Joan is perhaps not a story for the theatre of Shaw, after all. It is a fairy tale pure and simple, or it is nothing—an inspiring and lovely fairy tale for the drunken old philosophers who are the children of the world. It vanishes before the clear and searching light of the mind as a fairy vanishes before the clear and searching light of dawn and day.[9]

This dismissive attitude toward the positive qualities that Joan had represented a decade earlier continued throughout the 1920s. A case in point is offered by *La Passion de Jeanne d'Arc*, which the Danish director Carl Theodor Dreyer made in France in 1928 and distributed in the United States shortly after it was completed. Dreyer was the first director to eliminate the spectacle of court and battle and to deal exclusively with the trial and burning of the heroine. By the late 1920s, Joan's story evidently seemed less pertinent as an example of heroism and more useful as a means to consolidate traditional authority in response to a disruptive female. As Thomas Doherty found in his study of Hollywood film during World War II, images of the First World War and of war in general had been demythologized by the end of the 1920s.[10] The previously admired combat genre, with its magnificent battles and glorious deaths, was altered so as to promote peace, which consequently lessened the appeal of Joan of Arc's warrior persona.[11]

Joan of Arc and European Cinema in the 1920s

La Passion de Jeanne d'Arc was an international coproduction that recognized the importance of the American market. At one point in the film's preproduction, the American actress Lillian Gish was engaged to play the title role eventually given to Renée Falconetti.[12] *Exhibitors Herald and Moving Picture World* featured a full-page advertisement for the film in early 1928 inviting the "Attention of Critical America." The photograph in the ad pictures a soldier in the foreground, but behind him a bishop with his head in his hands looks through an arched window to see a tiny praying Joan of Arc in the distance. A second page of the advertisement depicts an agonized, tonsured Joan at the stake as she reaches for a cross held up toward her. The text describes the film as "an inspirational portrayal of the most dramatic episode in the life of one of humanity's amazing characters." The film itself is extremely powerful as the result of its unusual style and structure. For the most part, asymmetrically composed close-ups of Joan and her judges that carry little narrative information but tremendous emotional weight are intercut but untethered by any shot/reverse shot sequence. The visual challenge is matched by Dreyer's decision to rely heavily on the verbal text of the trial through intertitles.

Dreyer expended a great deal of effort in writing the film. He employed the author of a contemporary biography of Joan, Joseph Delteil,[13] and adhered closely to the actual trial records. Dreyer chose to begin his film with the end of the romance quest, with its characteristic distortion and inversion. Since nothing of the clear-cut, successful mission is shown in the film, this wide-eyed, baffled Joan of Arc does not fall from noble heights, but instead is targeted for inexplicable reasons by a merciless church and state. Much of the film depicts Joan's confusion and agony when she realizes that her trust in the authorities has been betrayed. At the same time, the film stresses that Joan's judges are not guilty, since Joan operates within a prophecy that attributes all her actions to divine intervention. As the film comes to its climax, Joan's accusers are tearful and ashamed as they watch her relapse and take Communion for the last time. Because the humanization of the authorities happens here, rather than after the burning, the priests' ordeal is privileged in the narrative. Joan is a tool used to test their humanity. Joan's apocalyptic immolation, which usually elevates her to heroic status by revealing that she is who she claims to be, is less important in narrative terms. By reconfiguring the story in this way, Dreyer illustrates here, as he does in much of his work, that evil resides not in individuals but in institutions that thrive by repressing those outside them.

The potent effect of *La Passion de Jeanne d'Arc* results from both the words taken from the trial records and the film's extraordinary cinematic space. The rooms built for the film are not square nor are lines plumb, so that

Joan (Renée Falconetti) faces her accusers in *La Passion de Jeanne d'Arc* (Carl Theodor Dreyer, 1928). (Collection © 1989 MOMA, The Academy of Motion Picture Arts and Sciences)

people seem to fall out of the frame from instability. The world of the film is literally out of kilter. Joan's suffering and the agony of her accusers seem to be caused by the distorting pressure of the institutions, represented by low passages and arches that make the characters continually stoop and twist. The irregularity of the film's space also suggests that Joan of Arc's redemptive agony and ascension are far from normal human, much less female, experience. The rapid, dynamic cutting of the extended burning at the stake, which ends the film, reduces Joan to a symbolic shadow, through which the witnesses to her extraordinary death see (and viewers of the film are told) that Joan is the "incarnation of eternal France."

Dreyer's film was not widely seen in the United States when it was released, but certain women of the time reacted violently to it. The columnist Louella Parsons reported that two hundred "smartly dressed women" walked out of the premiere of Dreyer's film in Boston (where it had been presented under the auspices of the Junior League, with an introductory speech by the esteemed actress Eva Le Gallienne). Parsons concluded that the women did not like "gruesome subjects . . . and did not care for the cruelties."[14] The American poet H.D. was both astounded and appalled by the film. She characterized the work as "remorseless." All viewers, she wrote, have Joan of Arc in the "secret great cavernous interior of the cathedral (if I may be fantastic) of the subconscious"; Dreyer's Jeanne is not "our" Jeanne but a "much, much better, more authentic Jeanne." As much as she finds to admire in Dreyer's work, H.D. is repulsed by the cruelty of a representation in which Joan experiences no transcendence, of a portrait that she deems to be outside of "human consciousness."[15] These women would have grown up with the spunky and inspired Joan of Arc of children's literature, popular song, and film of the first decades of the century. Their responses to Dreyer's pathetically victimized Joan indicate how the heroine's status had changed in just ten years.

In the same year that Dreyer made *La Passion de Jeanne d'Arc*, the *Exhibitors Herald and Moving Picture World* carried a small article, headed "Special to Exhibitors," saying that the church was incensed because "Joan of Arc" was to be screened in Notre Dame Cathedral in Paris.[16] Blame was laid on the proposed use of electric light in a space that had known only natural and candle illumination. The film in question was not, I believe, the Dreyer work that has found such fame but a film by Marc de Gastyne that is only now being revived, *La Vie merveilleuse de Jeanne d'Arc*.[17] The making of Gastyne's film and its exhibition in France received far more governmental support than did Dreyer's project. For the making of this film, the contemporary Joan of Arc statue in front of the cathedral of Reims was temporarily removed in the interests of authenticity, and the French army provided costumed extras for the magnificent battle scenes. Although the film's premiere at the Paris Opéra was attended by the president of the Republic, the film has received little attention in comparison with the amount continually given to Dreyer's work.

Aspects of Gastyne's film relate to Dreyer's contemporaneous work and play a part in the post–World War I transformation of Joan of Arc. *La Vie merveilleuse de Jeanne d'Arc* opens with a quote from Jules Michelet that appeals to sentimental nationalist feelings. The nineteenth-century French historian begs the viewer to remember that "our country was born of a woman, her tenderness, her tears, the blood that she shed for us." Rather than the militant Joan of the First World War or even Dreyer's martyr, this film's Joan of Arc is lively and earthy. The almost maternal Joan is sexualized through her enjoyment of a marriage proposal and a coquettish personality that charms the king's court. Furthermore, Joan is said to "seduce" the army into action during a vivid shot/countershot sequence in which close-ups of the heroine's emotion-laden face are alternated with those of her captains. While the wearing of armor usually signifies readiness for battle and unity with soldiers, this Joan's glittering cuirass distances her. The sequence of the battle for Orléans that follows her enticing self-presentation to her men is extraordinarily dynamic, with Joan appearing throughout as a mascot with dramatically flying hair and banner. Yet once the fight is won, Joan's reaction is not that of the victorious soldier. She sits alone in her room and exudes regret for the end of the excitement as much as for the carnage of war. In the end this Joan is a sweet peasant girl who would return home if she could, but is resigned to her role as scapegoat for "wronged France," which she accepts and endures with touching emotion. Although both Dreyer's and Gastyne's films were made in Europe and received limited distribution in North America, they expanded Joan's meaning in the United States to include ignorance and pathos.

Two years after the French films appeared, Bertolt Brecht set the first of his three Joan of Arc dramas in the United States.[18] *St. Joan of the Stockyards* of 1930 relates the story of a Salvation Army lieutenant in Chicago named Joan Dark, whose conviction that moral elevation is more important than food causes her to become the strikebreaking pawn of evil industrialists. When Joan realizes that physical deprivation affects moral behavior and that she has betrayed the workers with her naive pacifism, she dies of a broken heart and is canonized by the stockyard barons. Brecht's Joan is not only pitiful but a negative force. Joan Dark is well intentioned and energetic, but her failure to use common sense, which is due to a lack of intellectual rigor, makes her worse than useless. At the end she cries: "Oh, goodness without consequences! Intentions in the dark! / I have changed nothing."[19] The play's emphasis on the trial not only rationalizes the fate of the illogical, disorderly female but also helps to explain the reasons for the declining relevance of the Joan of Arc figure in the modern industrial United States.

The decade that followed Brecht's play and coincided with the beginning of the Second World War saw a minor resurgence in Joan's presence in books, plays, poetry, and popular journalism. A perusal of titles and study of key texts suggest an interest in incorporating Joan into larger narratives that do not end in her death. A case in point is Jehanne Orliac's *Joan of Arc and Her Companions,* published in the United States in 1934. In order to contextualize Joan and to understand her "everyday humanity," the story is told through the eyes of others and puts particular stress on Charles VII's mother-in-law, Queen Yolanda.[20] While Joan dies betrayed and alone but still courageous and inspirational, the book concludes by describing the ongoing lives of Joan's friends and family. Another example of this kind is the better-known contemporary American play by Maxwell Anderson of 1936 called *Joan of Lorraine.* (The play was produced on Broadway almost a decade later with Ingrid Bergman in the lead role.) The actors play actors in search of the characters they are to play in a Joan of Arc vehicle. The play is not about Joan of Arc and her life but about the heroine's right to her title as such. Finally, the RKO film studios planned to film Shaw's *Saint Joan* with Katharine Hepburn in 1933, until the rights to the material were refused when the producers insisted on shortening the play. Shaw then wrote his own screenplay, which he intended to film with Elisabeth Bergner, who had played Joan in Max Reinhardt's German version of *Saint Joan* in 1924. Shaw's interpretation of history collided with that of the Vatican, however, and his project was stopped before filming began when the *New York Times* publicized the church's ban on Shaw's work.[21] Shaw's script took advantage of the unique properties of film by showing simultaneous action and the spectacle and warfare that the play could only suggest. As in his play, Joan's story would have been framed by the king's dream, in which Joan and everyone who is part of her story are all equally ambiguous players on history's stage.

Joan of Arc in the 1930s

References to Joan of Arc in the cinema of the 1930s are circuitous. The films that mention Joan in this period vaguely attempt both to deal with the

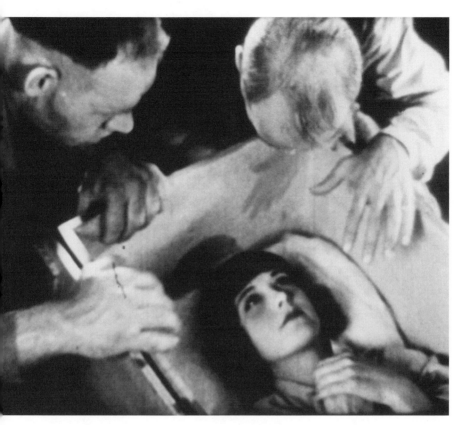

Monica Bannister as the deceased Joan Gale about to be reincarnated as a wax Joan of Arc in *The Mystery of the Wax Museum* (Michael Curtiz, 1933). (The Wisconsin Center for Film and Theater Research)

difficult consequences of having empowered women in World War I and to imagine the relation of women to war in the future. There are numerous films with implied references to Joan, such as the 1930 *She Goes to War*, directed by Henry King. This film is set in the First World War and contains an uncomfortable mix of trench warfare, romance, and comedy. The socialite heroine named Joan Morant goes overseas during the war to find that she can step in to save the day when a supply sergeant becomes inebriated, and also serve bravely under a man who is her social inferior at home. Despite the vast class difference between the two, a romance ensues between the socialite and the working-class soldier. To continue her relationship

Joan of Arc in a wax museum in *House of Wax* (André De Toth, 1953). (Author's collection)

successfully, Joan must sacrifice both the independence and social status that she had enjoyed as a wealthy woman.

A pair of films from 1932 and 1933 use Joan in a less charitable fashion. *Cock of the Air*, produced by Howard Hughes, relates the tale of a Parisian cabaret singer named Jean d'Arc who is asked to leave France because she distracts army officers. In a convoluted plot, she agrees to leave her native land to marry her American boyfriend and manages to save his career by this sacrifice of her own livelihood. In a scene that was cut from the film, Jean d'Arc lies on a bed, naked but for a suit of armor, while her fiancé approaches her with a can opener. This provocative sequence (which did find its way into a musical number by Busby Berkeley in *Golddiggers of 1933*) suggests that the sexualized female is not permitted to be a warrior. A similar lack of regard for the Joan of Arc figure occurs in the horror film *Mystery of the Wax Museum,* directed by Michael Curtiz. A demented wax museum owner, whose collection and skilled hands have been destroyed by fire, steals bodies from a morgue, which he dips in hot wax before displaying. One of his victims is a Joan Gale, who is never seen alive in the film but whose corpse is featured as the museum's Joan of Arc. Since no one knows what Joan of Arc looked like, simply the name Joan and the distinctive haircut appear to be enough to doom the woman. In 1953 André De Toth made a film with a similar plot featuring another inert Joan of Arc (played by Carolyn Jones), *House of Wax,* which also starred Vincent Price.

The urge to control the woman warrior's story finds its apotheosis in the only Johannic film of the 1930s, *Das Mädchen Johanna* of 1935. Gustav Ucicky's film was the only Joan of Arc film to be made in Germany. While there is little chance that this film was released contemporaneously in the United States, the specific ways it reworks Joan's story suggest reasons for the heroine's disappearance in the Second World War. The sole German Joan is represented as the passive front for the real power of the unfairly maligned Charles VII. Joan speaks incessantly of her desire to return home after the king's coronation, which she anticipates primarily for the chance to wear her ornate, closely fitted suit of armor. This vapid Joan is introduced by the fascist Charles as his instrument, to whom he gives the privilege of burning at the stake. Preparing for her death, he intones, "Dead, she will be a martyr. She should be glad for this." Joan models an ideal for women in war by serving mindlessly when called but returning home or disappearing when she is no longer needed.

By 1938 Joan had become less a subject of historical fiction than an icon of self-sacrifice. Just before the start of World War II, Mervyn LeRoy produced *Dramatic School* with an all-star cast. This film is one of the first of a series of contemporary stories that use the dramatic role of Joan of Arc to symbolize selfless dedication to a career in the theater. Here a poor understudy gives up her wealthy boyfriend when she is given the chance to make her mark by taking on the role of Joan. The fiancé courageously releases the actress from her commitment when he recognizes her immense talent. This use of Joan of Arc as an iconic character in contemporary performance was often imitated. After *Dramatic School,* Joan frequently became a means to display thespian skills and was less associated with actual women or with the historical figure.

With the approach of the Second World War the symbolic role of women in war had changed. The simple existence of the solid Joan of earlier decades, whose resolved life had made unstable times seem survivable, was no longer current. Women in the United States had achieved the vote by 1920 and Joan of Arc had come to represent not only women's rights in the world but a willingness to suffer to assert their claim to them. It no longer seemed safe to summon forth any female body during war and, by endangering it even symbolically, make it heroic and an object of veneration. In addition, Joan's authority and iconoclasm could not be used directly to involve women in the war without risking too great a success.[22] During the war, any reference to Joan of Arc was disguised, and many cinematic references to women in the military bore the mark of ridicule. Film titles such as *The Admiral Was a Lady, Skirts Ahoy, WAC from Walla Walla,* and *Never Wave at a WAC* suggest something of the shift in the relation of women to war. Joan of Arc's virgin warrior status and her devotion to her quest were clearly inappropriate. In the war films of the Second World War, if women were not the butt of the joke, they were valued for their looks first, then for their skill in the factory, and finally for their desire to return home. Although evocations of the woman warrior no longer conferred any sense of female power, references to the saint were not entirely pointless. The study of Joan of Arc in World War II reveals how the image and persona of the heroine were reformulated to suit the needs of a nation facing war abroad and social transformation at home.

5   The War Years

Between Us Girls, Joan of Paris,
and *Joan of Ozark*

The heightened technological sophistication and the larger
scale of the Second World War guaranteed that a medieval icon such as Joan
of Arc would have to undergo a major transformation in order to serve as a
tool of propaganda. After the First World War, Americans had become comfortable with technology and come to believe that it was safely harnessed and
integral to the American way of life. In this age of the home appliance,
women were recruited for war work with posters reassuring them that industrial machinery was as easily mastered as the vacuum cleaner and
sewing machine.[1] The sophisticated advertising of American consumer culture and the products themselves temporarily eased the feelings of inau-
thenticity that had plagued the beginning of the century and led to medievalism. In larger terms, the Second World War was defined by extreme
examples of good versus evil that made the rituals and iconography of
chivalry seem anachronous and superficial.

Although World War II was ruled by the discourse of rationality, the horrors of combat apparently were still better endured when encapsulated
within mythic structures, and Joan of Arc's story was indeed revived. On 21
August 1944 the *New York Times* ran a large photograph on the front page
depicting the monumental equestrian statue of Joan in the center of Orléans, with the caption "Americans pause in Orleans beneath the statue of
Joan of Arc, the base of which had been damaged by shellfire." Such oblique

95

references to Joan were part of the effort to recruit women during the war. Of particular interest in this regard are three films made in 1942: Henry Koster's comedy-drama *Between Us Girls;* a contemporary romance drama directed by Robert Stevenson called *Joan of Paris;* and the musical comedy *Joan of Ozark,* directed by Joseph Santley.

The United States entered World War II on 7 December 1941 and until the fall of 1942 appeared to be in danger of losing a war for which it had not been prepared. The government had to depend heavily on propaganda to recruit civilians to work, conserve, and fight. Franklin Roosevelt had established several divisions for the control and dispersal of information, but his trepidation about seeming to be manipulative in an antifascist war delayed the propaganda process. After a State of the Union address in which Roosevelt declared that the war would be fought at home as well as abroad, the Office of War Information (OWI) was formed in mid-1942 to oversee the dissemination of material by other government agencies, the media, and advertising. The War Advertising Council took particular aim at women, whose labor was needed in the war effort.[2] By the 1940s, the potential influence of popular culture was fully understood and employed. Since 80 million people, or two-thirds of the population of the United States, went to the movies every week, the OWI recognized that Hollywood should be the focus of greatest concern and effort.[3]

By this period in the history of American film, the job of the OWI had been considerably eased by the Production Code of the Hays Office. The code, which had been in place since 1930, had forced Hollywood to conform to and finally internalize its rules: wrongdoing must be punished; no profanity, slang, nudity, or sex was permitted; and respect must be shown for religious and government institutions. Accustomed to censorship as it was, Hollywood adhered for the most part to the OWI's frequently revised manuals and tolerated its participation in story conferences and even its alterations of scripts and rejection of certain films.[4] Roosevelt had asked that the media stress the values of the home front and the American way of life. Great care was to be taken with foreign subjects and with any depiction of the war that made it look easy or glamorous. Consequently, the tone created for the Second World War was serious, practical, and specific. Unlike the earlier war's evocation of medieval history, allegory, or Joan of Arc, the films, posters, and popular literature of this war told people how to conserve, ration, and work in factories. With all these compunctions to represent only the "normal" in movies, Joan of Arc enters the discourse of women and World War II in roundabout ways.

Notably fewer posters were used in this less imaginative war. The images that did appear in the public domain usually employed the contemporaneous and banal specificity of the photograph, as opposed to the more vivid drawings and collages of World War I. While the presence of new media such as radio and the newsreel made posters less necessary, the propaganda poster's sincere and open approach also limited its appeal for this more cynical generation. A typical poster of the time showed a pretty mother and daughter in frilly aprons happily canning food, captioned "We'll have lots to eat this winter, won't we Mother?" The OWI had decided that the American people wanted to see attractive, successful people in a prosperous, democratic country cheerfully doing their bit for the war by making small sacrifices.[5] For women at home, the work of the war had to be seen to be pleasant and normal, although it appeared to consist chiefly of keeping a stiff upper lip while maintaining the American way of life. The propaganda that sent these messages through cinema and advertising had the double task of persuading its audience to participate in the war while producing profits for the sponsor.

One of the few allegorical posters of the Second World War reveals how profoundly the targeted audience had changed since the previous war. This recruitment poster displays a row of seven soldiers in the lower third of the image, each wearing a uniform from one of America's wars, as far back as the Revolution. At the top of the poster is a Greek-gowned young woman with a laurel-leaf headdress against a pneumatic surface bearing stars and stripes.[6] In contrast to the many similar figures of the First World War, which were monumental and serious, this woman is distinctly modern in her physiognomy, styling, and pose. Looking like the girl next door in costume, the model seems self-consciously aware that she is dressed to represent a Victorian concept of the moral superiority of women, while knowing that this image is no longer current in the face of woman suffrage, relaxed social mores, and economic realities. The weight and majesty of history borrowed by this poster are a poor fit for the women of this time, who had

World War II poster by A. Parker (1943) encourages "victory gardens" and home canning. (The George C. Marshall Research Foundation)

actually been allowed to enter the military officially when they agreed to abide by conventional sex roles. In the earlier war gender was linked to morality and women stood above the fray as either pacifists, happily inferior colleagues, or sweethearts. By the middle of the twentieth century, the ideological meaning of woman in relation to war had changed.

Women in the Second World War were essential to the Army, Navy, Air Force, Marines, and Coast Guard, where they worked by the hundreds of thousands. At the same time, however, an ideal of Woman as the imagined stake of war was ever more necessary in the global technological economy. By midcentury, warfare was seen less as a glorious, chivalric endeavor than as the means by which power is maintained. Jane Gaines notes how the highly sexualized body of the film-star pinup came to be the idealized object in relation to which the soldier of the Second World War identified himself as virile, aggressive, and heterosexual.[7] The women who would have stayed at home in the earlier war to play this role were now likely to be in uniform themselves. One of the few overt references to Joan of Arc during the war was *Daredevil Comics'* "Pat Patriot: America's Joan of Arc," who was introduced in August 1941. Armed simply with the strength of her fists and snug-fitting clothes, this singing, dancing superheroine was a sharp departure from the images of girlfriends and mothers that were carried in the Great War. In the past, when idealized war offered its own rewards, women were inspirational and allegorical rather than potentially challenging.[8] The rules and rituals that controlled female behavior in this later war give evidence of the discomfort that real women warriors caused. Regulations stipulating that orders from women to men had to be filtered through another male, or rules encouraging enlisted women to have social relations with officers, separated women from their male counterparts. In addition, who could take seriously military groups called WASPS, WAVES, and WACS?

Examining the shifting representations of Joan of Arc between the First and Second World Wars reveals that public images of deeply ingrained notions about male and female roles are flexible and prone to rapid alteration in times of crisis.[9] The most important task of propaganda in World War II was the creation of a self-sacrificing collective populace from a nation of individualists at a time when isolationist sentiments were widely held. Propaganda had to make the country's responsibility to the principle of democracy more important and desirable than personal independence. Owing to

Pat Patriot, "America's Joan of Arc," appeared in *Daredevil Comics* in 1941.

changes in the social roles of women, connections between Joan of Arc and female sacrifice that were obvious to previous generations were not made. In fact, the only historical figure called forth in the Second World War for female emulation was Molly Pitcher, who was known and named for hauling water to soldiers. The preferred image was the home-front heroine, who recalled the older virtues of the household angel of the nineteenth century, who suppressed her individual desires in the interests of family and country.[10] In early 1943, the radio program *Uncle Sam Speaks* defined the female ideal in terms from an earlier generation. America was asked, "Ever stop to wonder why Liberty is represented as a woman? Why not a man? Because in every age, women have held the torch of freedom so their men could have their hands free to work and fight."[11]

The return of American women to this self-sacrificing ideal of woman-hood was envisioned as a performance. The waning of traditional definitions of feminine behavior and maternal instinct was a source of anxiety by mid-century.[12] One method for returning women to conventional roles was through the ratcheting upward of the standards for the model wife and mother, which was carried out by advertising and the selling of ever more sophisticated but not necessarily time-saving domestic tools.[13] Another mode of entreaty was through the family, by appealing to women to help the men who made life worth living. Ideally, the self-sufficient woman would be humbled just enough to preserve passively sexual femininity. Women had to realize that while their efforts were temporarily necessary during the war, these new tasks were not meant to replace the duties of wife and mother. The confidence that resulted from women's labor was attacked in popular representation with the theme and motif of the softening of the hard exterior. For example, rather than valorizing the protective qualities or efficiency of Joan of Arc's armor, as reflected in the business suit or industrial overalls worn by working women, popular culture prized glamour. The various female personas that women could adopt for different areas of their lives were envisioned as so many masquerades in the performance of femininity.

An article in a *Woman's Home Companion* of October 1943, headed "Be-grimed—Bewitching or Both," described four women war workers who were taken to Hollywood to be made up, dressed, and photographed for the magazine. These were the New Women of the 1940s—responsible, proud, straightforward, and feminine without being too seductive.[14] In a similar vein, the patriotic role of women during the war was increasingly conceptualized as the attainment of beauty via consumption. One advertisement for lipstick claimed that it "symbolizes one of the reasons why we are fighting . . . the precious right of women to be feminine and lovely."[15] Mary Ann Doane has noted the degree to which women were kept in the habit of consumption during the war (even when the objects themselves were not available) through marketing strategies such as "Miss Hollywood Junior" dresses that were based on the clothes worn by stars in films.[16] The complications that ensued for the streamlined, glamorous woman created by the many mixed messages are investigated in a 1942 film directed by Henry Koster called *Between Us Girls*. Although this film is a contemporaneous romantic comedy, the presence of Joan of Arc, or rather the playing of the role of Joan of Arc, focuses the film. In addition, the leading performance in the film, which is an exuberant layering of roles, becomes the object of critical attack in the reception of the film.

Between Us Girls begins with the applause for a performance of Queen Victoria and the return of the actress playing the role to the home where her sophisticated mother lives with their elderly but spry housekeeper. The three women (Diana Barrymore, Kay Francis, Ethel Griffies, respectively) live in contented self-sufficiency. While the daughter has been on tour, however, the mother has become romantically involved, and has apparently told her suitor that her daughter is a twelve-year-old child, away at boarding school. Being the confident, impulsive dynamo that she is, the Barrymore character plays along with the game by dressing up in schoolgirl clothes, complete with middy blouse, braids, and a favorite doll. The daughter also rashly decides to play an alcoholic vamp, supposedly the girl's aunt, when she is caught practicing for the part of Sadie Thompson in *Rain*. The audience for the various characters is the gullible friend of the mother's fiancé (Robert Cummings), who fawns over the "little girl" and is appalled by the drunken "aunt's" behavior. Battles over the control and availability of the women and the proper female role escalate to a level near chaos. The turning point is a fistfight initiated between the Cummings character and a bully's father by Barrymore as a child. When Cummings conducts himself "like a general," Barrymore the woman feels guilty, falls in love, and is thrown over a bridge into a river after being spanked by the duped Cummings.

After an ellipsis of uncertain length following her punishment, the Barrymore character appears on stage in a Joan of Arc costume that echoes the short skirt and knee socks of her adolescent persona. At the moment when she realizes that the man she loves is in a soldier's costume on stage with her, the actress launches into a speech about the weakness of women. While she chatters about her will belonging to heaven, the supernumerary boyfriend, struggling to lift his helmet's visor, proposes marriage. This request happens to come in the middle of a sentence: ". . . if asked for self-sacrifice, I'll say . . . ," so that Joan of Arc's "Yes, yes, yes" becomes the response of a now acquiescent woman giving up her career for marriage. Just as the

Diana Barrymore as Joan of Arc in *Between Us Girls* (Henry Koster, 1942). (The Wisconsin Center for Film and Theater Research)

final lines of the film are spoken, a title appears asking the viewer to buy war bonds.

The end of *Between Us Girls* abruptly conflates the sacrifice of Joan of Arc, the reversal of the lead character's trajectory, and the participation of the film's real audience. The collapse of narrative levels that unites the fictional world and that of World War II subtly equates women's war work with the deeds of the heroine. This blurring of roles recalls Joan of Arc's Amazonian persona, in which independence and success are permissible until the return of the male reestablishes the conventional couple.[17] Other attempts were made to assuage anxiety over the fate of the couple at the war's end, including popular songs set to silly tunes such as "Pop Goes the Weasel" or "The Man on the Flying Trapeze." A typical lyric reads:

> We're the WAACs and everyone a soldier,
> To class we go, no rifle on our shoulder,
> But we work to send a man who's bolder.
>
> . . . .
>
> We don't tote guns or bayonets,
> Our powder comes in compact sets.
> We're petticoat soldiers,
> Wacky WAACs![18]

When the seriousness of women's war work had to be diluted, the sentimental and respectful songs of the First World War that evoked Joan of Arc were no longer appropriate.

The unexpected reference to Joan of Arc at the end of *Between Us Girls* also confers retroactive meaning upon the sequence of the film in which the Barrymore character rehearses the role of Sadie Thompson. Some of Sadie's lines seem to be taken from a melodramatic play about the trial of Joan of Arc: "[You are a] terrible witchburner"; "What kind of Christian are you?"; "You believe in torture, you know you're big and strong and you've got the law on your side." The anger at the injustice of the fate of the once independent woman bursts through only momentarily but memorably. The OWI analysis of *Between Us Girls* adds another layer to the demise of the independent woman. In the "Personal critical information" section of the analysis the reviewer has an extreme reaction to the masquerading female star. Under "Acting" the reviewer wrote: "Satisfactory except on part of Diana

Barrymore"; under "Direction": "Good save for the latitude allowed Diana Barrymore"; under "Camera": "Good but not sufficiently expert to conceal Diana Barrymore's facial defects." The *New York Times* called the film a disaster because of Barrymore's incompetence.[19] Barrymore's much maligned performance is unquestionably highly energetic and self-conscious. Yet the OWI review that denigrated Barrymore and the film for being "exaggerated and unreal," despite the conventional ending, pinpoints a characteristic that is typical of the films of the 1940s. Dana Polan has described the typical film of the decade as a contradictory narrative that introduces but fails to reconcile multiple possibilities.[20] The Barrymore character in *Between Us Girls* is written and performed as a mass of contradictions in physical characteristics, behavior, and desire. The very aspects of the character that are frustrating also acknowledge the difficult situations in which women found themselves in relation to the Second World War. Although Barrymore's incarnation of Joan of Arc is brief and fragmentary, it ends the film and grounds the war experience in a fixed historical moment. In addition, Joan hovers over the narrative as a mythic figure whose cyclical story reassures the audience that manifestations of female power are followed by submission.

A more specific and immediately crucial task of wartime propaganda was the recruitment of women to work in the thousands of industrial jobs left vacant by men when they left for the European or Pacific theater. The task of convincing the mothers and older women who were necessary to the production of war material was especially difficult because the message contradicted the recently formulated post-Depression ideal of women in the home. The traditional Joan of Arc was inappropriate for this task because the freedom attained through a job had to be envisioned as temporary. Thus paid work was sold to women as a novelty, as if it had never been experienced before, but was close enough to housework to be easy. By March 1943 more drastic recruitment measures were needed: "Every idle machine may mean a dead soldier," the "slackers" were told. Leila Rupp quotes two appeals that seem to contradict some of the grounding assumptions of the female role in consumer culture: "Women can stand a lot, and actually they are workers by tradition. It is only in recent years, and mostly in the United States, that women have been allowed to fall into habits of extraordinary leisure"; and "Are you so blinded by 'women's rights' that you have forgotten that nothing but WORK ever earned them? Are you being old-fashioned and getting by just by being a 'good wife and mother'?"[21] The mixed message was also apparent in one of the few posters of the time, which shows a woman working with her hands with the words: "Women in the war; WE CAN'T WIN WITHOUT THEM." The form of the address, in which women were evidently not part of the "we" that are the United States, is supplemented by the visual composition. The poster features a large tubular object that looks like a bomb in the forefront, while a woman whose bowed head makes her anonymous occupies only one-sixth of the image, as she uses a tiny power tool to make the big explosive device. The recruitment campaign was successful, to judge by the remarkable increase in the number of women, particularly white, married, middle-class women, who took jobs during the war.[22]

Steps were taken to ease the contradictions created by demanding that women work while implying that they were not suited to do so. The Magazine Bureau of the War Manpower Commission advised that popular literature about women working in essential jobs that previously had been held by men had to include a romance in order to appeal to women and to make men accept female workers. In any instance in which women were independently strong in what was described as an "Amazon economy," the story was to be distanced in either a utopian science fiction mode or a historical one.[23] Thomas Doherty finds that any representation of successful women during war called for "dexterous manhandling . . . [that would] channel and constrain whatever revolutionary spirit it unleashed." He writes further of a need to deny the reality of the violence and agony of battle by contextualizing the war.[24] The Joan of Arc drama would seem to have been an ideal vehicle because of its temporal distance from the current conflagration, the distractingly ornamental quality of the medieval, and the emotional and literal self-sacrifice of the heroine. Apparently perceptions of women had changed so drastically that Joan's strength as a warrior made her too threatening to be used during this war. As Michael Renov has suggested, the dominant cultural issue had shifted from class conflict in the First World War to sexual difference in World War II.[25] The desperate need for female labor to supply the war only confused and complicated gender problems already present.

In 1942 Robert Stevenson made *Joan of Paris,* which responded to many of the problems and demands of the war through an adaptation of the Joan of Arc narrative in a contemporary setting. In spite of the film's title and the

World War II poster for the War Manpower Commission shows women's role in the war (1942). (The George C. Marshall Research Foundation)

multiple references to the heroine in the film, not every reviewer made the connection between the Joan of the story and the medieval warrior. In his positive *New York Times* review of the film, Bosley Crowther described Michèle Morgan's Joan as a "dreamy French Girl . . . a modern namesake of St. Joan, a little Parisian barmaid who emulates her patron saint in a small way."[26] The diminutives of this review suggest the more prevalent reaction: the film was criticized as phony for making the exploits of the Free French into a love story centered on a woman.[27] The fact that the film ends with the death of a lowly waitress causes what *Variety* called "too mild a climax without the generation of the tragic note intended."[28] The *New York Post* ran the most negative review, which attacked the excessive technique of the film, the bad timing that destroyed suspense, and the failure of the film to be spontaneous, as "in life."[29]

Joan of Paris is a typical Hollywood melodrama that fits into a category of wartime films that confronted the possibility of independence for women, such as *Flight for Freedom* (Lothar Mendes, 1943) and *Five Graves to Cairo* (Billy Wilder, 1943). In this subgenre, women affect their worlds, accept the consequences of their actions, and are either neutralized through romance or sacrificed in death.[30] Other films to which *Joan of Paris* might be compared are Fritz Lang's *Manhunt* (1941), in which a heroine's death concludes her espionage activities; and *Casablanca* (Michael Curtiz, 1942) and *Since You Went Away* (John Cromwell, 1944), in both of which lovers sacrifice their personal happiness for the war effort. Yet *Joan of Paris* is a more complicated film because of its connections to the Joan of Arc story. The stakes involved in destroying a second Joan of Arc are considerably higher than those involved in eliminating a wartime Everywoman.

Joan of Paris begins as five Royal Air Force flyers are shot down over occupied France, which has been represented briefly by a montage of neon lights and ebullient showgirls. The men overtake German soldiers, find French clothes, and plan to meet in a Parisian church run by Father Antoine, the boyhood priest of the French leader, Paul Lavallier (Paul Henreid). One of the flyers is wounded and is followed by a Gestapo agent. Meanwhile, Paul acts as a decoy so that his friend can escape to their sewer hideout, before he himself becomes the object of the enemy's search. Paul then randomly seeks cover in the room of a waitress named Joan, with the quickly invented excuse that Father Antoine asked him to give her money to buy a new dress.

Paul does not realize that he hands Joan a bill marked by the Gestapo in order to track him. Joan mentions in passing that an English spy in Paris is to be shot soon. Paul sends a message to this effect to Father Antoine via Joan, telling him to contact the spy, who knows the whereabouts of British intelligence in France.

Paul and Joan quickly fall in love and she is entrusted with contacting the British agent, the elderly Mademoiselle Rosay. The two women barely evade the Gestapo, which has traced them through the marked bills. The women return to Paul and help him escape, although by the time he has killed the enemy agent who has been following him, the hour of the flyers' rendezvous has supposedly passed. Mademoiselle Rosay is murdered and Joan is discovered by the Gestapo leader in her room with a note from Paul. Joan agrees to lead the Germans to the other four flyers if she and Paul are saved. Allowed to see Paul in the church where he has hidden, Joan has a change of heart and tells him to meet his comrades, who have waited for him to complete their flight. Joan then leads the Gestapo on a wild goose chase through the sewers, emerging in time to see the rescue boat roar away. Joan is shot for her role in the affair.

The connections to the Joan of Arc story are plentiful, starting with the stranded flyers' decision to meet at the cathedral on the Place Jeanne d'Arc in Paris. As Paul leaves the cathedral, just before he meets Joan, he passes behind the large statue of an armored, kneeling Joan of Arc in the square. This and other scenes evoking the saint are accompanied by ringing bells, reminiscent of the means by which Joan of Arc claimed to have received her orders. In a later segment Paul boosts Joan's morale by showing her the cross on the back of his dog tags, which symbolizes Lorraine, Joan of Arc, and the Free French. Finally, he reprimands her for alluding to France as a "conquered country," saying that Joan of Arc would never have uttered such words. In addition, the structure of *Joan of Paris* strongly echoes the organizing principles of the Joan of Arc story, which legitimizes the heroine's self-sacrifice.

Joan of Paris's quest begins when she encounters the injured Paul shortly after he miraculously escapes from the cathedral, when the malevolent German agent is distracted by a little girl. Looking from the closet in Joan's room in which he is hidden, Paul first sees Joan talking to her statuette of Joan of Arc, praying for the dress and hat that have tempted her from a store

Paul Henreid looking for help from Joan of Arc in *Joan of Paris* (Robert Stevenson, 1942). (Author's collection)

window. She seems to wait in a state of expectation for Paul to initiate her martyrdom. He does so by using her desire for beautiful clothes to win her allegiance and to get a vital message to the priest. When Joan returns from the cathedral and then the shop with what is described in the black-and-white film as a red frock, this French Everywoman has become an essential instrument in the fight for her country.

Once Paul and Father Antoine find the address of the British agent in Paris, they are faced with the problem of contacting her. During their discussion, Joan is seen mounting the steps from a God's-eye view, in the tradition of women on staircases approaching their fates typical of the Hollywood woman's film. Joan is unmistakably the heaven-sent innocent who can act without raising suspicion. The priest sends Joan on her quest with a note to deliver. While carrying out her mission, Joan is betrayed by one of her own when the storekeeper from whom she buys the dress informs the Gestapo that she paid with the marked bill. As a result of this treachery, Joan and the saintly Mademoiselle Rosay are chased by the Gestapo and Joan returns to Paul with a wound that is similar to the one inflicted on Joan of Arc herself. After Mademoiselle Rosay provides Paul with the information he needs to escape, she is killed and her death forces Joan to embark upon her own mission.

When it becomes apparent that Paul cannot go to the hidden flyers because he is being followed, Joan assumes the task of informing the men about the rescue plan. She saves the flyers, only to return to her room to find that Paul has left a message saying that he was too late to escape. She hides the note before the Gestapo leader comes in, but he finds it and gives Joan a chance to save Paul and herself by betraying the soldiers. Joan faces her statue of Joan of Arc and decides to recant to save herself from a terrible death. Joan tells the Gestapo leader that she must perform the deed her own way. She approaches Paul in the cathedral, where he is praying before a stained-glass window depicting Joan of Arc. Before she can tell him her plan, a glance at the saint's image convinces her not to go through with her deception. Instead she tells Paul to go to the other flyers, who are waiting for him. Bells ring as he leaves, saying "God bless you, Joan" to the two Joans who have become one in saving him. After delaying the Germans long enough for the men to flee, Joan defiantly tells the leader that France will defeat him just as the flyers have done. Joan's final scene occurs in a prison chamber with Father Antoine at her side. She kneels and prays in the submissive posture of her Joan of Arc statue before being led out of the cell. After a gunshot is heard, the screen is filled with planes flying through clouds as the flyers escape, thanks to the divinely inspired Joan(s).

Joan's death and the emotions it evokes are not as simple as they first appear. As noted earlier, Joan of Arc's strength as a warrior derives from her virgin state. Like the Amazons with whom she is identified, Joan can succeed in battle only by controlling her sexuality. In the original Amazon narratives, the women warriors were murdered so that the killers could absorb the warriors' power. In the Renaissance descendant of this story, rape was substituted for murder so that the pillager secured a mate in addition to a victory. This earlier reworking of the myth facilitates a film like *Joan of Paris,*

Michèle Morgan in metallic raincoat in *Joan of Paris* (Robert Stevenson, 1942). (Author's collection)

in which Joan of Arc is resurrected as a figure of passive good rather than subversion. Likewise, much of the propaganda of the Second World War advised women to be both aggressive at work and acquiescent sexually. In light of this duality, the one anomaly of *Joan of Paris* in terms of its Joan of Arc origins becomes significant. The night that Paul and Joan spend together is elaborately developed and crucial to the outcome of the film. After Joan returns home, wounded from her quest, the couple fall into each other's arms. The following shot depicts Paul shaving the next morning and Joan begging forgiveness of her statuette. Showing no regret and offering the misery of her wartime life as an excuse, Joan asks to be punished. Since Joan and Joan of Arc are fully identified by this point, the speech is a self-address that makes the heroine a willing participant in her own destruction. Yet in this Joan's martyrdom, the self-renunciation carries no weight, since her act is absorbed by the heroism of Paul and his flyers.

The Joan of the film follows in the footsteps of her patron saint. Although the actions and sacrifices of the two are meant to be analogous, the divergences place the film firmly in its wartime context. Joan of Paris is paged by men to assist with their mission and she confides to Mademoiselle Rosay that she prefers to remain ignorant of the men's exploits. The unmarried activist replies that Joan's self-deprecating attitude is sure to win her a husband. A wartime viewer of the film might have felt that to participate in the war effort leads to happiness in marriage and makes one a heroine. But the nature of this heroism is indicative of women's roles in World War II. Joan dies so that a small group of soldiers can continue with their mission under the assumption that their skills are more valuable than she is. In retrospect, one recalls the opening of the film, in which identically costumed showgirls from Paris's more risqué nightclubs are blacked out as an urgent voice announces the downing of the plane carrying Paul Lavallier. Just as these women are abruptly eliminated without further trace in the face of the all-important war, the film concludes that women are expendable in the war effort. In addition, although the priest tells Joan that she will live on when France is free, it is fairly certain that while "Paul Lavallier" will appear on statues and in the records, Joan's name will never be engraved in stone.

One of the more unusual films to call upon the story of Joan of Arc is the 1942 film directed by Joseph Santley called *Joan of Ozark*.[31] This musical comedy stars the former vaudevillians Judy Canova and Joe E. Brown. Canova is depicted on a production card for the film, which features a collage of photographs of her in various costumes, as having a "really unique style, [she is] a regular gal and a swell trouper . . . a hillbilly Mata Hari." In overalls, gingham shirt, and pigtails, Canova plays a girl who inadvertently shoots a pigeon that is carrying a message between Nazi spies working in the United States. When she becomes a national heroine for the lucky shot, the head of the spy ring orders her killed as an object lesson to all who may want to emulate her. The German leader works out of a nightclub, and when two theatrical agents bring in a showgirl they want to promote, he demands that they first bring him Judy. Simple country girl that she is, Judy will not capitalize on her patriotic service and insists on staying where she belongs. The agents persuade her to come with the invented story that they are G-men and that she will be a "G-woman" called Agent H2O, whose job is to masquerade as a singer at the club. The bumbling agents have no idea that the club actually is a spy headquarters. Once at the club, Judy is covertly assigned two real G-men after she has had to use jujitsu to defend herself against a Japanese would-be assassin. As an entertainer, Judy is a star, singing songs like "Pull the Trigger" and "Lady at Lockheed" with a bevy of beautiful backup singers. Finally, after a circus of mistaken identities and foul-ups involving real versus fake government agents, Judy is to be killed in the act of christening a bomber. Judy misses when she throws the bottle, however, so that the bomber flies off with the explosive champagne attached. Judy then follows in another plane and retrieves the bottle, which she throws into the ocean. It lands on a Japanese submarine. She parachutes down and captures the enemy commander by the nape of his neck to return as a heroine once more. The film ends with Judy back in the hills, married to her agent with a flock of children dressed exactly like their parents.

Any film that stars Judy Canova is, as the *Hollywood Reporter* describes *Joan of Ozark*, a "Canova vehicle."[32] With her gawky manner, huge grin, loud voice, and slapstick mannerisms, Canova invariably played herself and Hollywood saw no point in attempting to cast her otherwise. Her character in this film is named Judy rather than Joan. After her heroic gesture, she is told that she will be "like Joan of Arc—Joan of Ozark," implying that she is a few steps away from the original. The film stresses the inadvertent nature of Judy's success and the fact that her supposed heroism is purely random. Even when one accepts *Joan of Ozark* as a crazy musical comedy, the reference to and transformation of the French heroine into a hayseed hillbilly is an interesting stretch.

While the homely Judy becomes an entertainer only by virtue of her accidental heroism, she finds her greatest success singing and dancing in the nightclub. She sings songs about "doing okay, the American way" and doing what she can even though she is not a man. She is self-conscious about her looks, remarking that she is not pretty enough to be a spy. Her stage is a highly stylized factory set that seems to be made of huge Tinkertoys. The chorus girls are dressed in costumes that resemble jumpsuits worn by industrial workers, although they are of a shiny, armor-like material that is accented with plaid and polka-dot shirts that often leave the midriff exposed. The beautiful, smiling performers in the background provide the film's most

Judy Canova doing her best for the war effort from afar in *Joan of Ozark* (Joseph Santley, 1942). (The Wisconsin Center for Film and Theater Research)

appealing role models. These glamorous women work in factories but are content to stay out of the spotlight. There is little doubt that women would never aspire to the heroic status of the funny though unattractive Canova, who most often appears in the publicity material in the baggy overalls and work boots that make her appear both childlike and masculine.

Joan of Ozark's mockery of the Joan of Arc persona both recalls the story of the woman warrior and makes light of it. The peasant roots and connection to the land are turned into the hillbilly cliché that makes the film's title so absurd. In a most unusual transformation, Joan of Arc's "voices" become Joan of Ozark's voice; Judy's yodel has the uncanny ability to carry for miles across fields when she calls her family to dinner. All heroic activities are reduced to accident or incompetence, and her buffoonery eliminates any threat. Although Judy crows that "pulling a trigger is good for the figger," she is almost grotesque as she showers in a bathing cap and baggy towel and bats her eyelashes wildly in her attempt to be glamorous. *Joan of Ozark* can also be seen as an attempt to negate the appeal of individualism, which has traditionally defined American character but is detrimental to any war effort. While Joan of Arc's actions are remembered for their spontaneity and originality, these characteristics were under attack by the propaganda of the Second World War, which had to erase differences in ethnicity, age, class, and rank in order to facilitate cooperation.

The war years saw a number of films in which women were associated with the military in order to involve them in the American effort in the most useful way. Female characters performed as nurses, as drivers, or in factories with the general attitude expressed in the song sung in *Swing Shift Maisie* of 1943 (Norman Z. McLeod), "The Girl behind the Boy behind the Gun." In the same year, the much acclaimed *So Proudly We Hail* (Mark Sandrich) was released with one of the few serious representations of women in the military who form close bonds and operate competently and successfully. The heroine of the film is played by Veronica Lake, whose signature hair style, with one eye hidden behind cascading hair, was so widely imitated that propaganda had to be devised telling women in factories to pull their hair back from their faces. With perhaps the most subtle evocation of the name of Joan of Arc possible, Lake and her co-star, Paulette Goddard, are called Joan O'Doul and Olivia d'Arcey. The fates of the two, however, model a notion of female heroism that is not far from that suggested in *Joan of Ozark*. Goddard plays the attractive chorus girl, a role Manny Farber referred to when he described the film as continuing the "snide movie attitude toward women [in which] theater owners get their cheesecake in hunks so great that much of the movie hinges on Miss Goddard's black nightie."[33] The Lake character completes the couple by sacrificing herself (not for her country but in revenge for her boyfriend's death) by running with a grenade into a group of Japanese soldiers.

If Joan of Arc had any but the most indirect of places during the war, it is that suggested in a poem that appeared in 1941 in the *New York Herald-Tribune*. In the first verse of a longer work, "Prayer to Jehanne of France," Joseph Auslander concentrated on what he imagined to be Joan's fiery and passive death, while suggesting that she was self-sacrificing, childish, good-looking, and vacuous. He used the archaic, distancing spelling of the name to connect the mythic heroine to what was expected of American women during the war.

> O Jehanne, with the trumpets in your name,
> By all the lilies of the Oriflamme,
> By all the faggots and the final shame,
> By all the burning voices at the Tree,
> By all the visions that we cannot see,
> By all you were that we can never be,
> By all the little lambs, by every lark
>
> . . . .
>
> By all your simple strength, and by the few
> Straight words like light, and by the dream that grew
> In your gray well-spaced eyes until you knew
> The work you had to do—[34]

In the Second World War, the title of the popular World War I song "Joan of Arc, They Are Calling You" was no longer pertinent. Rather than an inspirational, talismanic figure whose existence gave hope for victory and redemption, only a shadow Joan of Arc haunted the period of the actual fighting of this midcentury war. The heroic, successful Joan of Arc was a vaguely fictionalized character to be performed at one remove or as "of Paris" or "of Ozark." After the changes in women's social and economic power since the earlier war, most ramifications of the Joan of Arc persona had become undesirable. Only the most abstract hint of patient self-sacrifice and final submission were valued.

⊷⟴ 6 The Return of the Maid

The Miracle of the Bells and *Joan of Arc*

In 1948 the first major studio film about Joan of Arc was made in the United States since the release of Cecil B. DeMille's *Joan the Woman* in 1916. When Victor Fleming started production on *Joan of Arc* for Sierra Pictures, he was in competition with the Joan of Arc projects that *Variety* reported to have been in progress at all the major studios in 1946.[1] David O. Selznick had already found his Joan in Jennifer Jones and had commissioned a script by Ben Hecht for a film that was never made.[2] What could explain this sudden surge of interest in Joan of Arc? Jean Bethke Elshtain has observed that World War II caused a shift in the rhetoric of war. The concept of war as a gloriously chivalrous enterprise had certainly faded before the beginning of the Second World War. Yet it was only the earth-encompassing debacle of the Second World War that fully revealed that war was not simply a means of asserting power but an unpredictable force beyond human control. The resultant postwar sense of vulnerability in the early years of the Cold War may explain the attraction of Joan of Arc's defiant and iconoclastic persona.[3] Given the nature of the films about Joan that were both made and planned, however, the motivation for reviving the story seems to be of a different sort.

Joan of Arc was not used during World War II to recruit women as military personnel or as industrial workers, despite her success as a propaganda instrument during the First World War. Perhaps the fear that women would take their economic and social power to heart if inspired by as uncompromising a figure as Joan made the heroine too risky to use. After the war the popular press was filled with images and stories of women who were thrilled to return home to their families or to the supportive clerical jobs that they "really wanted" when the men returned to "their" jobs.[4] Yet at the same time, articles began to appear about the loss of femininity in American women, who were described as increasingly unstable and dangerous.[5] In the cinema, the capable Rosie the Riveter type had evolved by 1945 into characters more like the neurotically independent Joan Crawford in *Mildred Pierce* of 1945 (Michael Curtiz) or the perverse Barbara Stanwyck in *The Strange Love of Martha Ivers* of 1946 (Lewis Milestone). The growing use of psychiatry both in everyday life and as a cinematic motif helped to blame the logical social repercussions of war's end on the behavior of women who refused to be either docile wives or ever-present mothers.[6] Films epitomized by *Possessed* of 1946 (Curtis Bernhardt) and King Vidor's *Beyond the Forest* of 1949, which featured two of Hollywood's most notoriously autonomous actresses both on screen and off, Crawford and Bette Davis, respectively, subjected women to excessive medical control and, often, death.[7] By the end of the war, *Life, Time,* the *Saturday Evening Post,* and *House Beautiful* had begun to berate women for letting their country down during the war. This ill-deserved belittlement has been interpreted as an attempt to create a sense of inferiority in the women who did not want to leave their rewarding jobs or their military positions after the war.[8] A more subtle tactic was the compensatory one of equating the heroism of Joan of Arc with the sacrifice of women's briefly held power. Female heroism was redefined to encompass the faithful service to and inspiration of the returning soldier.

The way a figure like Joan of Arc was employed after the war can be seen in the 1948 film *The Miracle of the Bells,* directed by Irving Pichel and based on a best-selling novel by Russell Janney. The convoluted story of the life of a young woman, dead of tuberculosis from the start, is told in flashback, from the hearse carrying the coffin, by her cynical, secretly adoring theatrical agent (Fred MacMurray). The inordinately good Olga (Alida Valli) had come from Coaltown to win the film role of a lifetime and then to die upon completing the part. Her story is magnified by the agent, in tandem with her priest (Frank Sinatra), to inspire her little hometown and persuade the film's producer to build a pulmonary research center. In the book, which was written with a film in mind, the role that Olga wins is in a movie called *The*

Garden of the Soul, while in *The Miracle of the Bells,* the role was changed to Joan of Arc and is the centerpiece of the film.[9]

In 1948 an article by one of the film's scriptwriters, Quentin Reynolds, appeared in *48* magazine called "It Isn't in the Book: How Joan of Arc Got into *The Miracle of the Bells.*" The film's producer, Jesse Lasky (who had produced DeMille's 1916 *Joan the Woman*), asked that the role within the film be changed so that the enacted scenes would give vivid evidence of the superiority of the actress. A first attempt envisioned Olga as a nightclub singer who would have to bid her soldier boyfriend farewell and then deal with his death in "a good schmaltzy heartbreak sequence." The next choice was Camille, which Ben Hecht, the co-writer, rejected as being too dreary and failing to show that Olga is a "great woman, a pure and wonderful woman . . . [with a] spiritual quality." The idea of Mother Cabrini was quickly eliminated, but Joan of Arc was approved immediately and a treatment was drafted by Hecht, who had previously written an entire Joan of Arc script for Selznick. The concept of Joan of Arc soon dominated the film's production; Joan's death scene was used to test hundreds of actresses for the part. The casting of the role became a public event, and the original book's publisher conducted a series of polls concerning who should play the Joan of Arc role. Readers were split between using a Hollywood star and an unknown, but the latter won when the film's producers decided that "Hollywood girls couldn't do it" or were not young enough for the role. When RKO's vice president in charge of production, Dore Schary, saw the twenty-four-year-old Italian actress Alida Valli in another film, the role was cast. Valli was new to American audiences but had already had an extensive career in European films. In addition, she had been decorated for heroism during the Second World War as a member of the Italian underground and thus carried the cachet of authenticity. The production's vaunted devotion to realism was said to be evident in Pichel's careful attention to detail of location and costume, realistic performances, and the re-creation of the square in Rouen on a Hollywood back lot. In his dedication to making the Joan of Arc sequences as genuine as possible, Pichel resurrected for Valli the armor worn by Geraldine Farrar in DeMille's *Joan the Woman.*[10]

Joan of Arc's presence in *The Miracle of the Bells* begins when an actress's selfish behavior on the set of the Joan of Arc film-within-the-film reveals to the director and crew that she is unworthy of the role. The pure and simple

Olga, who performs only because her dying father implored her to make people happy by singing and dancing, sets her heart on winning the part that is both her reward and her fate. Olga persuades her agent to let her audition for him privately in an unusual scene in which her apartment is transformed cinematically into the courtroom in which Joan confronts her prosecutors. This scene is a second-level narrative in which the space of the film shifts five hundred years in time without cues. Olga-as-Joan enters a courtroom and responds to the questions of men dressed as medieval priests and soldiers. She speaks movingly and humbly about being a simple peasant who would rather be at home cooking and sewing but must obey the voice of Saint Michael. She declares in her halting English that she will happily do God's will and speak the truth even if she burns for it. Although this scene ostensibly has been inserted to show Olga's thespian skills, it institutes both formally and thematically a correspondence between Joan's and Olga's devotion to divinely ordained feminine roles, and the fate to which this common bond leads.

The analogy between the two women is cemented by the double death scene in which Olga burns as Joan one day and expires in the contemporary narrative the following afternoon. In Joan's death scene, as Olga is tied to the stake she affirms that people should continue to dream of truth and justice because there is still kindness in the world. She pardons everyone and implores them to keep her in their memories as an inspiration. The demise of the two women is equated when a character solemnly reveals that Olga died because the actress insisted on doing Joan's final scene even though she had been quietly ill for many months. Indeed, the decision to have Olga's lungs fail because of coal dust echoes Joan of Arc's death from smoke inhalation on the fiery stake. Olga continues to play Joan on her deathbed, saying that because she is her people, she had to complete the film for the residents of Coaltown. It was perhaps the equation of the two deaths that led the reviewer for *Time* to write that the film's "box office gross should be a fair measure of the depths of U.S. pseudo-religious depravity."[11] After the star's demise, the esteemed Joan of Arc film-within-the-film is not distributed. As a final gift to his beloved Olga, the agent contrives a publicity stunt involving the ringing of all the bells in Coaltown in order to enlist the power of the press to force the release of the film. In addition, for largely unexplained reasons, the film's producer donates the money to build a clinic in

Fred MacMurray encouraging Alida Valli to share Joan of Arc's fate in *The Miracle of the Bells* (Irving Pichel, 1942). (The Academy of Motion Picture Arts and Sciences)

Coaltown. Another result of Olga's death is an event that the townspeople and the press classify as a miracle. As the priest explains to the agent, the apparently supernatural turning of the stone statues in the chapel during Olga's memorial service was due to the presence of vast numbers of people in a church built on earth honeycombed by caverns left by mining operations. The agent persuades the priest to keep this information to himself because the wondrous happening will inspire the credulous public. Although Olga is dead at this point, the film continues to call upon the Joan of Arc story. The benign deceit involving the miracles around Olga's death suggests that Joan of Arc's voices were equally specious but can be used by those with knowledge and power. The miraculously moving statues give the townspeople a "glimpse of beauty" before they return to their daily lives.

Unlike *Time, Variety* loved *The Miracle of the Bells,* calling it "tremendously moving" and referring to Valli's Joan of Arc performance as "high artistry."[12] In fact, Valli's performance as an actress and her dedication to acting are the focus of the film. Not only is Valli's character written as a fairy-tale innocent who performs with emotional abandon, but the script tells the viewer as much. The agent praises her to the producer: "Not only her acting. It's . . . it's what's inside her . . . what shines out of her. It's something you don't see in the world often. Don't test it—don't buy it, but take your hat off to it."[13] The contradictions in the film were captured by Bosley Crowther in his review in the *New York Times.* He called *The Miracle of the Bells* weak, limp, pompous, strange, and melancholic in comparison with the book. "Valli is evidently burdened with the notion that she is playing Camille, plus Joan of Arc, plus Olga Treskovna, yet not quite certain which she really is."[14] The sense that Valli's character is self-destructively conflicted is reinforced by lines in the film such as her giddy claim that the film's director is a "regular slave driver, but I love him for it. Oh, I feel as light as air." Although the film ends with Olga's voice-over words from the grave, "I am so happy. I did my job," exactly what Olga has accomplished is not obvious.

Uncertainty about both the value of what one had accomplished and what one's role was to be in the future occurs in Maxwell Anderson's *Joan of Lorraine* as well. Although the play was written in 1936, it was not produced on Broadway until 1946. *Joan of Lorraine* is not about Joan of Arc per se but about actors rehearsing a play about Joan of Arc and arguing about the relevance of the heroine and the nature of compromise. Sections of the play are devoted to establishing a sense of the great distance between Joan's time and that of the audience, as when the director twice requests in one short scene that pronunciations be investigated. Joan of Arc is not used as a heroine who can operate as a figurehead in any current political sense but is the focus of a psychological study of a confused woman.

The crux of *Joan of Lorraine* is the realization by the character who plays Joan, Mary Grey, that absolutes do not exist. This naive, even dim-witted character wants to play Joan as a girl in a fairy tale, whose life follows a well-known pattern. The rigorous director, named Masters, states the theme midway through the play: "We live by illusions and assumptions and concepts, every one of them as questionable as the voices Joan heard in the garden." As Mary learns this lesson over the course of the play, the action shifts back and forth between the present and the Middle Ages. Joan is first encountered at home, praying: "Oh, most sweet God, you must see now that too much was asked of me, more than I could do. You must see that it is better this way, most sweet God—that I stay with my own people and live quietly at home."[15] Soon after this scene, Joan's brothers boldly enact what they will say to the king. When Joan is directed to imitate her brothers, she says:

> Oh, if I could speak large and round like a boy, and could stand that way and make my words sound out like a trumpet,—if I could do that I could do all the things God wants me to do. But I'm a girl, and my voice is a girl's voice, and my ways are a girl's ways. If only I were a man! If only I could shout like a man!"[16]

This inept female warrior cannot start her quest without her uncle, and when a soldier observes, "Why, you're a little girl, Joan. Just a little girl," she replies, "Didn't you know it?" Joan describes the experience of her voices as making her feel like a girl in love, and finds that her last thoughts in this life are of her wardrobe: "I wanted a black dress when I left Domrémy, but I had to wear that old, red patched one."[17] Mary Grey's Joan of Arc in the play is a stubbornly stupid woman whose battles with the church over her proper role make her relevant in the postwar years.[18]

In addition to the delayed production of Anderson's play and Hollywood's renewed interest in depicting Joan after the war, the first of three similar photo essays produced for the *New York Times Magazine* over the next decade appeared.[19] "Saint Joan in Eight Moods" appeared in January 1947 as a two-page spread that featured a brief, ambiguous text and eight photographs of various actresses either posing in Joan of Arc costume or in their performance of the role. Sarah Bernhardt, in a publicity photograph for the 1890 Barbier *Jeanne d'Arc*, wears peasant dress and is described as being forty-six years old while playing the eighteen-year-old Joan. The 1909 production of Schiller's *Maid of Orleans* with Maude Adams, the "darling of the American theater," posing in armor and long hair, was featured next, followed by a portrait of a sweet Winifred Lenihan in Shaw's 1923 *Saint Joan*. The final two photographs on this first page are armored poses of an ecstatically praying Sybil Thorndike and a pensive Elisabeth Bergner in 1924 and 1925 European productions of Shaw, respectively. The second page of the article carried only three pictures, the first of which is from DeMille's 1916 *Joan the Woman* and features a row of overdressed churchmen and a blazing pyre with a tiny Geraldine Farrar tied to the stake at the far right of the image. Below is a photograph in a similar scale showing Katharine Cornell on her knees in a chapel in a 1936 production of Shaw. The final photograph is double or triple the size of the other images and was the centerpiece of the article: Ingrid Bergman poses in her armor costume from *Joan of Arc*, with her helmet under her arm, looking downward thoughtfully. The caption states that she gave a "haunting vision of the magic of the role."

The short text that accompanied the photographs reinforced the sense of a spectral Joan who was "endowed with . . . magic" and who "has held captive the imagination of mankind . . . [inspiring writers] to tell her story, each in his own way, and give us a Joan who is different and yet the same." Joan's appeal derived from the fact and nature of her death rather than from her actions during life. The latter all but disappear in the description of her career: "She started from Domrémy on the mission which led to the stake in Rouen." She was a "tragic figure" and "martyr to a cause on which her devotion placed a saintly halo." Moreover, the title of Shaw's play, *Saint Joan*, which stressed the post–First World War canonization that was intended to subdue Joan's iconoclastic influence, was deemed to be "sufficient." This collection of images and the discourse around them portrayed many Joans of various ages, in different costumes and poses, in order to posit something essential and eternal about Joan of Arc as a heroine. At the same time, the reader was reminded continually that Joan was made by specific authors and directors. If, as Roland Barthes has suggested, myth consists of history that has been transformed into nature, the multiple photo essays about Joan may be seen as attempts to postulate that the historical Joan is a myth.[20]

By the end of 1948 at least three books had been published about Joan in the United States, each illustrating her postwar function. Etienne Robo's book, with its glamorous frontispiece, was translated as *Saint Joan: The Woman and the Saint* and was self-described as a portrait of "the child, the woman, the saint." Of particular interest is its dedication to "the women who during the war served in king's armies. St. Joan is their patron and model. A woman, and by nature gentle, she made war because she loved peace; warrior by vocation, she liked home life better than soldiering."[21] Making a similar point about women's roles after the war is the book by Frances Winwar called *The Saint and the Devil: Joan of Arc and Gilles de Rais,* which strives to reinstate the lines of difference between femininity and masculinity, even if it has to equate the latter with evil. A photograph of Bergman in *Joan of Arc* adorns the cover of one edition of the book, which was "especially rewritten for extra enjoyment of Sierra Pictures' epic film in Technicolor starring Ingrid Bergman." Preceding the letter from Bergman and the story of Joan's fiery death that introduce the book is the description of "Joan, Thrilling Maid of Orleans . . . bareheaded soldier, beautiful saint, spirited prisoner . . . the flaming heroine of France."[22]

The scholarly text *Joan of Arc: An Anthology of History and Literature,* by Edward Wagenknecht, introduces Joan in 1948 as a sensual contemporary figure through his dedication to Geraldine Farrar, "a photographically eloquent 'Joan,'" and the placement on the back cover of photographs of both Farrar and Bergman. The erotic language used to describe Joan, who is envisioned not as distantly historical but as present in the body of the beautiful movie star, suggests something new in the relationship between women and war. The historian Klaus Theweleit has analyzed the meaning of femininity in relation to war in the fascist *Freikorps* in post–World War I Germany in ways that are not entirely alien to other situations of the time. Theweleit notes in *Male Fantasies* that conventionally feminine qualities were deliberately devalued in an attempt to structure meaning into the Second World War. The female came to symbolize a horrifying, insatiable Other who bore the blame for postwar psychopathology. By the middle of the century, the very concept of the woman warrior had become an anomaly, so that Joan of Arc's recurrence after the war begs investigation.

Joan of Arc of 1948 was a product of Sierra Pictures, which was created by the independent producer Walter Wanger, Victor Fleming, Bergman, and her husband, Petter Lindstrom, to capitalize on Bergman's current popularity. Wanger, inspired by what were known as British quality films, such as Laurence Olivier's *Henry V* of 1944, intended to make an artistic and intellectual film that would appeal to mature audiences in the United States. Although Wanger initially envisioned *Joan of Arc* as a spiritual experience as well as a spectacle, and welcomed endorsements from religious leaders during production, by the spring of 1948 the film was concerned chiefly with action. Wanger had sought to make a film that would "stand the test of time," but RKO, the film's financier, insisted on "spears and swords and flames and blood and horses and banners and roughhouse and armor."[23] The integrity with which the film was initiated was reflected in Bergman's attitude toward her character, as seen in publicity for the film and in her later autobiography. In her book, Bergman records that upon hearing that the film would be made, she ran to a chapel and prayed, "Thank you, God. Now Joan and I will finally make it. And Joan, I just hope that I can do your story justice."[24] This expensive, church-approved prestige film was released to heavy press coverage and a marquee in New York adorned with an eight-story cut-out of a banner-wielding Bergman in armor that was lit with tiny mirrors and the fiery glow of 900 lights.

The script held by the Library of Congress indicates that the original *Joan of Arc* was 145 minutes long.[25] This document indicates that the film began with Joan of Arc praying in church, then returning home to discuss with her family the horrors inflicted upon the French by the Anglo-Burgundians. The attention to historical detail and the concern with causal structure continue with the inclusion of Jacques d'Arc's purported dream that his daughter would run off with soldiers as a camp follower. The many positive reviews garnered by the film indicate that this straightforward approach to the story was appreciated. *Variety*, in particular, praised the film as not only honest and dedicated but part of a new, education-oriented kind of filmmaking. A more ambiguous observation by the same reviewer noted that the film was "not to be interpreted, necessarily, as having bearing on the contemporaneous."[26]

Skirting the edges of Bosley Crowther's generally positive review for the *New York Times* was a similar hesitation in regard to the film's relevance. While Crowther found the film stupendous and pictorially magnificent, he claimed that it failed to come to life and offer a real understanding of Joan of Arc because Bergman was too physical. He wrote that "the mystery, the meaning, and the magnificence of the poor girl called Joan have just been missed."[27]

On 20 July 1948, *Look* magazine featured a cover with a medium shot of Ingrid Bergman on horseback in full armor with sword raised, against a pure-white background with the small-print caption "Ingrid Bergman: A Picture Personality."[28] At that time Bergman was involved in the initial stages of her affair with the Italian director Roberto Rossellini, which was to provoke her denunciation on the floor of the United States Senate in March 1950 and calls in the press for a boycott of her films.[29] In light of this complication, *Look*'s photo essay and article, which equated the heroism of Joan of Arc with the generic sacrifices of American women after the war, appeared at the last possible moment. The multifaceted piece conflated both narratively and pictorially Joan of Arc's life, the cinematic version of that life, Bergman's real life, and the life of the American housewife.

The essay begins by linking Bergman with Joan, the "legend," by quoting the actress: "I always felt I looked like Joan of Arc, who was a big peasant girl. And all my life I dreamed of playing her." Bergman is described as grave, expressive, warm, and fresh, and she is characterized as "just about everybody's idea of how the inspired peasant heroine must have looked." After a brief description of how the film came to be made (it was said to have been the result of Bergman's immense popularity and drive, the success of *Joan of Lorraine* on Broadway, and $4.5 million), more personal things about Bergman are revealed. Bergman is said to contradict the rules of Hollywood beauty and glamour because she keeps her hair in the Joan of Arc "soup bowl" fashion for the sake of comfort, and she has notably large feet, wears flat shoes and size 16 dresses, and has the hearty laugh and stamina of a Viking. She is quoted: "I look just like a lot of the girls back home in Sweden." After brief mention of her many awards and the kind civility with which she acknowledges her fans, her domestic world is discussed. Bergman's life at home, where she is known as Mrs. Petter Lindstrom and the mother of a nine-year-old daughter, is said to be "uncomplicated." Taking "great pride in her husband's career," Bergman "looks forward to Sundays—cook's day off—when she can sort laundry, fix Pia's clothes and try her hand at cooking." The entire family is described as frugal and hardworking, getting up at seven in the morning every day. Furthermore, Bergman drives to work in her inexpensive gray car and spends a mere five minutes having her makeup and hair done. Although the final paragraph of the essay relates that the actress likes the challenge of difficult roles and women who are not necessarily good, Joan of Arc is said to be her favorite part. The last line quotes Bergman: "Now that I've finally played her on the screen, I look back and think: It wasn't like acting at all. I understood what she said and did so well that I just became Joan and let her come to life."[30]

The juxtaposition of advertisements with the Bergman essay in *Look,* as is typical in popular journalism, complicates the text. The reader cannot help but absorb the influence of the five advertisements that face the pages of the article.[31] The piece begins on the left page of the spread with a large, dark close-up of Bergman in profile, leaning against a heavy door with eyes closed and hands grasping a huge iron knocker. The opposite page, which is seen first because of its location, shows a close-up of the same size of a nurse with a glittering "Pepsodent smile" who looks out boldly at the reader. This real Mary Louise Shine, R.N., had been selected as a model and in 1948 her face appeared in ads and on billboards across the United States, "inspiring young Americans to join the proud nursing profession." She is also described as being "the recent bride of a Chicago doctor." Turning the page of the magazine discloses three photographs that illustrate the article, two of which show a half-dressed Bergman being costumed and having makeup applied on horseback. Again on the right side of the spread, and this time with red added to the black-and-white image, is an advertisement for Mennen Skin Bracer that features a provocative drawing of a winking woman in a small, two-piece bathing suit and high heels, sitting with knees and one arm raised. The ad is directed to men, one of whom is drawn aggressively grinning and grasping at the woman at the bottom of the half-page ad, with the line "Its He-Man Aroma 'WOWS' the Ladies!" On the next page, in the same position on the far right, is an ad for hair brushes that features an upside-down head with dark hair streaming across the image. The woman's face, without a neck, features dark lips and closed eyes heavily made up. Opposite is a series of production photographs from the film, one of which shows

Bergman being tied to the stake by the film's director with a lit cigarette hanging from his mouth. The next two right-hand pages sell refrigerators and Kodak film, one with a photograph of a young couple and the hand-written text "Jim's folks have had their Servel since 1928 and it's still going strong! Naturally he voted for Servel. I fell in love with its new conveniences. Now it's Servel for us, too." The Kodak advertisement is a long-shot "candid" black-and-white photograph of four smiling young people at play, three sitting on the edge of a pier and one of the two men arranging them to snap their picture.

Throughout the five pages of an article that portrays the scandalous foreign actress Ingrid Bergman as an ordinary housewife and then links her with the medieval heroine Joan of Arc, whom she simply "becomes," is a significant array of messages. *Look*'s advertisers celebrate a woman who chose women's work, nursing, and marriage to her superior, and a woman who subsumed her identity in that of her husband and his parents in the purchase of an expensive household appliance. Interspersed among these images are pictures of passive sexuality and mindless beauty, ending with an image of two young heterosexual couples having old-fashioned innocent fun as directed by one of the men as he arranges the world before him.

Joan of Arc and Joan of Arc were the basis for *Look*'s examination of Bergman as an actress. The photographs and captions in the essay stress the production of the film and the ways that the film re-created history. On the first page of the piece, headed "Bergman as Joan," the caption says, "For the prison scenes in *Joan of Arc*, two days of Technicolor tests and a new kind of makeup were needed to make radiant Ingrid Bergman look pale and wan." The next page is a large photograph of Joan in extreme long shot, wearing full armor, with a caption saying that her "armor, hand-made of aluminum, weighed 20 pounds." The same spread contains two smaller candid shots, one of Bergman being dressed in armor, its leg pieces held up by garters, and another of Bergman being made up on a horse, which is being held for her while a man leans over "to give Bergman some last-minute smudges." The final page of the main article features a large photograph of preparations for a battle sequence, captioned: "On the sound-stage battlefield, the armor-clad star stands by between takes as her 'soldiers' prepare to storm the fortress of Tourelles.in the Siege of Orleans. About 400 of the 4000 extras used in *Joan of Arc* took part in this sequence." A much smaller photograph shows the scene from the film. As noted above, another photograph depicts Bergman encircled by ropes and chains by a determined director, with a cigarette, which bears the caption "Fleming shows executioners how to chain Joan for the burning at the stake." The final image, of Bergman in costume looking down on the "crowd gathered for the martyrdom scene" with an 8mm movie camera in her hand, explains the large-print heading on the page: "Joan's armor and martyrdom left Bergman untired, with energy for her movie hobby." This amalgamation of real life, performance, historical events, and fiction—all mediated via the popular press—would have sent a powerful message to the postwar readers of *Look*. Bergman's and Joan of Arc's work were shown as being secondary to the real labor of the men around them. The essay suggested that women's roles are performative and superficial on several levels. Women were to maintain their beauty via consumer tools, take the back seat as a matter of course, and feel that this behavior was not only natural but akin to a meaningful sacrifice.

Superimposed on the last photograph, showing Bergman filming a scene in which she as Joan would logically appear, is the advice: "Turn the page for *Joan*-inspired fashions." Just as Bergman performed Joan in the raiment of the heroine yet was also a domesticated Everywoman, the *Look* reader could also "be" Joan. The costumes for *Joan of Arc,* designed by Barbara Karinska, won the first Academy Award given for costume design. Unlike the DeMille film and other Joan of Arc vehicles, which took pride in the use of medieval texts to achieve authenticity in armor and costume, this version turned to a designer who specialized in idealizing the female body. Karinska's goal was not to re-create the era or aura of Joan of Arc but to accentuate the line of the thigh.[32] Thus *Look*'s two-page "Joan of Arc fashions" feature was less anomalous than it might appear. As the text says: "First rushes on *Joan of Arc,* starring Ingrid Bergman, revealed its fashion importance. Colors alone are so impressive that Burlington Mills will high-light Joan of Arc shades for fall. *Look* chooses close-ups with costume ideas which will undoubtedly influence clothes this fall."[33]

The pages that make up the feature are divided into quarters, each containing a schematic drawing of the accoutrement, the name of the item, and a small photograph of Bergman in the film. The first section is pure fashion, with the word "gloves" followed by "Joan of Arc's silver armor includes gleaming gauntlets. John Frederics sketches gauntlet gloves—in leather or

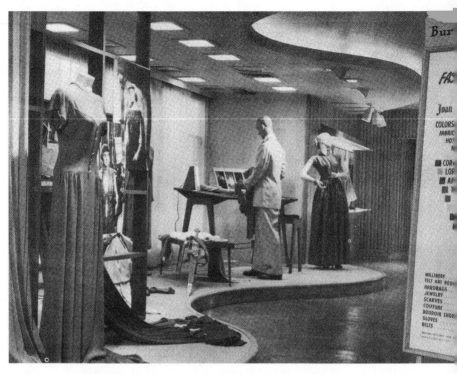

Promotion of Joan of Arc fashions (1948). Brochure designed to encourage the clothing industry to incorporate Joan of Arc motifs. (Author's collection)

wool for daytime wear, in satin or brocade for evening." The photograph shows Bergman holding up her hand as if modeling her gauntlet. The next item is more to the point, as "helmet hat" is followed by "The unwieldly [sic] helmet of 15th century warfare is brought up-to-date as a casually smart hat that has a high, snugly fitting crown, juts out abruptly in front [sic]." The photograph depicts a pensive Bergman in the helmet with full visor extended. The drawing shows a woman in a modified baseball cap that is only remotely similar to the helmet. The lack of conviction in the drawing and design and the misspelling and garbled grammar imply that little care was taken in promoting the concept of Joan of Arc fashions. However, the gesture of bringing Joan up to date and outfitting contemporary housewives in feminized evocations of warrior wear are consistent with the rest of the article. Women wearing chic, modern, nonutilitarian versions of what were

Look Predicts a Rash of
Joan of Arc
fashions

First rushes on *Joan of Arc*, starring Ingrid Bergman, revealed its fashion importance. Colors alone are so impressive that Burlington Mills will high-light Joan of Arc shades for fall. LOOK chose close-ups with costume ideas which will undoubtedly influence clothes this fall. John Frederics' sketches show how.

Feature on Joan of Arc fashions in *Look*, 20 July 1948. (Copyright 1948 by Cowles Magazines, Inc.)

helmet hat

The unwieldly helmet of 15th century warfare is brought up-to-date as a casually smart hat that has a high, snugly fitting crown, juts out abruptly in front.

called Joan of Arc's mail sweater, shoes, hat, sleeve effect, or cape were domesticated versions of the woman warrior, whose mid-twentieth-century task was to be the fashionable wife and mother.

On 14 November 1948, just four months after the *Look* article and four months before Bergman left the United States for Italy, *Life* ran a cover story on *Joan of Arc*. This ten-page essay could not have differed more from its predecessor in its complete lack of extratextual reference. Even allowing for the fact that *Life* generally had a more refined visual style than *Look,* the devotion to *Joan of Arc* of five uninterrupted spreads privileged the piece. The photo essay carries the reader through the film by way of a series of production photographs, with rounded corners that make the images resemble film frames. A brief text intelligently and critically introduces the historical Joan of Arc, the history of Joan's literary appearances, and the film's background, while praising both Bergman and José Ferrer and criticizing the Technicolor. The image of Bergman on horseback on the magazine's cover is supported by the text, which describes Joan of Arc as charming. However, the charge that she was "a simple-minded, stubborn country girl . . . tangled in intrigues beyond her comprehension" is difficult to connect with Bergman's Joan and the images from the film. With ever larger photographs and smaller captions, the essay moves through the beginning of the mission, the siege of Orléans, the coronation, the trial, and the stake. The piece ends with a full-page image of a glamorous Bergman tied to the stake, with eyes closed and head back in the tradition of the ecstatic Saint Teresa. The essay seems to be more a serious advertisement for *Joan of Arc* and the Bergman star persona than an article about the film that would connect to the experiences of the magazine's readers.

By June 1950, RKO had released the shortened, 100-minute version of *Joan of Arc* that is known today, after Sierra Pictures had met with foreclosure. Matthew Bernstein has noted that the failure of the original film was due not to any problems inherent in the film but to unaccounted-for changes in the audience after the war. On one level, the young people who had been the most ardent moviegoers simply spent less time at the movies now that they had started having families and were buying more consumer goods to fill their new houses. A more profound change in the postwar audience was an increasing cynicism that lessened the inclination to be manipulated by the extensive promotion that surrounded *Joan of Arc.* The self-reflexivity of

Anderson's *Joan of Lorraine,* as well as its questioning of the woman warrior's integrity and strength, were far more current.[34] In any case, by 1950 Ingrid Bergman had left the country as an adulterer, with a child born out of wedlock, and clearly had rejected the subservient position celebrated by *Look* just two years earlier.

Unlike the original film, the shortened version does not start with Joan's early life to provide a sense of causality and character, but uses the film noir tactic of working backward from a fixed, morbid end.[35] This change in the order of narration of the events of Joan's life was in keeping with a normal postwar tendency in film to soften the all too present effects of suffering and death. In general, the films of this era were characterized by either an ambiguous story that tried to transcend pain while acknowledging it, as in melodrama, or a rigorously unsentimental and controlled narrative, as in the combat film, that made death seem to make sense.[36] The shortened *Joan of Arc* has much in common with both genres. In her book about the combat film, Jeanine Basinger presents what she calls an archetypal example of the type.[37] From item 1 through 14 on her list, *Joan of Arc* actually follows the pattern: credits unfold against a military insignia followed by a dedication; the mission is begun with a sense of the unfitness of some members; the group has a commentator; the hero's leadership has been forced upon her; a military operation is begun and unfolds with movement and repose in the presence of the enemy; military iconography is displayed; conflict rages but rituals from the past and daily life soothe; members die and a climactic battle leads to resolution. However, *Joan of Arc* also contains visually anomalous moments when raw emotion erupts from narrative control. Near the end of the film, for example, Bergman is dressed in black, against a black background in an unusual long take of a high-angle close-up that isolates her tear-stained face into the very image of suffering. Whether for the irrecoverable losses of the war or for what women seem to have lost after the war, Bergman's tormented, crying Joan of Arc is a palliative for the postwar experience.[38]

The abbreviated version of *Joan of Arc* of 1950 begins in the present with a male voice-over that is identified with the Roman Catholic Church. The voice-of-God narration ultimately posits that the church benignly manipulated Joan to make her what she has become by speaking and giving value to her story. The first shot of the film reveals layers of superimposed candles and ringing bells as the camera tracks toward a cardboard image of the altar of St. Peter's Basilica in Rome. At the same time, in a condescendingly reverent tone, the voice-over declares, "In the year of our Lord 1920, with holy rite and ritual, Rome makes its uttermost reparation to one who five hundred years ago stood heretic accused before her enemies." This voice-over treads a delicate line by identifying itself with the institution that sanctifies Joan with all its visual splendor while verbally separating itself from the actions of the church that burned her in the first place. The ecclesiastical institution, which is not identified as Joan's adversary, becomes "Rome," while Joan, who has yet to be introduced, is merely "one." By beginning the film with the canonization, the church glosses over its negative role and begins to abstract the moral it has placed on the heroine's story. This postwar version of the life begins with a conclusion that leaps past the suffering at the stake to the "happy" ending celebrating Joan's sainthood. The film suggests that the church takes pride in having given Joan the chance to die as a virgin (rather than a warrior) martyr. This reworking of church history is given the stamp of authenticity by the film's official historian, Père Paul Doncoeur.

The film's frame story starts as the hands of a monk open a large white book that contains Joan's life. This reversal of events continues in the next scene, which elides Joan's death and the epiphany and introduces Joan as a victim at the mercy of the ecclesiastical court. This characterization creates pity for Joan and leads the viewer to identify with the sympathetic tones of the voice-over. The voice-of-God narration interrupts the narrative six times throughout the film, not to provide information but to reassert its control. Although it is conventional in historical films to use a voice-over to summarize information that cannot be easily visualized, the film depends entirely on the male voice to convey factual matters. The hovering voice speaks with omniscience of the past and the future, in addition to correcting the statements of the characters within the story. Whenever necessary, this authoritative speech reinterprets the aspects of the plot, particularly involving gender, that cannot be changed without altering the basic line of the Joan of Arc story. The voice functions to speak for the emotional, inarticulate Joan and to continually reiterate the glory of her martyrdom.

After beginning with the trial, the film turns back to Joan's innocent youth. The voice-over introduces Joan as a "half-literate child" and declares that God called her to save France. (Even the invisible and already powerful narrator is hard-pressed to convince the viewer that the womanly Ingrid Bergman is a child.) The voice-over speaks for God in place of the female saints, and Joan reacts tearfully with a self-deprecating litany of questions. As she considers her task, there is an inordinate number of references to her father, who in both history and legend has almost no importance. Joan introduces herself as the "daughter of Jacques d'Arc"; the king's agent, General de Baudricourt, responds that her father should box her ears to put her in her place; and Joan's uncle is fearful that Jacques will not forgive him for having aided Joan. The script does everything possible to counteract the strength that Bergman brings to the role. As Joan, she repeatedly states that "there is nothing in [her]" and she would prefer to be at home in her "proper place" with women but that she must obey her heavenly Father. In speaking with soldiers, she reiterates that she is an inferior female and apologizes for usurping a man's job. She is an amalgam of female stereotypes, acting stupid and helpless at one point and later nagging the men to stop cursing. Professing to know nothing about war, doubting the victory at Orléans, and tearfully refusing to acknowledge her success before the people of the city, this Joan is scarcely recognizable.

In its attempt to fit Joan into traditionally feminine roles while maintaining that these subservient roles are heroic, the film characterizes Joan in contradictory ways. She is pious and naive to a fault: she fails to understand the court jester's implications regarding her relationship with her two male escorts, and she orders all women to be removed from her camps, under the assumption that they are all prostitutes. Yet later, when Joan is forced to say farewell to her soldiers, she relates to them in maternal and sexualized ways. On the one hand, Joan chastises the rough General La Hire as if he were her small son for not saying his prayers. Then, as the handsome aristocrat Alençon kneels before her to express his undying devotion, she looks at him passionately before turning away. Near the end of the film, after the coronation and a string of victories, Joan despairs over the corruption of the king and decides to continue on her own. She stands at the altar of Saint Denis to give up her shining armor in a symbolic gesture and swears to rid France of the English. During Joan's grasp at independence, the voice-over again intrudes to provide the rational explications that the perplexed Joan is apparently incapable of giving. The voice declares that Joan must endure agony but that her demise "will bring her more than her highest

Ingrid Bergman in *Joan of Arc* (Victor Fleming, 1948). (Author's collection)

imagining, greatness and glory for France, and for her, peace, and such shining eminence as few in history have ever attained."

Continuing the film's conservative trajectory, Joan spins yarn with the wife of her captor after her arrest at Compiègne. The men whose roles she has usurped put her back in her place while her fate is decided elsewhere. Just before Joan's capture, the British Warwick and the English sympathizers among the French put the threat posed by Joan into a political context. The former enemies become human and comprehensible, so that the only issue in the trial is Joan's adoption of male apparel. Joan tells her judges that she wears men's clothing because she lives among soldiers and because God told her to do so, but that she would abandon it if allowed to hear mass. Although her allegiance to her male dress and all it stands for is not strong, trousers continue their protective function while Joan is imprisoned with rapacious guards. The film makes it evident that Joan is killed not for the heresy of claiming direct communion with the divine but for wearing inappropriate clothes.

The scene in which Joan awaits her death, in the unusual dark high-angle close-up described earlier, is her moment of strength. Joan reasserts that she did hear voices and that she would rather die and go to them than remain a victim of a corrupt church and state. Yet because of her previous passivity and her later acquiescence on the stake, this phase also illustrates her ultimate victimization. With the eroticized image of a beautiful, suffering Bergman chained to the stake on the screen, the voice-over says that her death is her "greatest triumph." The suggestion that women can do no better than to sacrifice themselves is further stressed by the clichéd death scene, in which a priest prays fervently while celestial voices sing and light streams from painted clouds. In view of the nature of Bergman's real life in the late 1940s, it is ironic that the actress should have played the meek saint of the Roman Catholic Church for American women as they struggled with changing social roles.

~~⇒ 7   **Looking for Joan of Arc**

Hedy Lamarr in *The Story of Mankind*
and Jean Seberg in *Saint Joan*

It is impossible to know whether images of Joan of Arc helped in any way to return women to their homes after the Second World War by making them feel heroic about sacrificing their independence. But it is clear that many women did quit their jobs.[1] Historians, particularly those working with women's history, continue to investigate how women's roles could have expanded and contracted so drastically in so short a time without confusing people and challenging deep-seated attitudes about gender and the sexual division of labor. Some argue that the trauma of the Depression followed by that of the Second World War was so great that women returned en masse to the imagined stability and reassuring domesticity of the home in the 1950s. Many of these same historians believe that the experience of the 1940s may have had delayed effects in the 1960s and 1970s, through children raised by mothers who had briefly known social and financial independence.[2] Other scholars, such as Leila Rupp, argue that behavior during the Second World War was typical of any war period, in which social mores are loosened and normally unacceptable behavior is allowed without causing permanent cultural transformation. After the war, images of Joan of Arc not only increased but were increasingly transformed along the conservative lines initiated in the 1940s.

In the 1950s, vicarious adventure in women's popular literature gave way almost completely to stories about babies, home, kitchen, and domestic affection.[3] However dissonantly, Joan of Arc's presence continued to grow. As we have seen, during the war Joan was all but absent, with only three articles about her appearing in popular journals between 1939 and 1945. Between the end of the war and 1949, Joan emerged more frequently and in magazines of wider circulation, such as *Newsweek* and the *Saturday Review of Literature*. During the 1950s, however, at least fourteen essays about Joan appeared, and the number grew steadily through 1970. In 1949 a book by Christopher Bick titled *The Bells of Heaven: The Story of Joan of Arc* directed interest toward Joan's childhood. Assuming that attraction to Joan was an adolescent phenomenon, Bick wrote that he wanted to make the story alive and pleasant by acquainting the reader intimately with the heroine. One-third of the book concentrates on Joan's childhood and an entire chapter is devoted to "the dream of Jacques d'Arc." In 1950 *Classics Illustrated* no. 78 featured Joan of Arc with a picture of Ingrid Bergman as Joan on horseback on the cover. The drawings inside show Joan as a voluptuous peasant who sits on her horse with an angry countenance, emoting in response to the voice bubble in the sky: "My voices tell me to stay here!" As is typical in this format, the enthusiasm of the illustrators was directed to the spectacle of the torture scenes as well as the fire, smoke, and agony of the stake. Overall, the blend of factual history and contemporary attitudes is humorous, as when two girls smirk like teenagers in a typical comic book of the time, saying, "Commander of the army! Ha! Ha!"

In mid-October 1951 the second of the three *New York Times Magazine* features about multiple Joan of Arcs appeared.[4] This photo essay was inspired by the newest production of Shaw's *Saint Joan* on Broadway in 1951, with Uta Hagan in the lead role (just as Bergman's appearance in *Joan of Lorraine* in 1946 led to the first version of the feature). The brief essay that appeared with the photographs describes Hagan as "the latest in a long line of actresses who have tried to re-create the heroic Maid of Orléans." The text claims that "Joan of Arc's brief and tragic life has fascinated historians, novelists and playwrights for centuries, each offering his own interpretations of the forces and spirit that moved her." The essay perpetuates the gender division in which women try to "be" Joan, while men give meaning to her. The implication that there is a Joan of Arc essence to be found and that each attempt is a variation on the evanescent theme is evident in the essay. Nowhere is it suggested, here or in the many other texts surrounding Joan's appearance in the 1950s, that the return to Joan of Arc's trial might have been connected to the hearings of the House Un-American Activities Committee.[5]

A quotation from Shaw dominates the *Times Magazine*'s authorless text about Joan, which bears the awkward title "Seven Ideas of Joan." Shaw had prefaced the published versions of his play with an extended interpretation and reconsideration of Joan's relation to the institutions of her day. Attacking what he saw as misinterpretations of her life, Shaw was convinced that the entire story was far more down to earth than mystical. He stressed that everything Joan did made sense, and that if she had not claimed to have been directed by saints, she would have been received as a successful general like any other. Shaw's claim can be dismissed as intentionally polemical, since Joan's unsubstantiatable voices are the crux of her longevity. Without the voices that simultaneously beg explanation and give reassurance that strong women are unstable, Joan most likely would be of little interest.

The images that accompany the brief essay differ from the previous Joan of Arc photo essay in their consistency with one another. This feature is one page in length, rather than two, so that the photographs are uniformly smaller. The actresses featured are the same but for the addition of Hagan and the elimination of Geraldine Farrar and Elisabeth Bergner. The chronology is irrelevant, with Hagan in 1951 followed by Winifred Lenihan in Shaw of 1923, Sybil Thorndike in the London premiere of Shaw in 1924, Katharine Cornell in the 1936 revival of Shaw, Bergman's 1946 *Joan of Lorraine,* Sarah Bernhardt as the 1890 Barbier Joan of Arc, and Maude Adams in a 1909 production of Schiller. The photographs seem to have been selected for similarity of pose, in which the actress appears to be divinely transported and unaware of the viewer's gaze. Each Joan is shown in an uncontextualized medium shot, wearing either peasant dress or armor without a helmet, in dramatic profile or semiprofile with the face tilted either up or pensively down in prayer or meditation. Only Bernhardt stares out at the viewer.

Ingrid Bergman's performance in the well-distributed and familiar version of *Joan of Arc* released in 1950 quickly came to define the heroine in the United States and elsewhere. The popularity of the film, along with Bergman's celebrity, made the subject of the heroine ubiquitous in popular literature, journalism, and elsewhere through the decade.[6] Otto Preminger's *Saint Joan* and Irwin Allen's *Story of Mankind,* with Jean Seberg and Hedy

Lamarr as Joan, respectively, appeared in 1957. These two films, in which Joan spans the spectrum from Seberg's naive child to Lamarr's beauty queen, encompass many of the contradictions found in the representation of women that had come to the fore after World War II and were later debated in the women's movement of the 1960s and 1970s.

In 1951 four texts that represent the nature of the diverse interest in Joan of Arc appeared. The decade began with the first version of Martha Graham's dance based on Joan, called *The Triumph of St. Joan.* In one of the last two solo pieces of her career, Graham danced a part that seemed to unify the increasingly fragmented Joan persona, since it was described as being about "the Maid, the Warrior, and the Martyr." Rechoreographed for a group, the piece was presented as *Seraphic Dialogue* in 1955. This transformation was consistent with Graham's move away from politically specific work in favor of more universal themes. In contradistinction to the earlier unification of Joan, the revision splits Joan of Arc into separate abstract spheres in a traditional way so that the individual figure is replaced by a series of Virtues.[7] However, it is not particularly helpful to discuss the story or character of Graham's Joan with any specificity since her dances were not narrative. Yet it is notable that a feminist artist sought to embody Joan twice during the 1950s. Similar attempts to address or use Joan in feminist art and history were not made again for another two decades.

More typical of this contradictory period and almost paradigmatic in its form is the travelogue by Leighton Houghton called *In the Steps of Joan of Arc.* Houghton used Joan's story as a structure from which to launch anecdotes about his own life. While he profited from Joan's cultural resonance at the time, Houghton seems to erase Joan as a historical entity. He wrote that "highly intellectual modern writers [with their] sophisticated paganism and complex unbelief" were incapable of understanding the divinity of Joan of Arc. The ideal Joan was a symbol for the purity of those who, like the author, did not attempt to understand Joan as an agent since they recognized that she was a tool of the divine. Also appearing in 1951 were two marginal works that highlight the tension between the concept of Joan as an uncomprehending child and the image of Joan as a glamorous celebrity. A Brother Ernest chose to portray Joan as a sad, long-haired little girl in the tradition of the virgin saints in *Flames against the Sky: A Story of St. Joan of Arc.* At the same time, Anne Emery produced a *Joan of Arc* that featured images of a movie-star Joan on horseback and on trial who was surrounded by adoring monks. Throughout the remainder of the decade at least one essay or book appeared each year to argue the various positions that could be taken toward the heroine. Unlike the culturally specific meanings that attached to Joan in relation to women's roles during particular wartime periods, Joan of Arc's significance now fluctuated continually.

The title of the 1952 book by Mary Purcell, *The Halo on the Sword: St. Joan of Arc,* provides a neat image of the general attitude toward Joan of the time. This sentimental fictionalization of Joan's story is an extreme example of its kind, since the author felt that culture and Catholicism were synonymous. Purcell's vision of the relationship between Joan's story and the larger culture was defined by the image of the victorious sword encircled by a halo. This same logic explains why the warrior Joan of Arc was sanctified as a virgin martyr. An essay by Milton Waldmar of 1954 consciously returned to an investigation of the 1920 canonization by questioning how an excommunicated soldier could have become a saint.[8] Evidently ignorant of the history of the Catholic Church in this regard, the author concluded that Joan's value derived from the fact that she is dead. Only in defeat, tied to the stake, is she comprehensible as a female who recognized and died for the fact that she was nothing without the directing voice of God. Two books published in 1956 continued Waldmar's attempt to unite Joan's life with Christ's as a symbol of resurrection. A translation of *The Maid of Orléans* by Sven Stolpe, which was intended to encourage the people of Communist-occupied countries, discounted Joan's earthly actions. She was painted as a mystical mirror of Christ, whose life was prophesied and who was to be remembered for doubting, recanting, and dying as a broken martyr. Frederick Cook's young adult book, *Young Girl of France and Other Stories,* made Joan the mirror of Christ by finding analogies between Joan's victorious ride into Orléans and Christ's Palm Sunday entrance into Jerusalem. The stress on the mystery of Joan of Arc stifled the inquiry about the anomalous aspects of her story. Cook absorbed Joan into already significant narratives through the Christ analogy, and through the invention of a maternal drive that reconfigured Joan as the Florence Nightingale of the Hundred Years' War.

Serious, scholarly investigation of Joan of Arc was carried out at this time by the renowned French medievalist Régine Pernoud. In 1955 her work was translated and published in the United States as *The Retrial of Joan of Arc.*

The review of the book in *The Commonweal* carried the title "Maid of Honor."[9] While the reviewer of Pernoud's book was amazed by the numbers of witnesses who testified for Joan during the retrial of 1456, which resulted in nullification of the first trial, she concluded that there was "no accounting for Joan of Arc on a natural level." With pessimistic resignation, she all but dismissed Pernoud's book as another in an endless chain of books inspired by the inexplicability of Joan of Arc. The review of Pernoud's work in *Time,* in contrast, found Joan of Arc perfectly explained by *The Retrial of Joan of Arc.*[10] Beginning in medias res with Joan's capture, the critic said, "Stripped of armor, the soldier was seen to be a handsome, well-knit girl of 18 with short-cropped dark hair." After briefly describing the matter of the book, the writer revealed that "what actually brought [Joan of Arc] to the stake was her return to men's clothes after she had promised to give them up." He continued with examples of what various witnesses said, with the stress on Joan's plucky conviction and determination, and on the nature of her sexuality. The essay concluded that although the retrial found Joan wrongly condemned, she would have had to be burned because she was a "devilish nuisance." The final, Shavian line claimed that "saints have a way of being insufferable until they are good and dead." From Pernoud's wide-ranging book the *Time* critic extrapolated a message about the dangers facing women who challenged their cultural and sexual roles.

One of the more illuminating essays to appear during the 1950s was John Steinbeck's "The Joan in All of Us" in the *Saturday Review.*[11] The brief article was accompanied by two small nineteenth-century engravings, one showing Joan in front of her distinctively asymmetrical house in Domrémy surrounded by sheep, and the other featuring Joan on her knees with head bowed in front of a king. Steinbeck began, "It is a rare writer in any language who has not thought long and longingly of Joan of Arc as a subject." He discussed the great numbers of works written, the multiple approaches possible, and the fact that Joan's story allows each writer "some corroboration of his convictions, no matter what they may be." The gist of the essay was the utter impossibility of Joan's life. Steinbeck claimed that Joan's class should have prevented access to royalty and her illiteracy should have made her conviction easy for ecclesiastical prosecutors to win. He stressed that Joan simply could not have raised the siege of Orléans, since she did not have the bloodlines to command respect nor had she received the necessary childhood training. Steinbeck argued that "war was as carefully systematized and formal as ballet. Assault and defense were known movements set and invariable. War was no business for amateurs." Steinbeck concluded by saying that writers are drawn to Joan because she proves that dreams come true and miracles do happen, even though his own "sense of reality is outraged by her story." The central argument of the piece is that war is a mystical experience that is by definition unavailable to women. Furthermore, if women feel that they have been part of a war effort, they are to understand that their experience was, like Joan's, "a fairytale so improbable" as to have no bearing on the real world.

With Joan of Arc circulating in the culture at large as widely as she was, it is little wonder that she appeared in the consumer-driven 1950s in numerous children's books, as the theme of a coloring book, as a doll, and as a Halloween mask. The books, whether from general or religious presses, strove to create a Joan who was "lovely, glorious, young," and "so lovable, that we can still feel her charm across the long centuries."[12] At the same time that Joan's story was reconfigured in the adult popular press as mysterious and even legendary, the next generation was learning to see Joan as a Mouseketeer. In the early years of the century, to dress up in a Joan of Arc costume was empowering to some degree, whether the act was part of a suffragist rally or a masquerade. By the 1950s, it appears from the evidence in popular culture, Joan of Arc no longer signified courage, skill, or confidence. The child's plastic mask of Joan of Arc from the 1950s is adorned with a silver helmet, a gold mail collar, brilliant blue eye shadow, rouge, and red lipstick.[13] The dolls are all less than eight inches in height with a curious blend of a tiny face with Kewpie mouth and chubby cheeks and intricate and beautiful accoutrements of metal, velvet, and fur. It is impossible to know the degree of distribution or function of these dolls, but their existence indicates something of the nature of the shift in both the meaning and use of Joan of Arc.

An offbeat magazine of the era called *Fate,* which specialized in strange occurrences and sensational topics, featured on its cover a helmeted Joan of Arc with red lipstick who looked out at the reader seductively.[14] The article, "The 10 Proofs of Joan of Arc," was part of a tradition in which Joan was claimed as an occult figure, and was also one of the first representations of Joan as a femme fatale. In the same vein, Gerald Hopkins's translation of

Lucien Fabré's *Joan of Arc,* published in the United States in 1954, has an obsessive tone that was characteristic of the time. The writer described himself as having become Joan's "bond-slave. With an insatiable appetite he devoured the substance of every book" about her in an attempt "to [discharge] some of the debt which all men owe to beings of so rare a quality." After relating the history, the book ends with the disclosure that "the body of the virgin, who had been of all virgins most chaste, was revealed . . . in its utter nudity." A similar fetishizing tone is evident in an article by Richard Gilman in *Jubilee,* in which Joan is described in detail, down to an imagined "beauty spot behind her right ear." Gilman believed that Joan's value lay in her refusal to kill and that her battle cry was "Let those who love me follow me." While creating a Joan that resembled a film noir seductress who left scarred and ruined men in her wake, the author concluded that "the simple point is that [Joan] was a child."[15]

The simple, girlish Joan of Arc was present more often in the higher realms of American culture in the 1950s. Shaw's *Saint Joan* was staged twice in New York during the decade and appeared for the first time in the Modern Library series in 1956. Jules Michelet's *Joan of Arc* volume of his *History of France* of 1841 was first published in the United States in 1957. In 1953, Lillian Hellman translated and adapted Jean Anouilh's *The Lark,* which appeared on Broadway for 229 performances in 1955–56 with Julie Harris in the lead role. *The Lark* is constructed as a flashback from the courtroom, in which Joan remembers the events of her life while her accusers interpret them. Joan's experience becomes meaningful to the degree that it leads to recognition of the accomplishments of others. The most unusual aspect of *The Lark* is the alteration of the entire Joan of Arc story through a *coup de théâtre.* In the play within the play, as the pyre is being constructed, a character comes forward to note that the coronation scene has not been performed. In the name of efficiency, the glorious spectacle in Reims Cathedral, rather than the one at the stake, ends the play and disperses any potential tragedy.

The last of the three *New York Times Magazine*'s photo essays about Joan of Arc appeared in connection with the 1955 production of *The Lark* under the title "The Maid in Many Guises."[16] The brief text begins with the usual observations about and description of the many literary Joans, but it reframes the issue by asking, "What was Joan like?" The questions from the past about politics, military strategy, mysticism, and religion are replaced by more mundane and personal concerns. The quotations from Hellman report that this Joan was "deeply religious, a big, healthy, sensible girl, a sort of peasant type." She was "gayer, more fragile, less saintly." More to the point, the play's Joan is quoted as saying, "True miracles are created by *men* when they use the courage and intelligence God gave them." The nine photographs that dominate the two-page spread show nine women (all seen in earlier versions of the article) wearing either armor, peasant dress, or prison rags. Eight of the images are small, quarter-page photographs, while the picture of Harris covers close to half a page. Each figure is shown in long shot, with the majority contextualized against a salient background, and each is posed dramatically so as to stress some extreme sentiment of ecstasy, angst, or determination. In this essay about "guises" the artificiality of poses is stressed. Joan is "like" nothing in particular but can assume whatever role is given to her by the male authors mentioned, from Shakespeare to Anouilh.

The most extensive and conclusive essay to appear in the 1950s was D. B. Wyndham Lewis's "Joan of Arc" in the *Atlantic Monthly*. The piece was one of a series of biographical essays that investigated "that supreme crisis, that turning point, of a person who made history . . . the particular strands that give life and belief to [Joan's] career." Lewis constructed a woman who would be at home in a Howard Hawks film, "an extremely human being, possessed (the jolly, healthy wench) of a quick temper and a sense of fun; as essentially feminine, were such a comparison permissible, as Lola Montez, the standard adventuress-type." In the lengthy piece, Joan was imagined to be supernaturally inspired, following orders from Saint Michael and receiving "gentle encouragement and consolation" from the female saints. She was hearty and capable on horseback but also fond of beautiful clothes and attention. Lewis identified the defining moment of Joan's life as occurring on 6 March 1429, when Joan first met the dauphin, later Charles VII of France, at his castle in Chinon. Here Joan imparted to Charles what became known as the King's Secret, and whatever she said was so impressive that he gave Joan command of his army. Apparently Joan told the dauphin that he was the legitimate son of Charles VI, despite insinuations to the contrary by his Burgundian advisers and his mother, Isabelle of Bavière, who favored her daughter's English husband, Henry V. Thus, as Lewis writes, "Charles is, so to speak, Joan's creation."[17] In her own way, Joan produced a proper male heir.

In 1954, a French film called *Destinées* was released in the United States.[18] The three-part, omnibus film is about women and war, with one vignette based on the Lysistrata theme, a second section about an American woman who travels to Italy after the war to claim her husband's body from his Italian lover, and a third part that is titled "Jeanne." The episodes were directed by Christian Jacque, Marcel Pagliero, and Jean Delannoy, respectively. While the latter two sections are serious, *Variety* described the first as a "bawdy take-off . . . played as a farce and a sex-comedy."[19] The "Jeanne" vignette was a compromise on Delannoy's part. He and the French scriptwriter Pierre Bost had written an entire Joan of Arc script in 1947 but had been thwarted by Sierra Pictures, which produced its *Joan of Arc* first. Bitter about the American usurpation of the French national heroine, Delannoy declared that he would film only one brief, apocryphal episode in Joan's life that is not found in Fleming's film.[20] According to legend, during Joan's post-Orléans travels she encountered a group of young women who begged her to pray with them around the body of an infant who had died before being baptized. At Joan's touch, the baby breathed just long enough to be christened and thus was enabled to rest eternally in heaven. This maternal episode breaks all the rules set for the virgin warrior. "Jeanne" opens with a title declaring that "what woman wants, God wants," and features female characters almost exclusively. Of particular note is the aural presence of Saints Catherine and Margaret, who are privileged by both the repeated use of close-ups of the listening Joan and by a remarkably high-angle iris-in on Joan when the saints speak to her for the last time. Diverging from their usual role, these saints are puppeteers who force Joan to carry out their will. Because Joan fights her destiny, she is not a sacred figure symbolizing the rebirth of France. Instead, upon sacrificing herself for a child, she assumes the role of a mother who fulfills her natural function and disappears.

The film begins by describing Joan's heroic deeds and foretelling her approaching failures. She first appears while haranguing her saints and showing herself to be headstrong by swearing to complete her quest with or without divine participation. When the voices fail to respond, Joan, played by the mature French star Michèle Morgan (who had been Joan of Paris twelve years earlier), appears to be more frustrated than heroic. The fact that Joan

Michèle Morgan listening for her voices in *Destinées* (Jean Delannoy, 1954). (Courtesy of the Centre Jeanne d'Arc, Orléans)

is seen only as a grown woman facilitates the later assumption that she is, by nature, a maternal figure. While lying by a tree in a meadow, Joan is called upon by the village women to save the soul of a child. Although she hesitates, Joan succumbs to the will of the priest and accepts the task. Joan goes so far as to make a pact with her saints: she will give up further assistance from them if they will save the infant. The scene of the baby's resurrection is a confusing set of quick shot/reverse shots and eyeline matches. Just as Joan asks the saints to intercede, a man's face appears at an upper window and his shadow eclipses Joan at the moment of the miracle. When the infant opens its eyes, a surprised Joan looks up at the man's face. When Joan self-deprecatingly surmises that the child must not have been dead in the first place, a priest reassures her that God indeed acted through her. What appears to be a heroic, self-sacrificing deed becomes the rationale for Joan's death at the stake. As she stands among the mothers in the dark cellar and brings the child to life, Joan opens herself to the charge of sorcery. More to the point, Joan's abandonment of her source of power in exchange for the eternal soul of a baby makes Joan the willing instrument of her own death. When she is no longer a threat, she can be safely classified as the generic mother of her country.

Only after the miracle with the child do the men of the town volunteer to accompany Joan on her mission. As she and her soldiers prepare to go to Compiègne, the man who witnessed the miracle gives Joan a sword and the priest provides her with a standard. As Joan and her men leave the village to fight, a woman with wild hair and tight clothes, the antithesis of the virginal Joan, attempts to accompany the soldiers. When the men push the harlot from the cart into the mud, the woman curses Joan and her troops. When her curse comes to fruition in Joan's capture at Compiègne, the woman's desires indeed mirror God's will and make sense of the initial intertitle, "What woman wants, God wants." As the female who stays in her place, away from war, the sexual woman insists that the transgressive Joan be punished by death in order to erase the ambiguity caused by her challenging life.

It was not long before the superficially warrior-like Joan of Arcs typified by Michèle Morgan and Ingrid Bergman blended with the sexual, homebound woman who has the final say in Delannoy's film. While Bergman epitomized an emotional but strong kind of femininity in her Joan of Arc, by the middle of the 1950s the very concept of the woman warrior seemed irrelevant.[21] By the late 1950s, concern with female heroism had been replaced by what Betty Friedan called the "feminine mystique." While women continued to work and receive the intellectual, moral, and practical educations that would result in the women's movement of the next decade, the discourse of proper female behavior was another matter. Domestic concerns with children, home decoration, physical appearance, and the suburban community dominated popular journalism, which pictured the ideal home as a place that kept women in childlike isolation and served the corporate man as an almost Victorian respite. The cinema of the period, in its struggle to retain audiences increasingly drawn to the convenience and the live dramas of television, revived the war film as a genre full of action that could not be duplicated in a TV studio. The new war hero, however, epitomized as early as 1949 by John Wayne in *The Sands of Iwo Jima* (Allan Dunn), was no longer the individualist outsider who saved the day but the corporate man who sacrificed himself and his humane responses for the good of the group.[22] In addition, war itself was no longer envisioned as a glorious endeavor, but as one that was rife with contradiction and incompetence.[23] With women pictured safely at home once more, the iconoclastic female warrior Joan of Arc seemed to have outlived her usefulness as a sacrificial heroine.

The July 1956 issue of *The Atlantic* provided an example of Joan of Arc's shifting status. The featured article of the month, "The Nun and the Dramatist," consisted of a series of letters and texts chronicling the relationship between George Bernard Shaw and the abbess of Stanbrook. While *Saint Joan* was naturally mentioned, the main focus of the conversation was Catholic versus Protestant issues; yet the cover of the magazine featured a modern painting of Joan of Arc by James Avati. The mood of the picture is lugubrious, with muddy purples and charcoals scarcely penetrated by sickly yellow splotches of light. Several barely sketched soldiers stand in the far background, holding banners and weapons. In the foreground, in medium shot, stands Joan of Arc wearing burnished armor with strong highlights across a breastplate shaped in a female form. Joan herself resembles Doris Day with curly blonde hair and cute, well-made-up features. Given the substance of the magazine article and the painting itself, Joan is simply the cover girl.

An echo of *The Atlantic*'s use of Joan appears in the 1957 film *The Story of Mankind*, directed by Irwin Allen. The film, in which the Joan of Arc segment is the longest and most detailed, is based loosely on the popular classic history of 1921 by Hendrik Van Loon. Deemed by one critic to be "so bad that it's funny," the Technicolor extravaganza is structured as a court case in outer space before a white-bearded Deity to decide whether humanity should be allowed to destroy itself with the hydrogen bomb.[24] The defense, the Spirit of Man, played by Ronald Colman, and the prosecution, Vincent Price in the role of the Devil, offer examples of good and evil, respectively, to make their cases. The fifty-six "historical" vignettes, each from two to five minutes in length except for the ten-minute Joan of Arc segment, range from the depiction of cave dwellers to documentary footage of World War II. While the argument is presented with some seriousness, the film seems cynically aware that it offers little more than a display of movie stars, including Hedy Lamarr (as Joan), the Marx Brothers, Peter Lorre, Virginia Mayo, Agnes Moorehead, Charles Coburn, Cesar Romero, John Carradine, and Edward Everett Horton. Each bit of casting is stranger than the last, with Lamarr's sultry Joan heading the list. *Variety* wrote that "Hedy Lamarr is miscast as Joan (yes, of Arc)"; *Newsweek* described the casting as "the weirdest . . . ever committed. Among other oddities, Hedy Lamarr turns up as Joan of Arc."[25] Despite the apparent gravity of the Joan of Arc segment and others, the tone of the film is epitomized by Groucho Marx's scenery-chewing portrayal of Peter Minuit. Overall, the casual acting style, the 1950s version of historical dress, and the garish color deliberately mock the idea of history. *Newsweek* quotes the director as saying that "history is still something like hearing a joke for the second time. The punch has gone out of it. So we have added a gimmick."[26]

The story of mankind consists more or less of the tales of uncontextualized individuals who were either good or evil. History's great men are balanced between the positive and the negative, with Nero and Attila countered by Moses and Lincoln. Virtually all women who have achieved power, including Helen of Troy, Cleopatra, and Marie Antoinette, are exemplars of corruption, their fame based on betrayal, seduction, or malice. Moreover, when men are wicked, blame is shifted to the ubiquitous and barely dressed cave women, Native American maidens, and slave girls. Queen Elizabeth I alone cannot be made to symbolize evil, so not only is she the film's one middle-aged, homely woman, but her story is credited to Shakespeare. With the sole exception of Elizabeth, women whose deeds have forced their entry into history are voluptuous, dimwitted, and weighed down by the heavy makeup and hair styles of the 1950s.

The high visibility of Joan of Arc as a positive figure in the decade before *The Story of Mankind* presented the filmmaker with a dilemma. The film's solution was to have Joan's story related by the Devil as an example of the evil done *to* her by her judges. Joan is reduced to a minor figure in her own story and she is connected to the wicked women who crowd the film. The structural parallels among the women are strengthened by the resemblance between Lamarr and Virginia Mayo, who plays Cleopatra as an apolitical temptress. Cleopatra's claim that she knows nothing of war resonates in the later scene in which Lamarr's similarly made-up Joan struggles vainly for words as she watches her soldiers fight. The Devil himself sums up the film's attitude toward women in reassuring the Spirit of Man, in reference to Cleopatra's death, that it is "natural" for men to kill women.

The Joan of Arc segment begins with a discussion between the Spirit of Man and the Devil, the former wearing a contemporary business suit and the latter sporting anachronistic morning dress. As in Fleming's *Joan of Arc,* Joan's story is spoken by institutional male voices. The two men lounge on the branch of a tree while the Devil presents Joan's demise as the fate of an unfortunate victim whose function is to symbolize the evil of the Inquisition. An apparently mute Joan of Arc first appears in the ruins of a woodland chapel mugging in reaction to a deep, authoritative voice that seems to come from above. In the scene that is meant to portray Joan's innocent girlhood, Lamarr's vacuous expression, tight dress, and red lipstick are contradictory. Lamarr's Joan is less the youthfully energetic vehicle of the divine than the erotically passive object of the camera.

Lamarr's Joan of Arc appears to be not only disconnected from her life but physically uninvolved in her quest, which the viewer learns of through the Devil's description of soldiers who are seen marching toward battle. The Devil's statement that Joan persuaded the king to give her control of his army is increasingly hard to believe since Joan is struck dumb repeatedly by Saint Michael's heavenly voice. Hedy Lamarr's rendition of Joan of Arc reaches its apotheosis as she stands still, her hair undisturbed by protective head gear, holding her sword firmly by the blade. This mundane and almost subhuman version of Joan of Arc blends the iconography of the virgin warrior with the body of the beauty queen. The absence of irony in the cast-

Hedy Lamarr posed for martyrdom in *The Story of Mankind* (Irving Pichel, 1957). (Author's collection)

ing and performance of Lamarr contrasts with the extravagant use of the Marx Brothers, for example (imagine Harpo as Sir Isaac Newton). The film can only conclude that Joan of Arc is an impossibility, since women are sex objects and the maiden warrior must possess the shield of virginity.

Joan speaks in the film once she has become a doomed victim on trial, although, as the reviewer for *The New Yorker* pointed out, she "uses a kind of baby talk as evidence of the saint's virtues."[27] Still coded as a female of the 1950s through the cut of her clothes, elaborate makeup, and careful hair style, Joan argues briefly but passionately that her voices are real. However, since the viewer has not seen Joan actually do anything that would challenge the church and thus make her death meaningful, her convictions carry little weight. The Devil seems to be right in asserting that an innocent Joan of Arc died as a victim of corrupt men. Her story is about the victory of evil over good, in which, as the Devil declares, Joan's burning is the result of "greed, selfishness, and above all, lack of faith." The interpretation of Joan of Arc's life in *The Story of Mankind* eliminates the anomaly of a female hero. At the same time, by associating Joan with her historical sisters through appearance and through the inclusion of all their stories in a single narrative, every female known to history is condemned for combining sexuality with an overt expression of power. In fulfilling a destiny outside of her given role, even Joan of Arc must be catalogued under evil and killed under an order conceived of as natural.

Changing concepts of what is natural have shaped the representation of Joan of Arc in the cinema since the late 1920s. During the First World War, when Joan was a distant and metaphoric icon, Joan was played by the most popular stars of the day. After the disillusionment of the First World War, with its concomitant revelation of the relativity of even the most sacred cultural ideas, Joan of Arc was ever more understood as a potentially threatening iconoclast, particularly in relation to gender. By the late 1920s, the very casting of the role of Joan of Arc bore the signs of a culture that had become uncomfortable with a woman warrior. The French carried out the first of the Joan of Arc casting searches for Gastyne's *Vie merveilleuse de Jeanne d'Arc* in 1928. The filmmakers requested not an actress but a horseriding brunette girl of medium build with French parents. Over the producer's choice of his glamorous girlfriend, the star Louise Lagrange, the unknown Simone Genevoix was given the role. As noted earlier, Irving Pichel, undecided whether his martyred actress should be played by a Hollywood name or an unknown, conducted a series of polls in 1948 before choosing the unfamiliar Alida Valli as his star in *The Miracle of the Bells*. The most notorious search was instigated by Otto Preminger in preparation for his 1957 version of Shaw's *Saint Joan,* for which a film trailer hailed a girl who embodied "sincerity, honesty, [and] a fanatic devotion" and manifested a "being" rather than a style.[28] In the course of a 30,000-mile tour Preminger personally auditioned 3,000 young women from among 18,000 aspirants; he finally chose Jean Seberg, an eighteen-year-old girl from Marshalltown, Iowa.

A public search for Joan of Arc is, first and foremost, a marketing ploy. The discourse that surrounds these quests for the perfect girl to embody Joan, however, raises questions about the cultural meaning of Joan of Arc in relation to notions of femininity and performance. While the criteria for playing Joan usually include a solid, forthright appearance, directors also ask for the purity, honesty, and valor of the saint. This attempt to typecast Joan spiritually can be traced to a long tradition in the theater in which women, once they were allowed onstage in the late seventeenth century, were assumed to be presenting themselves rather than acting.[29]

In the history of the cinema, the identification of histrionics with femininity created an opposition between the authentic actress of quality and the artificial, showgirl type. The former is typified by Ingrid Bergman, whose value as an actress was perceived as coming from her failure to act. The director Sam Wood made this point in saying that "when she plays a love scene she blushes real blushes. And when her cheeks get pink you can see it on the screen because there's no make-up to hide it. It's a beautiful sight to see."[30] It was just this quality of not seeming to perform but expressing real emotions that allowed the professional Bergman to play Joan of Arc. The degree to which actresses, and in particular powerful American stars, were deemed deficient in authenticity and more like the showgirl is evident in the fact that when stars played Joan in the American cinema after the Second World War, they all spoke with a foreign accent. Besides the Swedish Bergman, only the Italian Alida Valli, the Austrian Hedy Lamarr, and the French Michèle Morgan in *Joan of Paris* filled the role. The accented voice was a continual, subtle reminder that American women were not up to playing Joan of Arc.

The conviction that Joan of Arc could be played on the American screen only by a select group of women, whether foreign-born or nonprofessional, attests to a continued trepidation about the role and its implications. The sophisticated and experienced film director Otto Preminger looked to spiritual typecasting as opposed to professional capability when he cast Jean Seberg in *Saint Joan*. In the classical Hollywood mode of filmmaking in which Preminger worked, everything that appeared on the screen was understood as a sign in a system assembled by production designers, camera operators, directors, and editors. While a performer's physical characteristics and mannerisms were used in this construct, inner qualities such as chastity and honesty were irrelevant as such. In this system, placing a nonprofessional player in the role of Joan of Arc, amidst a cast of accomplished actors, can be interpreted only as a bizarre attempt to use the naif to channel the "real" Joan of Arc. Preminger later realized that he had "made the mistake of taking a young, inexperienced girl . . . and [wanting] her to be Saint Joan—which of course she wasn't. I didn't help her to understand and act the part, indeed I deliberately prevented her, because I was determined she should be completely unspoilt."[31]

Chosen as the Everygirl from among thousands of hopeful American teenagers, Jean Seberg was given the notoriously difficult role of Shaw's Saint Joan without the benefit of professional training or experience. The degree to which Seberg was conceived of as a medium through whom the spirit of Joan herself would enter is evident in the extensive press coverage of the preparation of the film. Seberg is presented as a vacuum who was under Preminger's constant surveillance to prevent her from being corrupted by the other actors as they intellectually prepared their roles. At the same time, the press was given access to all the superficial details of Seberg's life as Preminger made his film around her, from the fitting of her armor to the cutting of her hair to her self-conscious visits to the pertinent sites in Joan of Arc's life. Typical headlines from the plethora of press stories on the search: "Jean of Iowa to Joan of Arc"; "Jean Becomes 'Joan.'"[32]

The extensive mock-newspaper that was constructed for theaters as part of the publicity for Saint Joan suggested that the search for the unknown actress was the focus of the project. The paper's headline reads, "The Most Fantastically Successful Star Search in Movie History." Below the title are a series of photographs and a collage of headlines and articles that show the huge national interest in the process, as well as Preminger standing in front of a roomful of aspirants and Seberg being introduced by Preminger to Ed Sullivan on television. The three pages of articles designed for press use by local theaters contain stories titled "Talent Search Produces 'Joan,'" "Iowa Girl Gets Chance of a Lifetime as 'St. Joan,'" and "Talent Hunt." Each article, as well as every review of the film after its release, rehearsed the same banal information about Seberg's background as a normal high school girl in a small town who became, in the words of one article, "a real-life Cinderella." The section headed "School Promotions" adds another element to the search phenomenon in providing specific instructions for a "local Jean

Otto Preminger directs Jean Seberg in *Saint Joan* (Otto Preminger, 1957). (The American Academy of Motion Picture Arts and Sciences)

Seberg search." Although this feature and another headed "'Saint Joan' Hair-Do Fashions" are not uncommon in Hollywood press books, they suggest a new facet to the impulse behind Preminger's original search in relation to his concept of Joan of Arc. The local search is for girls with "talent and beauty" who are to send in their photographs, measurements, and talent background to be judged by "local beauty and talent experts." It seems that once the American Everygirl was given the chance to be Joan of Arc, Joan of Arc had mutated into a beauty pageant queen.[33]

Questions about the star search and Seberg dominated an article in the *New York Times* that was ostensibly about the absolute and highly efficient control over the film maintained by Preminger. The director claimed that in the two years he spent pondering the making of *Saint Joan,* he could come up with only four or five actresses worthy of the role. However, he wanted "something [*sic*] new and fresh and . . . wanted audiences to identify this actress only with Joan, not to identify Joan with an actress they already knew." Preminger's interest was less in Shaw's play than in the creation of his own Joan. That concern explains why, if he had been interested in Shaw's *Saint Joan* for twenty-three years, he failed to realize that Shaw himself had written a screenplay.[34] Preminger described Seberg as having "just the right innocence" and as having "shaped very well under instruction." When the interviewer suggested that the director sounded like Svengali, Preminger responded that he merely tried to "teach her to think." [35]

All of the film's publicity material, including posters, marquees, slides, streamers, valances, flags, and badges, featured the image designed by Saul Bass that is called "the symbol of Saint Joan." The symbol resembles a rough woodcut print of what is apparently the body of Joan of Arc viewed from just above the top of the legs. The lower part of one arm and the hand are also seen, with the hand holding the top of a broken sword, the bottom half of which lies on the ground by the feet. The symbol is generally seen with the title "Saint Joan," written in capital letters, with both ends of the *S*, the curved end of the *J*, and the second line of the *N* at the end of "Joan" written as pointed arrows. The crotch-level shot of Joan, the broken sword, and the serpentine letters suggest an aggressive approach to the film's topic.[36] On the same page of the press book, a poster is advertised that displays three photographs of the near-disaster in which Seberg was actually singed during the filming of the scene at the stake. The poster reads, "ORDEAL BY

Jean Seberg being tied to the stake in *Saint Joan* (Otto Preminger, 1957). (Author's collection)

FIRE—as it actually happened!" above the text: "These three photos depict the accident during the filming of the burning scene which almost ended in tragedy for Jean Seberg!" While the burning of Seberg was surely unintentional, it seems that such a gross error on the part of filmmakers would have been hidden rather than publicized.[37] The promotional use of the "remarkable 'burning' scene that almost ended in tragedy and became international news" was connected to the search phenomenon. In this material, Seberg, who was ever more closely tied to Joan of Arc throughout the film's production, was pictured as owing Preminger not only her career but her life.

The film's poster featured "the symbol" and the text in capital letters, "For the first time on the screen Otto Preminger presents Bernard Shaw's *Saint*

Joan starring Richard Widmark, Richard Todd, Anton Walbrook, John Giel-gud and Jean Seberg." A second poster used the same text along with a pho-tograph of an imposing, low-angle shot of the four actors surrounding a tiny Seberg wearing handcuffs and kneeling at the bottom edge of the image. The iconographic privileging of the male stars in both print and image was part of the film's ongoing publicity. The press book provided articles about the four men that stressed their theatrical pedigrees and the fact that three of them shared the European background of the film's Viennese director. Given this high level of training and theatrical experience in the classics, it is difficult to imagine that the error of casting an eighteen-year-old amateur in a film of Shaw's *Saint Joan* could not have been recognized. Shaw him-self wrote in his prologue of 1924, before writing his own screenplay in 1933, of what might happen in the filming of his play. He described how all the references to ideological issues would be eliminated in favor of the spectacle of battles and the coronation, concluding, "Joan would be burnt on the stage . . . on the principle that it does not matter in the least why a woman is burnt provided she is burnt and people can pay to see it done."[38]

Saint Joan was made in black and white and in the older, conventional screen size in order to lend a sense of seriousness to the project. Much was made of Preminger's courage in making the first cinematic *Saint Joan* and of his provocative experimental methods.[39] Not only did Preminger cast an unknown but he rehearsed the play on the set as if it were a theatrical pro-duction, rather than employing the usual method of completing shots out of chronological order and assembling them during the editing stage of pro-duction. Preminger also stressed that only 5 percent of the play's dialogue had been changed in the screenplay by Graham Greene, although 25 per-cent had been allowed. Preminger made clear in the film's publicity mate-rials and in interviews that he was concerned chiefly with integrity and au-thenticity in relation to Shaw's play.[40]

Bernard Shaw's interpretation of the story of Joan of Arc is straightfor-ward and quite different from the vast majority of Joan of Arcs that have ap-peared on stage and in print over the centuries. *Saint Joan* is not overtly con-cerned with the usual oppositions between good and evil, innocence and corruption, the individual and the institution, female and male, or Protes-tantism and Catholicism. Instead, Shaw presents characters who all act with conviction according to the system in which they believe. The play gives each

Poster by Saul Bass for Otto Preminger's *Saint Joan* (1957). (The American Academy of Motion Picture Arts and Sciences)

character the chance to explain and justify her or his actions; while Joan's value lay in her particularly courageous and uncompromising challenge to the religious and political powers of her day, her accusers were equally logical and sincere in behaving as they did. The particular interest of *Saint Joan* is described by Bertolt Brecht, who wrote three Joan of Arc vehicles himself, as the play's ability to "[dislocate] our stock associations" with familiar characters whose "opinions . . . constitute their fates."[41] Shaw strips the audience of preconceived notions about his characters, who have been understood as good and heroic or evil and cowardly, in order to reveal each player as an ordinary, contradictory human being.

The most drastic change made in the Preminger/Greene adaptation of *Saint Joan* is the splitting of the play's epilogue into three sections. The epilogue takes place in the dream of King Charles at some point after Joan is burned. Shaw uses this device to comment on Joan's immolation, the freedom death gave her, the eventual reversal of the sentence, the reverence Joan receives, and the duration of her memory. The film turns this afterthought into a frame story so that this second-level narrative involving Charles and Joan can continually explain the difficult aspects of Joan's life. The revelations about the end of Joan's life at the start of the film eliminate narrative tension and viewer involvement, so that what is meant to be sensational is reduced to mere information. These interpolated sections in which Joan is alive and full of banter take the sting out of her later death.

After the epilogue-turned-introduction, Joan is presented as a down-to-earth and imaginative member of the peasant community. She first appears, looking like an all-American teenager, stubbornly awaiting an audience with a general. By taking credit for the refusal of the village hens to lay eggs, she convinces the still partially pagan guards that her connection to God is real. Once she gains access to General de Baudricourt, she presents a plan of sound military sense. Ultimately, Joan's ability to make coincidence and common sense appear to be miraculous is understood to be the source of her power. In her particular historical moment, the merest hint of access to the divine was all the inspiration that her beleaguered countrymen needed to fight. The quest itself begins once Baudricourt recognizes Joan's sway over the soldiers and sends her to the king. True to form, she predicts and then witnesses a man's death, unveils the impostor in court, persuades the king to fight, changes the wind's direction, succeeds at Orléans, and attends the coronation. Although a great deal happens in a narrative sense, the film is devoid of drama since verbose explanation overwhelms the events themselves. Fully half of the film's seventeen scenes depict conversations in which Joan, in Seberg's modern midwestern tone, explains herself. Joan's contemporary significance is focused by three long conversations between Joan and her ally in the French army, Dunois. The point is made that while Joan preferred to die rather than compromise, the friendly and easygoing Dunois lived to win the battle for France. During the discussion, Dunois says that if he were fearless like Joan, he would be a good knight for a storybook but a bad commander. Since practical success results from working within the institution, the courageous and faithful Joan of Arc is to be understood as an inspiration and not as a model for emulation.

Midway into the film, the explanatory frame narrative of the king's dream is again activated to introduce and resolve the potentially spectacular aspects of Joan's final days. Warwick, the English captain who buys Joan and gives the orders to kill her, appears in order to describe the capture, trial, and death. He explains that his actions are a historical necessity meant for the good of England, and as a responsible soldier he cannot act in any other way. With the ironic acceptance of hindsight, he notes the paradox that his actions have the opposite effect and lead to the creation of the French nation. This apologetic foretelling reduces the viewer's expectations for a spectacular conclusion and eliminates any sense of opposition between good and evil.

Joan's familiarity with her supposed superiors, which is written into the dialogue, becomes startlingly contemporary through Seberg's expressions, voice, and jaunty acting style. Warwick is played as a sophisticated cynic, while the Archbishop archly mocks Joan for being "in love with religion," saying that he considers his bishopric to be little more than a particularly powerful job. The most anomalous contemporary touch is the secular attitude of the king and the archbishop toward the coronation. While the king childishly rejects the discomforts of the ritual, both are blasé about it. In a way that is inconceivable in the fifteenth century but appropriate to the twentieth, they dismiss the event as an empty show for the superstitious masses. The stubbornly sincere Joan looks ever more foolish in comparison with those around her. After the coronation, Joan's refusal to compromise and her talk of further miracles have lost their appeal in relation to the proposals of those who espouse the use of treaties to save lives and money. Joan's spirituality is now a liability and the church and state seem justified in trying to get her to accept the logical, commonsense position that would save her life. In a revisionist moment during the trial, the church claims that its objection is not to Joan's male dress but to the breaking of its rules. The film calmly makes the point that Joan's refusal to submit to its authority forces the church to rid itself of her.

Before the conclusion reverts to the frame story, Joan suffers in her cell, glorifies her cause with a brilliant self-defense, relapses, and goes gallantly to her death. An additional scene is inserted in which Warwick and his Burgundian assistant, whose loyalties are bitterly torn, discuss the rise of nationalism. While Warwick believes that Joan is merely a heretic and that all her miracles can be explained, he recognizes that she is the figurehead of a new, nation-centered worldview. In the final section in the king's chambers, Joan confronts all of her transgressors. While she excuses the English because they fought bravely for their country, she does not pardon Warwick, because he acted without conviction. The trial judge, Cauchon, the usual archvillain of the story, is presented as the scapegoat who was faithful to his office. Joan forgives her fellow warriors for abandoning her because they did so to continue the fight for France. Finally, the English soldier who comforted her during her last minutes by making a cross out of sticks appears for Joan's blessing.

This last anonymous soldier emerges out of eternity in order to share his awareness of all subsequent wars. He describes the rise of nations, laying particular blame on Germany for its role in international hostilities. This anachronistic reference is meant to put Joan's story in perspective and to challenge opinions about the relative good and evil of its characters and their accomplishments. Shaw's play ultimately defends all parties for acting according to self-interest. Regardless of her own interpretation of her motivation and otherworldly inspirations, Joan's victories are explained as being the result of sound military sense. While Preminger's film ostensibly reflects Shaw's message, the jarring dichotomy between the performances of John Gielgud as Warwick versus that of Seberg leaves the viewer with a different conclusion. At the very end of the film, Joan asks her former antagonists whether they would like her to return to earth. Their claim that the world is not yet ready for her makes clear that Saint Joan's value lies in her inspirational qualities and that the absolute that she represents cannot be integrated into the practical world.

The reviews of Preminger's *Saint Joan* were uniformly negative, with most of the blame for "turning Shaw into pshaw" laid on Seberg.[42] Nearly every review begins with and each one mentions the search for Joan, only to dismiss the results as a drastic error due to Seberg's lack of depth and ineptitude as an actor. Janet Winn in the *New Republic* even made the point that the famous short haircut that was to lend authenticity was inaccurate. To varying degrees, the critics mention Greene's "dismal," pro-Catholic adaptation of the Protestant play, the unimaginative staging and costuming, and the film's slow pace. In addition, critics were unanimously uneasy with the performances of the esteemed actors in the film. Some reviews simply noted that Gielgud, for example, was good; others said that the direction did not show the obviously talented actors to full advantage. Robert Hatch in *The Nation* claimed that "there is no point to the role as Miss Seberg has been taught to play it; and there is no more point to Richard Widmark's portrayal of the Dauphin as a half-wit boy from the Middle West." Janet Winn concluded that Preminger "deliberately set out to defy the play" in a distinctly uninteresting way by showing that the "plucky little lady who saved France [was right], and everyone else was wrong." Finally, *Variety* noted that Seberg's "interpretation may be a reflection of Preminger's concept of Joan."[43]

Preminger's notion of Joan was part of a general trend in the "evolution of a new Saint Joan," to use the title of a *New York Times Magazine* essay.[44] This brief interview with Seberg begins with a cynical description of how stars are made. The critic writes, "In a time in which turkeys are engineered, breast and thigh, to predetermined proportions of light and dark meat, and history is frequently arranged to happen . . . the subject is chosen, endowed with characteristics and merchandised." He then provides the usual description of Seberg's small-town life and discovery before letting the young Joan of Arc take over. In just two pages, Seberg reflects upon a number of disconnected issues, ranging from her failure to grasp Stanislavsky to her interest in the NAACP. In relation to Preminger she noted that she had to "figure out how much of [her] life [she] would give to Otto," and in reference to the accident on the stake that her "scars, unfortunately, are healing beauti-fully, . . . and so no one will believe it wasn't for publicity." All in all, the New Saint Joan paints herself as a particularly frantic and vapid American teenager of her time. Although Preminger's filming of *Saint Joan* failed at the box office and did not do justice to Shaw's play (or to Seberg), the over-all project of constructing a new concept of Joan of Arc succeeded quite well.

⤙⤝⟹ 8 · Conclusions

The Vietnam War and Afterward

Otto Preminger's *Saint Joan* of 1957 was the last feature film about Joan of Arc made in the United States in the twentieth century.[1] In view of the part Joan of Arc has played in the discourse of women and war throughout the century, the question arises: How does she figure in the Vietnam War? The closest approximation to an armored woman in the cinema of that war is Jane Fonda wearing a half-transparent breastplate in Roger Vadim's 1968 semipornographic science fiction fantasy *Barbarella*. Before 1978 almost no films were made about Vietnam, with the exception of John Wayne's *Green Berets* of 1968. Between 1978 and the Persian Gulf War in the early 1990s, a number of esteemed films specifically about Vietnam were made, including *The Deer Hunter* and *Coming Home* of 1978 (Michael Cimino and Hal Ashby, respectively), *Apocalypse Now* (Francis Ford Coppola, 1979), *Platoon, Gardens of Stone*, and *Full Metal Jacket* of 1987 (Oliver Stone, Coppola, and Stanley Kubrick, respectively). Women had almost no place in these films. If they appeared at all, they were the victims of violence or briefly shown as the wives and mothers for whom the war was fought. Neither in the films of the time nor in the cultural context surrounding the war and discussion of the war was there a place for Joan of Arc. Only with the Persian Gulf War, in which women were combatants for the first time, does the woman warrior resurface.

Despite the absence of feature films about the heroine after 1957, the 1960s experienced another Joan of Arc revival, in which the venues broadened and the focus narrowed. In 1968 Boston College held a two-week Joan of Arc festival that featured a production of the Honegger/Claudel oratorio, *Joan of Arc at the Stake*. The review of the event suggested that the festival was a response to the appearance of fifteen new books about Joan of Arc since 1960 and seven major theatrical productions in roughly the same time.[2] In addition to five television shows, including a 1967 Hallmark Hall of Fame version of Shaw with Geneviève Bujold, the usual array of juvenile literature that was characteristic of the second half of the century continued to appear. A typical book of the time, *St. Joan of Arc* by John Beevers, began with the claim that Joan was "no beauty and no scholar," but succeeded because of her "cheerfulness" and her "happy serenity." Joan's story was most often "astonishing" in this period, as the heroine became ever more a natural child with connections to higher powers. The French historian Jules Michelet's mid-nineteenth-century *Joan of Arc,* which launched the innocent peasant Joan, was first translated and published in the United States in 1957. Michelet's last words about the heroine, which were simply poetic when they appeared, gained new meaning when they were resurrected in the era of women's consciousness raising. The historian wrote:

> The deliverer of France could be no other than a woman. France herself was woman; having her nobility, but her amiable sweetness likewise, her prompt and charming pity; at the least, possessing the virtue of quickly excited sympathies. And though she might take pleasure in vain elegances and external refinements, she remained at bottom closer to nature.[3]

Joan of Arc was no longer used for war propaganda in the 1960s but on the logo for "Joan of Arc Sardines," as well as for a brand of kidney beans, a kind of cheese, and a pattern of sterling silverware.[4] In the early years of the twentieth century, when representations of angels sold corsets and Joan advertised cigars, there was little awareness that these commercial uses would rob the icons of their spiritual value. By the 1960s, Joan of Arc had become little more than currency in consumer culture. By the time of the Vietnam War, Joan of Arc had become kitsch, like other archaic figures who had been tainted by continual association with objects and ideas with which they had no real connection. While the other visual arts and much literature had reacted to this stripping of meaning by turning away from established visual imagery by 1960, only the most experimental and necessarily esoteric films could reject representation for abstraction.[5]

Joan of Arc appeared twice at the end of the 1950s in ways that suggest how separate she was from specific cultural significance, particularly in relation to war. In 1957 a poem titled "Buddha and St. Joan" appeared on the editorial page of the *New York Times*. The verse presents Joan as

> the mask of
> the Maid . . . cheeks aglow with the vigor of youth,
> she looks toward Buddha, rosy mouth
> calling to rouse him from passivity.
> She battles Fate, and he accepts it.[6]

The sensual language used to describe Joan's aggressive approach to such an unlikely candidate as the Buddha recalls Hedy Lamarr's attractive but dimwitted Joan of the same year. In addition, the juxtaposition of two such dissimilar icons creates a set of oppositions in which the female is active and the male is passive, but to no end. The temporal and cultural distance of the Buddha in 1957 America would have made Joan seem equally removed.

In 1958 *Time* magazine reviewed a scholarly essay titled "Joan of Arc: A Medical View," by John and Isobel-Ann Butterfield.[7] The piece was one of three on the "Medicine" page and was headed "The Trouble with Joan." The small accompanying image is a full-length nineteenth-century Joan in peasant dress who faces the viewer fearfully, with arms outstretched in a self-protective pose, while a winged male figure who floats behind seems to whisper intently in her ear. The original essay in *History Today* was an informed analysis of the possibility that Joan of Arc may have suffered from bovine tuberculosis. The authors chronicled the mysterious aspects of Joan's story, such as the voices and visions that she experienced and her survival of a leap from a tall tower, together with the symptoms of the disease that would explain the odd occurrences. The authors concluded that it was "not her visions and voices, but her courage, her intelligence, her ability to get big things done and her struggle for the independence of her mind which distinguish Joan and place her among the great women." The *Time* piece ended with this quotation, but its focus was epitomized by the title and the salvo in the opening line, "Was she hysterical? Was she insane?" While *Time*'s review accurately described the research, its dominant message was that Joan of Arc was troubled and "trouble."

The detached nature of the 1960s revival of a diminished Joan of Arc in relation to war and politics in the United States related to the trauma of both the movement for women's social and economic liberation and the Cold War. In addition, the therapeutic consumer culture described by Lears as beginning early in the century had fully flowered by the 1960s. The cultural malaise that marked the beginning of the century could be eased by a return to sacred symbols such as Joan of Arc, but by the time of the Vietnam War, the sacred had become banal. Joan of Arc could no longer provide ritual release or reassurance. Although Walt Disney never made a Joan of Arc film, when the heroine appeared in the 1960s the venue was most often a cartoon or children's show, such as the 1972 CBS show "The Torment of Joan of Arc" on the popular series *You Are There*. These light educational films were typified by picturesque drawings, brightly colored schematic maps, and Walter Cronkite's reassuring voice-of-God narration. One of the more serious references to Joan in this period occurred in the formation of an American branch of the relatively radical women's organization called St. Joan's International Alliance in 1965.[8] Since the Catholic Church's strength has often come from its ability to maintain an ahistorical relevance in the midst of an increasingly rational and legalistic society, the reference to Joan of Arc at this point is a conservative one.

This newly legendary Joan of Arc, who by this point resembled an earth mother more than a warrior, was popularized by the folk singers Leonard Cohen and David Allen Bliss, both of whom wrote songs in the mid-1960s titled "Joan of Arc." Bliss's song, the less known of the two, is a narrative ballad that insists that Joan was a simple country girl who "never owned a thing" and was inspired by nature both to "free this land again" and to give France a king. The lyrics celebrate the fact that Joan heard and followed her own voices in order to demand of the listener,

> When you walk alone in the fields of the summer,
> Where the green earth is whispering a song,
> Will you ride the high road leading afar
> And ride out to answer ev'ry wrong?[9]

This flower-child Joan is admired for rejecting strong men and kings to follow her own drummer, to the point of suffering "madness, a tomorrow of pain." The vague connection between Joan of Arc's idealism and absolute commitment to her cause and the rhetoric of the antiwar and civil rights movements occurs only in this one little-known song.

The more famous song by Leonard Cohen, from the 1971 album *Songs of Love and Hate,* is more indicative of the counterculture's relation to medievalism and to a woman warrior. Cohen's lugubrious "Joan of Arc" is an antiwar song that re-creates the heroine as an icon of essential femininity. This Joan is "quoted" in the second verse of the song as saying,

> I'm tired of the war.
> I want the kind of work I had before,
> A wedding dress or something white.

The principal event of the song is the burning at the stake, in which the flames are personified as a male who seduces and consumes the heroine because she is unaccompanied by a man. In a replay of the ancient Amazonamachie, the Fire says, "There's something in me that yearns to win / Such a cold, such a lonesome heroine." When he claims to love her solitude and pride, Joan responds by saying that she will willingly enter the flame as his bride.[10] Cohen's lyrics modernized the Joan of Arc that Ingrid Bergman played in 1948 for the women of the antiwar movement of the late 1960s and 1970s. After the Second World War, Joan's sacrifice was just slightly sentimentalized in order to help women's return to the home seem heroic, since the impetus to women's independence of the home had been largely war-driven. However, once the women's liberation movement provided a theoretical base for expanding women's roles in the public sphere, Joan of Arc was remade as a romantic heroine in the masochistic nineteenth-century mold. The transformation of the relationship between women and war over the course of the century is evident in the alteration of the World War I poster "Women of Britain Say—Go!" to the 1960s version, "Girls Say Yes to Guys Who Say No."[11]

The Joan of Arc revival of the 1960s was dominated for the first time by scholarly interest more than propaganda or popular culture images. In 1961 the French André Guérin and the American Jack White collaborated on a book called *Operation Shepherdess,* which sought to "rectify" the inaccuracies that apparently plagued historians. The writers wanted specific answers to such questions as who Joan's parents were, if she was a pawn in a political strategy, the nature of her sign to the dauphin, and whether she was actually burned or not. The impetus behind this detective work was the revival of the ideas of Pierre Caze, who had speculated in 1810 that Joan of Arc had been the illegitimate daughter of Isabelle de Bavière and Louis d'Orléans, and thus Charles VII's half sister, and that an impostor was burned in Joan's place.[12] In 1965 and 1966 two works argued for Joan's royal status: Maurice David-Darnac's *True Story of the Maid of Orléans* and Raymond Legrand's play *Jehanne Vérité*. In France, where these stories started, the royalization of Joan of Arc was almost redundant. In the United States, however, Joan's appeal has always come from the fact that she conquered kings despite, or perhaps because of, her peasant roots. The mode of scholarship that explained Joan's miraculous behavior began to eliminate her figural status in relation to the democratic, revolutionary United States.

The most typical of the scholarly texts of the 1960s was the influential book *The Judgements of Joan: Joan of Arc, a Study in Cultural History*. Charles Wayland Lightbody marveled over the numbers of books about his "gamine de France," around whom he purported to weave a coherent and enlightened history. Lightbody's scholarship included observations such as the fact that Joan's preferred name of "La Pucelle" (The Maid) means a kitchen servant, a kitchen pump, and a prostitute. This book relates particularly to the gender politics of the 1960s in light of the wealth of clichés used in regard to her. Lightbody writes:

> The more we study Joan, the more, in some respects, does she become an enigma. She has the charm of an enigma, of a sphinx. . . . The famous smile which crossed her face as she made her mark upon her paper of abjuration is like the smile of the Mona Lisa. . . . To some it is a sneer, to others the vacuum of an exhausted and vacant mind, to yet others, eternal wisdom.[13]

In the same year, Roger B. Salomon wrote an essay titled "Escape from History: Mark Twain's *Joan of Arc*," in which he claimed that Twain also liked Joan for being a "mysterious creature—living enigma—a phenomenon—a marvel." Salomon argued that Joan is a problem that cannot be explained because a female peasant simply could not have done what Joan did. But, since Joan resides safely and rationally in real historical documents, she can be adored as a jewel-like anomaly. The author quoted Twain with apparent personal relief: "It took six thousand years to produce her. . . . Her like will not be seen on the earth again in fifty thousand."[14]

In May 1971, near the 540th anniversary of Joan's death, the *Washington Post* ran a parody in its editorial section headed "France: Hot Time in an Old Town." The piece, which was reprinted from an in-house magazine of *Time,* was one of the few appearances of Joan in the popular culture of this era. The parody begins by identifying Joan in a square headed "Milestones" in the upper right-hand corner of the page: "Died. Jeanne D'Arc, 19, French warrioresse and clair voyant who in the brief span of three years rose from peasant milkmaid to power broker behind the throne of France, of the effects of burning at the stake in Rouen." On the opposite side of the article is a drawing that occupies one-third of the space. The image is a mock-*Time* magazine cover with a medium shot of Joan in the center. "Five Centimes" and "May 31, 1431" appear at the top of the image, "Jeanne D'Arc" appears at the bottom, and across the upper right corner, "End of a French Milkmaid." The Joan figure is a drawing by Michael Witte of a cartoonishly voluptuous woman wearing a tattered minidress with one shoulder strap falling off, who is tied tightly to a stake with ropes around her waist, surrounded by flames and smoke. Atop a pencil-thin neck, crowned with Jean Seberg–styled hair, the face has vacant, long-lashed eyes, a huge-lipped grin, and a nose shaped like Pinocchio's at his most mendacious.

The text itself is a mock-journalistic telling of Joan's story as if she were a contemporary student radical; one protester at her trial is described as a member of "SMS—Students for a Monarchical Society." Covering her background as if she were a twentieth-century American "educated in parochial schools," an interview segment reads in part as follows:

"Call me Jeanne," she said cheerfully, extending a manacled hand as I entered her cell. . . . For the first time in years, she wore women's clothes again—her tattered gown looked Givenchy to me—on orders of the court. I asked if she minded being burned. "I do," she said. "I'd much rather be beheaded seven times over. Fire is so hard on one's skin."

She discusses moving "from Phase Two to Phase Three of the Chinese guerrilla warfare concept" before slipping her gown off her shoulder to show how her wound had healed. The interview concludes, "In view of the nude-look fashions that Paris recently showed for the 1430 season, I thought it a pity that the Maid would not be able to wear them." The piece ends with jokes about the disposition of her possessions: her horse is sold to cover court costs and her armor becomes the centerpiece of a new museum. There is no overt point to the article other than its humor.[15]

The gender problems of the 1960s and 1970s that were manifest on all levels of American culture provide the answer to the question: Where was Joan of Arc in relation to the Vietnam War? The attempt to make sense of any war in progress is by nature a conservative gesture that returns to the past as a figural model. In the First World War, the woman warrior/child-at-the-stake Joan of Arc was simultaneously a symbol of the virtue of unselfish sacrifice for all and the touching embodiment of the women and children for whom war was symbolically fought. Enough of a shadow of this sentimental, utilitarian Joan remained for the heroine to be evoked during World War II and purposefully used afterward. By the 1960s, the female warrior had become a possibility who sometimes threatened to take the place in war once reserved for men or refused to stand as the symbolic stake of combat. Umberto Eco's observation that "Joan of Arc [was] a warrior as charismatic as Che" suggests an awareness of Joan's potential iconoclasm.[16] Several radical women artists were inspired by Joan in this period, including Meredith Monk, who choreographed *Vessels* in 1971 to blend Joan's story with modern New York (Joan was burned by a welder's torch in a church parking lot), and Patti Smith, whose poem "Jeanne d'Arc" envisioned a heroine desperate to lose her virginity before she died.[17] The more widespread attitude of the time was that expressed by the film critic Andrew Sarris upon seeing *Le Procès de Jeanne d'Arc*: "My pet peeve here is the subject, the Big Subject if you will, already done to death by Shakespeare's witchy strumpet to Shaw's bitchy saint. . . . [We are aware of] Joan's whole body, that temple of professional virginity, that Joan longs to present intact to her Bridegroom in heaven."[18] The irrationality of this response to Bresson's somber, restrained, highly respected film indicates that Joan of Arc had become a sensitive subject.

Joan of Arc's relative absence from representation in the United States during the war in Vietnam involved not only gender issues but broader political matters as well. In general terms, the war had no coherent narrative that could be performed before an audience at home. The entrance of the United States into the war had no cause that could be glorified, there was no enemy to be vilified, and there was no quest through which boys could feel that they had been made into men. In addition, the virgin warrior was inappropriate during a period in which "natural" systems of gender relations were in dispute. Susan Jeffords has described the discourse around the Vietnam War as directed toward the remasculinization of America. As ideas about gender roles were renegotiated, the opposition to feminine influences was discussed openly. Jeffords quotes a report of the Hoover Commission, writing after World War II, that while women could be trained as warriors, they should not be, because "it might seriously alter society's equilibrium, which depends upon a male-female or rather a military-nonmilitary balance."[19] The confusion surrounding the war in Vietnam, in which there was no clear enemy and the former audience for war was either refusing to be impressed or trying to join the action, explains why only one film was made about the Vietnam War during its duration, *The Green Berets* of 1968.

In the 1970s and 1980s, numerous films were made about the Vietnam War and its repercussions and not one of them referred to Joan of Arc. During this time, American women were moving closer to the role of combatant and actually fought in the Persian Gulf War of 1990–91. Joan of Arc's presence during this period followed a dual trajectory. While rigorous scholarly work increased, Joan also appeared with greater frequency in consumer culture. In 1982 Hans Mayer's *Outsiders* was translated into English with a serious consideration of how Joan of Arc inspired Shaw and Brecht by proving the relativity of all social, political, and gender rules. Ten years later, Harold Bloom edited a book called *Joan of Arc* for a series called Major Literary Characters, which includes criticism from the past two hundred years. The book allows the reader to chart the ever-changing response to Joan on the part of both the writers of the original texts and the critics who were attracted to the original work and to Joan for reasons of their own. From the evidence presented in the book, representations of Joan in art elicit rational textual and historical analysis in the 1990s, in place of the attack mode that dominated the 1970s. *Fresh Verdicts on Joan of Arc,* edited by Bonnie Wheeler and Charles T. Wood in 1996, presents historical, analytical, and sociological essays on a wide variety of related topics.

The intellectual interest in Joan was equaled by another resurgence of the heroine in everything from serious art to haute couture. The 1990s saw a major revival of a Joan of Arc vehicle every year, including the works of

Tchaikovsky, Schiller, Shaw, Honegger, and Verdi, in addition to an oratorio written by Richard Einhorn called *Visions of Light,* which is meant to accompany Carl Theodor Dreyer's 1928 film, *La Passion de Jeanne d'Arc.* While these Joan of Arc pieces were performed for many reasons, which may or may not have included interest in the heroine, they set her in the public eye, reviving interest in her story. Juvenile literature continued to appear, with the contemporary tone epitomized by Polly Schoyer Brooks's *Beyond the Myth: The Story of Joan of Arc,* which mentions Isabelle Romée's words at the rehabilitation trial and her vow to fight the notion that women are the cause of all evil. The medical community also maintained its vigil, declaring in 1982 that Joan suffered from "testicular feminization syndrome": she was a genetic male who looked and thought like a woman but had neither ovaries nor uterus. A sympathetic study reported widely in 1990 that Joan's voices may have been the result of epilepsy.[20]

An essay in *NEA Today,* the journal of the National Education Association, made clear in its November 1989 issue that Joan's contemporary cultural currency was complete. An article debating the ideas behind E. D. Hirsch Jr.'s book *A First Dictionary of Cultural Literacy* featured the banner headline "Who Is Joan of Arc?" and argued that not to know about Joan was to be culturally illiterate in the United States at the end of the twentieth century. Joan of Arc, the formerly enigmatic female warrior, had become a figure who could be understood in a logical way. Those who made films for young people believed that Joan was current enough to have a role in the 1989 film *Bill and Ted's Excellent Adventure* (Stephen Herek). This juvenile time-travel comedy also featured Genghis Khan, Freud, Socrates, Lincoln, Beethoven, and Napoleon. Joan is parodied along with her fellow legends in bogus publicity: " 'Totally HOT!!!' —Joan of Arc, Teen Martyr Magazine."

It is impossible to tally all the cinematic references to Joan of Arc in the films of the last three decades of the twentieth century. While there has not been a Joan of Arc film made in the United States for over forty years, there are innumerable references to Joan in American films and those made for international distribution. One finds the structure of Joan's heroic life and evocation of her iconography in *Supergirl* (Jeannot Szwarc, 1984), *The Nasty Girl* (Paul Verhoeven, 1989) and *The Little Drummer Girl* (George Roy Hill, 1984), which opens with a ten-minute scene of the film's contemporary heroine playing Shaw's Saint Joan before embarking naively on a career as a terrorist. The 1985 film *The Legend of Billy Jean* also uses Shaw's Joan, but in this case the play is present in the form of Preminger's 1957 film. *The Legend of Billy Jean* uses the Joan of Arc story in integral ways in its tale of a working-class girl who becomes an outlaw in reaction to sexual abuse. After seeing a scene from Preminger's film on television, the heroine adopts Joan's (or Jean's) androgynous look in her fight against gender and class oppression. The film ends with the burning of an effigy of Billy Jean.[21]

The Legend of Billy Jean was not the first movie to use an earlier film about Joan of Arc as a reference point. In 1962 Jean-Luc Godard used a scene of Joan's suffering face from Dreyer's *La Passion de Jeanne d'Arc* in *Vivre sa vie,* as did Philip Kaufman in his 1990 *Henry and June.* In both films the angst-ridden Joan as played by Falconetti is used as a sign of authenticity in an increasingly banal culture. Godard's Nana pitifully imitates Joan's tears in a heartfelt effort to find solace for the emptiness of her own life. Kaufman uses Dreyer's images more superficially to suggest that tormenting women is aesthetically interesting. A little-known film starring Ingrid Bergman's daughter Isabella Rossellini, called *Zelly and Me* (Tina Rathbone, 1988), tells the story of a poor little rich girl who finds the strength to survive in the voices on a record album called *The Child's Joan of Arc.* The film's credit sequence begins with close-ups of a child's drawings of Joan, including Joan listening to Saint Michael, the heroine on horseback assaulting the walls of Orléans, and Joan in flames. The simple story is told of a child who learns, through her brief relationship with a French governess, how to live with her cruel and disturbed grandmother. When the beloved Joan of Arc record is taken from the girl, the little heroine learns that she has internalized Joan's courage and strength.

Joan's wider presence in popular culture ranged from the light to the absurd. Joan was evoked in a positive 1993 article about Hillary Rodham Clinton in the *New York Times Magazine,* "The Politics of Virtue," which featured a full-page drawing of a haloed Clinton in armor. In another *New York Times Magazine* article, "Getting into Character," in which six writers were asked to dress up as their favorite literary characters, an armored Donna Tartt looked uncomfortable astride her horse. She described Joan's literary legacy and her historical deeds, concluding that Joan was rightly accused of witchcraft: she was "one of the greatest magicians that ever lived."[22] Joan's name and iconography invariably return every time short hair comes back in style.

The heroine even inspires fashion photographs, as in October 1991, when *Vogue* used the actress Michelle Pfieffer in Joan of Arc dress to model cross-shaped earrings, and in 1998, when the London designer Alexander McQueen created a line of clothes and a runway show based on Joan of Arc at the stake.

The heroine reached her apotheosis as a consumer icon in an advertisement in the early 1990s for a medical product that read: "Pick four women. Your best friend. Your realtor. Your boss. Joan of Arc. Statistics say that three out of four of them have suffered from a feminine yeast infection. Chances are, you have too."[23] In this list, Joan of Arc is clearly an aberration. Joan is evoked as an idealized woman with whom the reader may identify only to use a statistic that makes this identification unlikely. In addition, connecting Joan to a contemporary woman's problem pulls her out of her own time, making her as much an anomaly then as now. Finally, the ad draws the reader's attention to the one site that should link Joan with other women, only to show that she does not fit in. While the reader may be a realtor or a boss, no woman will be a Joan of Arc.

Woman warriors appeared in a number of films in the 1990s, including *Starship Troopers* (1997), Walt Disney's *Mulan* (1998), and *G.I. Jane* (1998). The most intriguing of these works is the Persian Gulf War film *Courage under Fire* of 1996, directed by Edward Zwick. The heroine, named Karen Walden, played by the popular actor Meg Ryan, is a captain in the army, a helicopter pilot, and a single mother. Her story is told posthumously from several perspectives as the army attempts to decide whether the actions leading to her death entitle her to be the first female recipient of the Medal of Honor. In *Courage under Fire,* as in the other films featuring woman warriors in the 1990s, the issue is not the woman's competence, which is taken for granted, but the question whether women belong in battle at all. Much is made of Walden's maternity, which should exclude her from war from the start.[24] While the film ends with a celebration of the heroine's honor and bravery, the question remains as to whose story has actually been told. As a character who is dead from the start, the heroine is less a subject than a device through which men concoct their own stories. In one scene in particular, a soldier who is dying of cancer and haunted by the memory of Karen engulfed in flames exclaims, "O Jesus!" using the very words attributed to Joan of Arc as she died. In the end, the sacrifice by fire of the film's ostensible heroine is less for her country than for the redefinition of American masculinity.

Neither Joan's military strategy nor her saintly gifts guarantee her continual presence in the United States for the foreseeable future; the fact that she was both female and a successful warrior do. An essay on the editorial page of the *New York Times* in 1994, "Women without Hair: Lost or Found?" was inspired by the national discussion surrounding the admittance of the first woman to The Citadel, the military officer's training college in Charleston, South Carolina. In particular, the essay reflected on a judge's ruling that the woman, Shannon Faulkner, was to have her head shaved to one-eighth of an inch, like all the other cadets. The writer of the piece, Catherine S. Manegold, began by writing, "It is not the hair. It's the hair *thing*," before describing how witches had their hair shorn in the belief that their hair held mystical powers. She reflected that despite the fact that Joan of Arc shocked her cohorts by cutting her hair, she has usually been represented over the centuries with a flowing mane. The medieval scholar Ulrike Wiethaus is quoted: "Men felt very comfortable when they cut off women's hair. . . . But when women did it themselves—like Joan of Arc—the men just freaked out." Other examples of hair cutting are noted, including the shaving of French women who had been involved with Germans, the Old Testament correlation between cutting the hair of captive women and rape, and the bald pates of the feminist artist/activist "Riot Grrrls." Finally, Faulkner herself is quoted as saying, "It's just hair." The article concludes, ". . . it will grow back." [25] This essay makes the point that the emotional and social significance of women's hair is disappearing, along with all the other qualities assigned to females that have disqualified them for the military.

Although women warriors are now legally mandated, an essay in the *New York Times Magazine* in late 1997 revealed how much has yet to change. The cover of the issue, titled "Women in the Warrior Culture," states outright, "The larger issue for the military is not what to do about adultery, harassment or even rape, but whether being a good soldier depends on being an aggressive male." The article itself, by Richard Rayner, bears the more specific title "The Warrior Besieged," and highlights quotations at the top of each page: ". . . Military life may correctly foster the attitudes that tend toward rape"; "This idea of female marines? . . . It's a bunch of bull, man. They cause trouble and they can't do the work. It's why we call recruits *girls*." This long article comes to a nostalgic end by describing a classic Air Force officer: "flight helmet tucked under his arm, [he] is the last of a breed, the embodiment of an ancient and soon-to-be outmoded masculine sense of military purpose and perfection." Just before this conclusion, the author describes "America creating its own Amazon warrior myth, the equivalent not so much of Boadicea, or the one-breasted soldiers who fought Achilles in 'The Iliad,'" but rather the Soviet fighter pilot of World War II as seen in "a Soviet realist movie, riding into town at the head of a Red Cavalry troop, then heading out again three days later, leaving behind the child to which she'd given birth."[26] Where is Joan of Arc in this prophecy? Why refer to a little-known British warrior queen, the Greeks, and an irresponsibly maternal fictional character when Joan is so much more familiar and specific? Appearing as it did in a year that saw the first monument ever built to commemorate the 1.8 million women who served in the United States military (the Women in Military Service for America Memorial in Arlington National Cemetery), the essay was perhaps a reaction to the end of an era.

Now that women are actual combatants and their service is fully recognized, the woman warrior Joan of Arc no longer functions symbolically as she did in the First and Second World Wars. Joan's medieval aura, which was so useful during World War I as an evocation of past glory and mystical self-sacrifice, surfaced chiefly as an inspiration for fashion during the Vietnam and Persian Gulf wars. The domestication and infantilization that characterized representations of Joan of Arc after World War II simply became irrelevant as women armed themselves for battle. Consequently, the twentieth century's final films about the heroine, Besson's *The Messenger* and Duguay's *Joan of Arc*, are occupied less with the relation between women and war than with Joan of Arc's psychological state and the visualization of the supernatural. It is certain, however, that Joan of Arc's hold on the American imagination has not faded.[27] One can only imagine what new voices will be inspired to speak in the twenty-first century by the enduring visions of Joan of Arc.

Appendix

Visions of the Maid, 1429–1895

Joan of Arc and her first chroniclers existed in a world in which issues of feminism were alive as they were not to be again until the late eighteenth century and again in the twentieth century. The famous *querelle des femmes* of the fifteenth century was sparked by the two-part *Roman de la Rose*, begun by Guillaume de Lorris about 1230 and completed by Jean de Meun in 1275. Lorris established the courtly tradition in which the Lover longs to pick the Rose in the garden of Love and is hindered and helped by various allegorical forces. By contrast, Meun's completion of the poem is, among other things, a virulent attack on women, and particularly on the aristocratic glorification of women. The outcry caused by this work, which rivaled *The Divine Comedy* in influence, reached its pinnacle in the fanatical tract by Guillaume Postel, "The Very Wonderful Victories of the Women of the New World. And how they should govern the whole world by reason, and even those too who will be Monarchs in the Old World."[1] Despite the fact that Postel's Joan of Arc is often confused with the messianic Italian visionary known as Mère Jeanne, this early work reveals that Joan's presence in her own day was not so anomalous as it appeared to the twentieth century.

The women of the Middle Ages had the dubious benefit of the first major Christian theological theorizing about the role of women and marriage. This reaction to the secularizing of Europe while the church established its dominance resulted in a rational relegation of women to secondary status. Subsequently, women with something to say took advantage of the rampant heresies of the time, from the mysticism of antinomianism, which cast rules aside, to self-deification. Gnosticism in particular attracted women for its elevation of the female figure of Wisdom, its revolutionary egalitarianism, and its numerous self-appointed women prophets. An important aspect of all medieval religion was the presence of female visionaries. Not entitled to speak from either a royal or a literate position, these women soared above scholarly distinctions to direct and ecstatic connection with the divine.[2] As an unruly woman, the female visionary was a subversive figure of protest, whose absolute allegiance to her visions widened options for all women. In her expression of repressed female anger, however, the visionary woman also reconfirmed the hysteria of what was thought to be the womb-ruled sex.

By the time Joan of Arc achieved legitimate visionary status in the early fifteenth century, the church had redefined the pagan roots of the mystical experience as heresy. Consequently, cultural definitions conflated the female visionary and the witch. Both were possessed, had the ability to read the thoughts of others, were able to fly, and bore mysterious wounds. Unless completely surrounded by male followers, holy women had become threatening.[3] This transitional time, between the Middle Ages and the Renaissance, was a reactionary one in which the outsider was punished as an inherent challenge to authority. As Mary Douglas suggests, during times like these, in which the social system is loose, power exists in those who are a source of disorder. She describes Joan of Arc as a "legitimate intruder . . . a peasant at court, a woman in armor, an outsider in the councils of war." Joan stands in an ambiguous, interstitial zone that projects unconscious power for being outside of authority.[4]

Hans Mayer's claim that Joan is "something that is no longer and not yet" may well be attributed to the absence of any representation of the Maid made from life.[5] Although one wants to believe in the enchanting, helmeted stone head owned by the Musée d'Orléans, which was once thought to be a portrait, or the single strand of dark hair ensconced in a wax seal, the fact remains that the visions of Joan have all been imaginative constructs. Even the first image of Joan, made by Clément de Fauquembergue on 10 May 1429, two days after the victory at Orléans, was drawn before the artist had seen Joan. This topheavy, chinless Joan with long wavy hair and a décolleté gown is overwhelmed by her banner and the huge sword that she carries backward in her left hand. Otherwise, Joan appears in tapestries and miniatures, such as Martin Lefranc's *Le Champion des Dames* of 1451, as a fantasy derived from hearsay, memory, and classical and religious icons. The unimposing stature, the long hair, and the sweeping dress, with or without hints of armor, derived from the first image continue through the sixteenth century.

The apparently inconsequential Joan of Arc of these contemporaneous images belies the fear that led to Joan's burning at the stake. To the English, Joan was a Medusa figure who literally froze men on the battlefield. She enters the chronicles of the duke of Bedford in 1433 as a "disciple and limb of the Fiend." In the Burgundian chronicles of Le Fèvre de Saint-Rémi as well as the writing of Pope Pius II, Joan finds her first major niche as a tool of political conspirators. Her position as commander is seen as such an absurdity that it was thought that "after-ages are likely to regard it with more wonder than credulity."[6] Even her first and one of her greatest advocates saw Joan, if not as a political weapon, then as a providential force. Christine de Pisan, who had refuted Jean de Meun's misogyny in *Le Dit de la Rose* in 1400, came out of retirement to celebrate Joan in the *Ditié de Jehanne d'Arc* in 1429. In lines such as "This is God's doing: it is He who guides her and who has given her a heart greater than that of any man" (XXVI), she simultaneously elevates women and reveals an inability to transcend the hierarchy in which Providence keeps women in their place.[7]

The championing of Joan by a writer as important as Christine, along with the widespread reaction to Meun's misogyny, kept the Maid in the cultural mainstream. Christine's popular poem introduced several productive elements to the Joan of Arc persona. The poet gravitates toward Joan's androgyny, describing her as "the champion who casts the rebels down and feeds France with the sweet, nourishing milk of peace, here indeed is something quite extraordinary!" (XXIV). In view of the rigid sex role divisions of the time, this image introduces an element of irreconcilability that comes to be Joan's trademark.[8] In addition, Christine equates Joan with the Virgin Mary as co-saviors of both humanity and France. Joan's virginity, so essential to her value as a woman warrior, elevates her to a divinity hailed in tones usually reserved for Mary: "Blessed be He who created you, Joan, who were born at a propitious hour! Maiden sent from God, into whom the Holy Spirit poured His great grace . . ." (XXII).

The views of Joan as providential and as a political tool found their natural home in the English chronicles that culminate in Shakespeare's *Henry VI, Part I* of 1592. Even after the Treaty of Arras had reunited Burgundy and

France in 1435, the skeptical Burgundian historians gave Joan her divinity but retained a hostile tone toward her "unseemliness," manifested particularly in her choice of male dress.[9] At a time when women sat on the thrones of England, Scotland, and France, the skewering of a powerful female must have been something of a release. Edward Hall's chronicle of 1548 and Raphael Holingshed's of 1587 form the two poles of Shakespeare's Joan. While Hall attributes her virginity to her "foul face" and abhors the French for allowing their victory to come through a "chambermaid in a hostelry, and a beggar's brat [who was] an enchantress, an organ of the devil, sent by Satan," Holingshed's description is fairly flattering, despite his attribution of her power to the devil. Shakespeare, who may not have written the entire play in question, creates a brave and dignified Joan before turning her into a cruel, deceitful virago who bargains with the devil before claiming pregnancy and promiscuity in an attempt to escape her fate. This is a Joan to be taken seriously, as evidenced in her magnificent final curse:

> May never glorious sun reflex his beams
> Upon the country where you make abode;
> But darkness and the gloomy shade of death
> Environ you, till mischief and despair
> Drive you to break your necks or hang yourselves![10]

Although Joan's purported affiliation with the devil surfaces from time to time, the thematic connection with biblical and classical heroines dominates her history. As a prophet, Joan was legitimated as a shaman with the right and power to redefine her people. In specific terms, although the idea of France as a nation had been recognized by the aristocracy since the fourteenth century, Joan gave the peasantry the crusade mentality to see France as a holy realm.[11] Thus it seemed natural to equate Joan with Judith, Esther, and Deborah, even though only the latter was a warrior and the others achieved their ends by traditionally feminine wiles. On a broader level, Joan's story often is connected metaphorically with the athletic contest as it represents a struggle with evil. In the moral battle, Joan resembles the weak, unsexed Christian maidens whose righteousness is rewarded with victory.

In 1549 the influential *Mirouer des femmes vertueuses* was written anonymously to present women with two models: the gentle, patient Griselda and the valorous, miracle-working Joan of Arc. About the same time, the painting that has come to be known as the Hôtel de Ville portrait recast Joan for the next three centuries. She appears to be a bourgeoise in fancy dress, with only a sword to identify her as Joan of Arc. Perhaps the most interesting aspect of the portrait is the panache, the feathered headdress tied under the chin, a symbol of victory that heretofore was worn only with male garb. As this first of the enormously influential images of Joan gazes knowingly at the spectator, many questions are raised concerning Johannic iconography. The painting actually contains the well-known sword, with its five engraved crosses, that was found on Joan's advice buried behind the woodland church of St. Catherine de Fierbois. While clearly a phallic substitute, the sword, as carried by Catherine, Margaret, Judith, and other female liberators, is also a tool of separation. It not only cleaves one into two to create binaries but is a symbol of generation that suggests parturition.[12] In this latter regard, Joan's graceful but deliberate grasp of the sword is somewhat threatening. Just as Judith, who liberates her people and remains chaste, is described in the language of eroticism and stands for the danger of female sexuality, the sword-carrying virgin warrior Joan can suggest the potential for reproductive power.

The great anomaly of this portrait is the dress that Joan wears, in view of her choice to die rather than give up her trousers. Joan apparently understood the iconography of power and seemed to know that since the time of Homer the transformation of the hero had been achieved through armor. Shining like the stars in imperishable metal, the burnished armor of the hero bestowed divine status. Further, the armor of the maiden has complex significance owing to its connection with the patriarchally aligned Athena. The aegis by which Athena is recognized differs from that of Zeus, her sole parent, in being adorned by the head of the Medusa. Freud described this symbol in relation to what he perceived to be the mythical dread of female reproductive power: "This symbol of horror is worn upon her dress by the virgin goddess Athena. And rightly so, for thus she becomes a woman who is unapproachable and repels all sexual desires—since she displays the terrifying genitals of the mother."[13] Separated from the maternal, both Athena and the armed Joan are presumed safe and fit to enter the male war game. In addition, the armor of the virgin warrior literally contains the chaos that is woman and becomes a powerful and magical symbol of good as opposed to the evil of disorder.

The significance of a woman in armor is complicated by its contrast to the inherently leaky nature of the female body.[14] In the manner of Saint Tuccia's miraculous watertight sieve, armor makes the porous female body impermeable so that it can represent virtue in the male value system and prevent the threat of pregnancy. Joan of Arc's well-known lack of menstruation further solidifies the symbolism in which life-giving blood stays inside rather than leaking and questioning the valuation of rigid boundaries. Finally, the fact that the watertight sieve is an impossible ideal removes the armored female from any connection with reality and freezes her on Virtue's pedestal. A last anomaly can be found in the apparel worn by Joan in the Hôtel de Ville portrait. A closer look at the dress reveals a stony hardness to the regular folds of the skirt, while the design of the sleeves and neckline suggests the joints of a suit of armor. The metaphor of the armed female as virtue is so strong that the encasement of the female body need only be suggested to elevate it from the individual to the abstract.

Joan of Arc in full armor inevitably evokes the Amazon warrior. While Joan was still alive, Perceval de Boulainvilliers sought to understand Joan's extraordinary achievements by comparing her with the athletic Amazon queens Atalanta and Camilla. In 1497 Philip of Bergamo claimed to have seen Joan, yet he described her as the legendary hunter Diana, complete with bow and quiver. Perhaps most indicative of the power of this mythic image is the naming of Joan of Arc. Joan called herself La Pucelle, or The Maid, and gave her last name as Romée when pressed, since girls in her part of Europe used their mothers' names. Yet Joan is referred to exclusively in the Diana/huntress/moon goddess mode, through an alteration of her father's name, Darc, which neatly suggests both crescent and bow.[15]

Because of her influence on the representation of Joan of Arc, the Diana figure demands careful scrutiny.[16] Appearing in the *Iliad,* the *Aeneid,* and Ovid's *Metamorphoses,* the "lady of the bow" is a cruel and unforgiving goddess whose aloofness and ambiguity have come to define the androgyne. Her careless beauty, childlessness, and rejection of all men but those of her own choosing reflect her autonomy and her obsession with the hunt. The eroticism and the subversiveness of this figure, which is based on the preChristian notion of a virgin as a young woman who is free to choose her lovers, cannot be underestimated. Not coincidentally, Amazon narratives usually end with the Amazonamachie, in which the women are massacred and their valor is absorbed by their male conquerors.

Tales of Amazon tribes in Africa were of great interest in sixteenth-century Europe. Later, the more rational Renaissance transformed the death-dealing virgin warrior into a romantic heroine, as exemplified by Ludovico Ariosto's Bradamante and Torquato Tasso's Clorinda. These warriors achieved success on the battlefield but were prone to languishing otherwise, as symbolized by the removal of the helmet to reveal a cascade of long hair. In fact, an influential bronze monument of a kneeling Joan of Arc in armor, with hair reaching down her back, was built in Orléans in the early sixteenth century, and was copied by Peter Paul Rubens in 1620. Here chastity is no longer represented as a rejection of men but as an invitation to the Christian concept of ideal love. From the sixteenth century onward, the classical warrior Joan of Arc is armed for practical purposes alone and she wears her hair long to signify her eventual return to womanhood. While this powerful Amazonian iconography permitted Joan's entry into culture as one of the Nine Worthies, all of whom could be understood and appreciated within patriarchy, this image is most culpable in the erasure of the eccentricities and challenges that make Joan intriguing.

Joan of Arc's passage into the seventeenth century, almost two hundred years after her death, finds her ever more similar to the women of the period. Although many artists recalled her religious and warrior roots by showing her awkwardly holding her sword or banner and by making her resemble a combination of an Amazon and an opulent Judith, her face is characterized by the big eyes and the small mouth that were considered beautiful at the time.[17] In a number of engravings, typified by the 1647 illustration by Gilles Rousselet for a text by the Jesuit priest Pierre Lemoyne titled *La Gallerie des femmes fortes,* Joan's fantastic armor and affected pose prefigure her demise as a serious figure over the next two centuries. Lemoyne's text is equally important in the changing conception of Joan of Arc, and is of interest for its attempt to avoid misogyny while using theological language. Primarily, Lemoyne refutes the Amazon image as sexist and inadequate to the divine Joan. In line with the Neoplatonism of the time, Joan's connection to the deity puts her into an angelic and androgynous zone far from the battlefield.[18]

Lemoyne's book was part of a new Joan of Arc vogue that was connected with the early seventeenth-century Wars of Religion between Catholics and Protestants. The Catholics chose Joan as their patron; Cardinal Richelieu had her portrait painted on the wall of his palace and La Fontaine made a pilgrimage to her statue in Orléans. Joan's support of the monarchy, along with her violent and spectacular life and death, made her a valuable figure-head in this explosive era. The Huguenots despised Joan, both for her alle-giance to church and king and for the contemporaneous representations of her as a plumed and posed lady of the court. In the early days of the Wars of Religion, numerous representations of Joan were destroyed along with the "fairy tree" in Lorraine that had inspired Joan and her followers. It was not until the nineteenth century that Joan was perceived and revived as a forerunner of the Reformation.[19]

The early seventeenth century seemed to be a propitious time for Joan of Arc's reputation. Edmond Richer wrote the first scholarly version of her life, *L'Histoire de la Pucelle d'Orléans*, in 1639, although it remained unpublished until 1912. Richer used the trial and rehabilitation records to vindicate Joan and condemn her accusers, a task continued by descendants of Joan's broth-ers, Charles Du Lys and Jean Hordal. In the middle of the century, the *pré-cieuse* Madeleine de Scudéry praised a virgin heroic Joan in male dress, while a Jacquette Guillaume wrote *Les Dames illustrées où par bonnes et fortes raisons il se preuve que le sexe féminin surpasse en toutes sortes de genres le sexe masculin.* In a similar mode, François Hédelin dismissed the humble vessel of divine Providence of the previous century in *La Pucelle d'Orléans* of 1640. This in-tellectual, salon Joan fights her narrow-minded prosecutors with words and dismisses the English Warwick's advances with a sophistication that asserts her equality. Yet Hédelin, in having an angel announce Joan's death by fire at the start of his play, introduces the childlike martyr Joan of Arc who appears through the end of the century as an unfortunate victim of the Inquisition.

The best-known work of the seventeenth century, both for its own sake and for Voltaire's later reaction to it, is Jean Chapelain's *La Pucelle, ou La France délivrée*. Commissioned by descendants of Joan's colleague, the bas-tard of Orléans and count of Dunois, the poem is a combination of allegory, romance, epic, and fiction in twenty-four cantos written over thirty years. The work returns Joan to the Renaissance Amazon mode, in which rever-ence overcomes physical love for Joan and greater stress is placed on the religious aspect of Joan's battles. Joan is most important in this poem as a martyr and saint so that Dunois can emerge as the hero. The work was immensely popular in its day, although its future reputation was prefigured in an immediate lampooning by the critic Nicolas Boileau.

With the Enlightenment, in which France followed England's lead, the monarchist Joan of Arc began to appear as something of a fraud. With her unquestioning devotion to the church and her peasant origins, Joan represented the superstitious confusion that was often referred to as the "spirit of the dark Middle Ages."[20] In addition, the epic, heroic aspect of Joan's story that had so enchanted writers of the previous century was rejected in favor of character study. In 1756 Voltaire wrote his *Essai sur les moeurs,* in which he praised Joan of Arc's courage but revived the much earlier notion of Joan as a tool of political conspiracy. In 1762, apparently as the result of a dinnerparty challenge after a mockery of Chapelain's poem, Voltaire wrote *La Pucelle d'Orléans* for the amusement of his friends. A rare Joan of Arc farce, this bawdy, clever parody of an Italian epic in twenty-one cantos of heroic couplets uses Joan's story to counter the church, the monarchy, and the nobility.

Although *La Pucelle d'Orléans* is a general attack in which Joan is only one principal player, the poem is important because Voltaire finally had isolated the crux of the Joan of Arc story—virginity as power. The poem, in which everyone is in love with Joan, even her magic donkey, is driven by an all-out, often hilarious attack on and preservation of the "rare jewel" of Joan's chastity. The popularity of this scandalous mockery was short-lived, however, because Joan was far too valuable a symbol of a unified France. Yet Voltaire's antimonarchist reworking of Joan's story, in combination with his elision of her terrible death, assisted her entrance into American culture several years later. By 1801, Friedrich von Schiller had redefined the use of Joan of Arc for the Romantic reaction of the nineteenth century, in which the desire for female equality was replaced by the urge to punish unconventional women.

A brief examination of the pronounced absence of Joan in the American colonies provides a background for the eventual explosion of her popularity in the nineteenth century. The position of women in Calvinist America is fraught with paradox. Even more strikingly than in medieval Europe, the spiritual equality between men and women at the heart of Christianity collided with social practice in the American colonies. Martin Luther's misogyny, which caused God's purported view of the inferiority of women to be codified into law, made life contradictory for Puritan women. Not only did these women come from a country dominated by myths and examples of female power such as Elizabeth I, but many of them must have possessed the same spirit of adventure and hunger for religious freedom and economic opportunity as their mates. The oppressive female role was bound to cause the problems manifested in the witchcraft trials in Salem.[21] Perhaps because of Joan's allegiance to Catholicism and the monarchy, her ready prototype does not seem to have entered the discourse of the trials.

The most marked elision of Joan of Arc in seventeenth-century America occurs in the trial of the antinomian heretic Anne Hutchinson. A religious reformer, Hutchinson left England in 1634. She was a middle-aged nurse-midwife and spiritual adviser to women before she attracted a larger group of both sexes with her discussions of grace, good works, and redemption. Reviving a heresy described by Paul (in Romans 6), she supported the free giving of grace and absolute assurance of salvation that validated female religious experience and undermined clerical authority. Just as Joan of Arc rejected the church militant in her day in favor of her voices, Hutchinson replaced the colonists' self-concept as a chosen people with the image of a mystical community of the elect.[22] In addition, Hutchinson's trial performance was remarkably similar to Joan of Arc's in its cleverness, its refusal of intimidation, its utter conviction, and its tendency to make fools of her accusers.[23] Like Joan, Hutchinson was defeated and excommunicated in 1637 after claiming direct revelation from God.

One of the more intriguing aspects of Hutchinson's story is the connection between her power and reproductive issues. Hutchinson herself had several miscarriages and an antinomian follower, Mary Dyer, had a badly deformed stillborn baby. Intimidated accusers perceived these "monstrous births," as well as the violent death at the hands of Native Americans suffered by the Hutchinson family five years after their banishment, as manifestations of evil sent by the divine to reaffirm the power of the church. In multiple ways, Hutchinson embodied female disorder that threatened the stiff Puritan hierarchies. Like Joan, Hutchinson shared the fate of the Amazon, with defeat at the hands of rational men.

Although Hutchinson's story is not so well known as Joan of Arc's, it acts for Americans as what Amy Lang calls a cautionary tale that "reenlivens the female heretic only to banish her once again." Hutchinson's tale may be about the individual versus authority whereas Joan's is about nationalism, but gender issues must be seen to reside at the heart of both narratives. Just as Joan disappeared into history in the guise of an abstract Virtue or an Amazon, Hutchinson quickly lost her individuality and became an instrument of Satan and another Eve or Jezebel. Most notably, Hutchinson is remembered as a statue in Boston, depicted with her arm wrapped around a child as she looks into the sky. Purely a fiction, since no representations of her exist and children play no part in her story, Hutchinson is domesticated as a visionary and a heroic mother to prove that even a notoriously dissenting woman can be put in her place.[24]

For all their similarities, Anne Hutchinson and Joan of Arc seem to share no discursive space. Revolutionary women called upon the distant Judith, Esther, and Deborah or the queens Elizabeth I and Catherine the Great, but never the woman who actually fought her own battles as the superior of her male compatriots. Until the English become the outright enemy, Joan's Catholicism and monarchism apparently exempted her from representation. Perhaps because of the ever-widening split between the public and private realms in late eighteenth-century America, females who acted outside the bonds of conventional female behavior aroused particular consternation. With men in control of economics and politics and women domesticated far from the city, the cross-dressing, virginal Joan would clearly threaten the American ideal as put forth by "Philanthropos" in the *Virginia Gazette* in 1790: "However flattering the path of glory and ambition may be, a woman will have more commendation in being the mother of heroes, than in setting up, Amazon-like, for a heroine herself."[25]

Nevertheless, Joan of Arc was used in both the American and French revolutions. This most sustained Joan of Arc vogue, which peaked during the First World War and continues still, is marked by a truly phenomenal amount of material from all over the world, which includes biography, fiction, poetry, drama, painting, sculpture, music, and film, not to mention innumerable popular culture references and ephemera. While many of the images already described continue to appear in various guises, the postrevolutionary Romantic Joan of Arc is transformed from a Virtue and Amazon to both a figure of erotic attraction and a pure, martyred child of nature. In effect, once Joan achieves a general revolutionary significance to which her monarchism and Catholicism are no longer relevant, she becomes more threatening as a potential model for all women. Reflecting the growing clamor for women's rights, nineteenth-century representations of Joan of Arc exhibit an often contradictory blend of nationalist and religious celebration and misogynist usurpation or dismissal of female power.

The country that was to see the American Revolution was, among other things, an amalgamation of Greek republicanism and evangelical Protestantism. An important aspect of republicanism was the presupposition of a sharp split between public and private worlds. The freedom and community that reigned in the public, male realm was supported by the love, faithfulness, and selfless labor of the private, female arena. In addition, by the middle of the eighteenth century the American businessman had given his allegiance to the economic sphere at the expense of the familial, religious one. This commitment further enmeshed the majority of women in domestic bondage, whether as slaves, homesteaders, or household angels. In this system, in which the higher moral stance of women was to compensate for the corruption of the individual man, the female-dominated church was depended upon to elevate the community. As a reaction to the mass exodus of men from the church, a movement of itinerant preachers, who advocated an inward-looking religion, challenged the failing established churches with what came to be known as the Great Awakening.[26]

This polarization between the public and the private, the masculine and the feminine, became one of the rhetorical supports of the revolution itself. The British enemy was identified with elegance and luxury, as opposed to the frugal and industrious American colonies. John Adams wrote of "public virtue" as the manly self-sacrifice and public spiritedness that would hold fast against the feminine depravity that threatened from the effect of both the Great Awakening and British dominance.[27] In this milieu, Joan of Arc came to play a role, since she had rejected traditional femininity in her choice of dress and in her forthright approach, and her female status made her a subsumable icon of truth and virtue. Furthermore, Joan was both a prophet and, more important, the fulfillment of a prophecy, so that her followers were envisioned as God's chosen people. In Protestant America, the Joan who had died in direct defiance of the Catholic Church was a good example of the weak raised to confound the strong.

Shortly after the American Revolution, the young English poet Robert

Southey felt provoked by Voltaire to write the epic poem *Joan of Arc*. This long, torrid work of 1793 introduces the secularized Joan who had become capable of standing for opposing causes. Southey envisioned Joan as an uncrushable exemplar of the human spirit and used her story to express a revolutionary socialism. Joan represented the natural as opposed to the industrialized world, and her connection to the earth linked her to the supernatural as well. The degree to which Joan had lost her historical specificity is evident in the fact that Southey gave Joan a lover who died in battle. Southey's poem is most important, however, for its manifestation of a major cultural shift in the overall perception of Joan of Arc. Southey himself told of the very moment at which English opinion toward the heroine seemed to change. At a London pantomime of Joan's story at Covent Garden, the audience apparently became so displeased by the ending, in which Joan was carried off by devils, that the script was changed to have her elevated by angels.[28]

In 1798 Joan of Arc first appeared in a play in the United States. The Irish-born American author of *Female Patriotism, or The Death of Joan of Arc*, John Daly Burk, uses Joan as a national liberator of her people against the common enemy of fifteenth-century France, eighteenth-century Ireland, and revolutionary America. As the spirit of liberty and justice, Joan is juxtaposed to the insensitive English, who demand servitude and provoke dissension. The play, which is peopled by characters named Lafayette, Rochambeau, and de Grasse, uses the battle of Orléans to evoke Lexington, Valley Forge, and Yorktown. Burk takes pains to make Joan's story antiroyalist. In the course of the play, Joan speaks of monarchy as an unfortunate but necessary transition in the upsetting of the English occupation, and during the coronation she speaks of symbolically crowning each French person, free and equal. However, history is at Burk's service in the recounting of Charles VII's actual failure even to attempt to save Joan of Arc. This was an aspect of the story that spoke directly to the American experience of monarchy. Before dying, the play's Joan sees into the future, which is embodied by the French Revolution and universal republicanism.[29]

Burk tended to see Joan's era as the advent of a new French order, a perceived childlikeness in the Middle Ages, and Joan as an uncorrupted noble savage. Despite the fact that women had been vital to both the settling of America and its revolution, so that Joan was less of an anomaly here than in most other times or places in history, Joan adheres to Puritan standards of femininity. In addition, the inherent analogy between the new country and the revolutionary Joan was enhanced by the stress placed on Joan's purity, innocence, and providential position. Burk's Joan ends by asserting her traditional femininity, saying that she would give up all the honor rather than lose "those timid, soft and virgin sentiments" that she had had to control in order to fight.[30] While the equally youthful American patriot Nathan Hale could live forever in the single brief statement "I only regret that I have but one life to lose for my country," Joan's vacillation on the boundary between life's richness and an honorable death dooms her to endless resurrection.

Whereas the United States discovered Joan of Arc's value for the first time in relation to its revolution, the French Revolution suddenly dismissed Joan and glorified Voltaire. Joan's status as part of France's Gothic past led to mass destruction of her purported relics and monuments, as well as the only disruption in the five hundred years of annual celebrations of the liberation of Orléans. Not long after this hiatus, however, Napoleon I perceived Joan's value anew and revived her as an anti-English symbol of nationalism. Up until this time, a decontextualized Joan had appeared most frequently in painted and engraved portraits, many of which illustrated written texts. But the nineteenth century began to insert Joan in historical tableaux. Although she appeared in battle and on the stake, for Napoleon's sake she was frequently envisioned in the middle of the coronation. In 1854 Dominique Ingres painted the influential coronation scene in which a radiant and fully armed Joan, seen from a slightly low angle and surrounded by kneeling followers, appears to be communing with the divine. Most notably, the period saw an increase in the numbers of naturalistic bronze equestrian Joans that exhibit a strength heretofore absent.

Perhaps the most important image of Joan created during this time was the statue made by Marie d'Orléans in the 1830s, in which Joan has negotiated the complex transition from Amazon to humble servant of God. This downward-gazing but robust Joan wears armor above the waist and a skirt below, and although she has a helmet and gauntlets, she has laid them aside. The sword she clutches to her chest resembles a cross, while her appropriately short hair is styled fashionably. The growing tendency to erect Joan of Arcs in city squares is evidence of the broader assimilation of Joan into French culture. Robert Musil observes that public statues, which are "made to be seen," "virtually drive off what they would attract. We cannot say that we do not notice them; we should say that they de-notice us, they withdraw from our senses." The apparent invisibility of these statues makes their influence all the more subtle.[31]

The first narrative twist in this new Joan of Arc vogue appeared in Schiller's *Die Jungfrau von Orleans* in 1801. Perhaps because of Joan's growing influence, or in reaction to the challenging writings of such people as Mary Wollstonecraft, Joan at this time was rarely seen without a lover, who eventually benefited from her death in the tradition of the Amazonamachie. Writing in reaction to Voltaire, Schiller is equally concerned with Joan's virginity, which in his work leads to her tragic fall. In the play, God has given Joan a magic helmet, which protects her until she falls in love with an English soldier named Lionel. She then dies a slow death, partially on the battlefield and partially in front of the court, presumably to make the most of her self-sacrifice. Likewise, Giuseppe Verdi's 1845 *Giovanna d'Arco* has Joan fall in love with the dauphin; in N. J. C. de Hédouville's play of 1829 both Dunois and the English Bedford fall for Joan; La Trémouille is the suitor in the 1870 opera by Jean-Joseph Olivier; while Tchaikovsky simply set Schiller's play to music in 1881.[32] Schiller also revived a Shakespearean vision of Joan as a supernatural force, whose link with the elements empowers her.

The most influential proponent of the natural Joan of Arc was the French historian Jules Michelet, who devoted one volume of his *Histoire de France* to Joan in 1841. His obviously Christian structure, which begins with the modest shack, passes through glory and honor, and ends on the crosslike stake, is somewhat secular. Whereas in pre-Romantic days, saintly beings occupied a higher zone and occasionally descended to provide mortals with assistance, the Romantic ideal is based in the earthly, the sensual, the human realm. The previously ignored fact that Joan was raised as a peasant became central to her appeal as a nationalist hero. Joan's story in this period is one of optimism in which her life proves that everyone is capable of heroic action. Of particular interest is Michelet's continuation of Voltaire's obsession with Joan's chastity. La Pucelle's power comes from her virginity because Joan and France are analogous in their femininity.

The new democracy in Joan's heroism, in which her humble and innocent virtue entitles her to what previously was available only to highborn and cultured people, marks the latest and most abiding alteration in her persona. Although she retains Amazon traits, such as the connection with nature and the pure, strong body, she is nonsexual. Whereas virginity is central to both, the Amazon chooses hers while the child is simply oblivious. Not coincidentally, the Amazon's relation to nature's wildest animals is replaced in the nineteenth century by a tendency to represent Joan with sheep. As Warner notes, Joan's absolute innocence and integrity at this time mask a despair that sees goodness as inevitably corrupted. In fact, Joan's "youth" is primarily a nineteenth-century invention: although Joan was only nineteen when she died, at nineteen she was fully a woman, and her companions at arms could expect to live only five or six years longer.[33] This notion of a childlike Joan erases ambiguity and incarnates an unchanging idea of goodness in an era that feared the flux of a vastly changing world.

The most profound revolution in the perception of Joan of Arc resulted from Jules Quicherat's five-volume translation from Latin into French of the full trial and rehabilitation records, *Procès de condamnation et de réhabilitation de Jeanne d'Arc, dite la Pucelle*. One of the first complete historical records about a single subject, this collection, which also includes chronicles, letters, literary works, and public documents, was established between 1841 and 1849. In this manifestation of the Romantic period's obsession with history, particularly with the wisdom and truth of the Middle Ages, Joan became known through her speech, her tone, her behavior, and the reactions of others to her in a way previously unimagined.

The liberal stance perpetuated by both Quicherat and Michelet was echoed in the Joan of Arc works by Alexandre Dumas *père* in 1842, as well as in the biographies of the 1860s by Henri Wallon and Marius Sepet. In England, Thomas De Quincy reflected the late Romantic fascination with Joan in an essay directly inspired by Michelet. This work was one of the first to concentrate on the brutal treatment and the unjust trial inflicted upon Joan. Although he is typically concerned with patriotism, liberty, and nature, De Quincy utterly disregards Joan's voices in his tale of martyrdom. On the other hand, Alphonse de Lamartine's biographical essay of 1852 is concerned particularly with the connection between Joan's voices and her noble peasant soul. Uncorrupted by dogma, the inner voice becomes an exterior phenomenon, the personal becomes political, and individual conviction and choice represent liberty for all.

At the same time, across the Atlantic Ocean, Ralph Waldo Emerson might well have been writing about the experience of Joan of Arc when he offered his version of "radical correspondence." Joan's well-known ability to find coherence in the ringing of bells, the flashing of sunlight, and the sound of celestial voices and her consequent self-obliteration and revelation of the divine manifest Emerson's belief in life as spiritual vision and the superiority of intuitive self-direction. Yet, in an essay titled "Woman," Emerson writes that woman is the ideal representative of manhood: she is "medium, not seer, oracle, not prophet . . . the model to the artist." Furthermore, Nathaniel Hawthorne, through a reference to Anne Hutchinson, elaborated the American attitude toward women who knew the "inward voice." Hawthorne described the burdensome nature of "public women," or "ink-stained Amazons" who wrote or spoke publicly, as unseemly and unnatural.[34] The United States, more than any other Western country, was afflicted by the myth of the Beautiful Soul, in which women were conceptualized as existing solely in the private realm as powerless repositories to be filled by culture. As Jean Bethke Elshtain notes, Martin Luther's masculinist theology eliminated the female images of the Madonna, the female saints, and the "mother church." Marian values of hope, compassion, dignity, and maternity had been dismissed by this time as nature to be overcome by culture.[35]

Although American culture at large still paid little attention to Joan of Arc, she entered through the growing momentum in favor of women's rights. In the Second Great Awakening of the early part of the nineteenth century, women were once again valued for their capacity for direct and emotional access to the divine. As in the antinomian scandals of Hutchinson's day, Calvinist predestination and notions of the elect were replaced by a belief in universal salvation. The Shakers, the celibate sect of Second Adventists who were brought to America by Ann Lee at the time of the Revolution, exemplify the strengths of women in the religious realm. The mystical Mother Ann was seen as the counterpart to Christ, in reflection of a God who is eternal mother and father. Given that Lee advocated celibacy out of sympathy for childbirth difficulties and the grief of infant death, it is no wonder that the sect included twice as many women as men.[36]

More specifically, nineteenth-century women seemed to feel a new ability to effect change. The American Female Moral Reform Society began in 1834 to battle male licentiousness, the double standard, and prostitution, with the latter being blamed entirely on patriarchal economics.[37] The society's goals, however, were not equal rights for women but the protection of children. This equating of adult femininity and virgin childlikeness now dominated Joan of Arc imagery, and is evident in Sarah Moore Grimké's 1867 introduction to her translation of Lamartine's biography of Joan. Grimké idealizes women as "more sensitive, more impressionable, more loving, [identified more with] imagination and . . . affections," and more capable of self-sacrifice.[38] In 1848 the feminist Elizabeth Cady Stanton praised Joan of Arc as a visionary whose prophetic spirit and powerful legacy could assist the movement for women's rights. As was typical in the time, Stanton declared women's need for both Joan's will and her religious enthusiasm.[39]

As is evident in the analysis of the twentieth century, periods of war have traditionally boosted the organizational powers of women and given them greater economic strength. The Civil War was no exception, as can be seen in the work of countless women abolitionists and of Harriet Tubman, who claimed she led her people to freedom by divine command. A seventeen-year-old Quaker named Anna Dickinson came to be known as "the Joan of Arc of the Union Cause," "the American Joan of Arc," and "the Joan of Arc of the Civil War." Dickinson often spoke of Joan as she visited hospitals, soldiers, and even the Congress of the United States. In a curious parallel to certain aspects of the Joan of Arc story, Dickinson publicly disagreed with the powerful but inept General George McClellan just before he was relieved of command. Perhaps the most interesting question raised by Dickinson's story involves her near absence from history. Had she died a virgin martyr rather than living to be ninety, might she have merited a place in history comparable to Joan's? The second major use of Joan of Arc during the Civil War was John Fentonhill's pamphlet *Joan of Arc: An Opinion of Her Life and Character, Derived from Ancient Chronicles* of 1864. A Richmonder, Fentonhill adopted Joan as a fellow southerner, who reacted aggressively when besieged by northerners. His Joan was not the child of most nineteenth-century biographers, but rather a combative warrior with complete commitment to her cause.[40]

Women's use of Joan of Arc in the mid–nineteenth century coincided with Joan's increasingly generic persona. In 1877 liberal Protestant women used Joan in their missionary work, invoking the power of "the voice, like that which followed Joan of Arc." At the same time, Roman Catholic women in search of equal rights formed a group called St. Joan's International Alliance.[41] By the end of the century, most groups in favor of women's rights had become allied with conservative groups. The Women's Christian Temperance Union, which expressed its secular concerns in religious language and used an image of ax-wielding Joan of Arcs destroying barrels of liquor, had become right wing. Yet this strident authoritarianism in the quest for moral reform and against domestic violence must be seen in the light of women's complete helplessness in the political sphere.

In an article titled "The Maid of Orléans and the New Womanhood," the American Isabel O'Reilly used Joan of Arc to mount an attack against the first women's movement in 1894.[42] Disturbed by the uncomfortable fact that Joan evidenced in history what women were to represent only in iconography, conservative women revalued Joan for her spinning ability, her pious childhood, and her celibacy. Joan became a model for Catholic women to the degree that she blended with female saints who simply did as God ordered them. Part of this conservative trend encouraged a return to the womanly model of the Middle Ages, in which art portrayed women as gentle, indulgent, and uneducated.[43] Joan of Arc was also increasingly identified with motherhood. An illustration of this phenomenon occurs in the representation of a statue of Mary before which Joan was said to have prayed in Vaucouleurs. This Queen of Heaven Mary, without a veil but with a crown and a regal expression, is shown in late nineteenth-century stained-glass windows suddenly holding a child. Likewise, an American poet eulogized Joan in wildly inappropriate terms:

> No more a mother's ripened love
> Shall feed her with its autumn balm;
> Nor her warm teemful bosom prove
> Young mother's first ecstatic calm.[44]

This need to connect Joan with acceptable images of femininity is further evidenced in numerous depictions of a domesticated Joan at her mother's knee. Although the cult of Joan was influenced by the contemporary cult of the child Jesus, as well as the social interest in children exemplified in the novels of Charles Dickens and Victor Hugo, a fear of the women's movement's devotion to the iconoclastic Joan was surely a factor as well.

The French representation of Joan was plagued by this same tendency to be adopted by both the right and the left, but with far greater stakes. After

France's defeat by Prussia and the loss of Alsace-Lorraine to Germany in the late 1870s, Joan became a serious symbol of national integrity. Her cult grew to monumental proportions that climaxed in 1878 at the centenary of the death of Voltaire, who was now reviled, partially for having dared to mock Joan, whom many French citizens considered a saint. At this time, Joan's childhood home in Domrémy was swamped with pilgrims, a statue and basilica were built in her woods, journals were started, and a national holiday in honor of Joan was instigated. One of the key documents of this era is Maurice Boutet de Monvel's children's book, *Jeanne d'Arc,* of 1896. Boutet de Monvel's tiny, modest, blonde Joan, whose male clothes are forced on her, contrary to her "innate femininity," boosts the morale of the soldiers, who are dressed in contemporary uniforms and whose banners are adorned with the names of Napoleon's victories.

The future of Joan's cult and the determination of who could claim her was resolved during the Dreyfus affair of the late 1890s. Both the Catholic Charles Péguy, who wrote several books about Joan, and the writer Anatole France worked on the side of Alfred Dreyfus to keep Joan the symbol of progress and of the free individual opposed to a crushing government. The reactionaries who accused Dreyfus of treason, led by Charles Maurras of the anti-Semitic Action Française, wanted to perpetuate a Joan who obeyed the established order and military rule without question. To admit that the government had wrongly condemned Dreyfus seemed an unacceptable admission of military weakness in a country so recently damaged by the Franco-Prussian War. The Catholic royalist reactionaries dominated in the battle for Joan of Arc and they largely held on to her through the twentieth century in France.

The intensity of the battle over the image of Joan of Arc in France at the end of the nineteenth century highlights the need to separate the French Joan from the American Joan in the twentieth century. While Jeanne d'Arc appears openly at the very highest levels of church and state politics in France, Joan is used in a far more subtle way in the United States. The manner in which Joan exits the nineteenth century in America is typified first by the plethora of biographies of her, among them Jane Tuckey's *Joan of Arc, "The Maid"* in 1880, Mrs. Oliphant's *Jeanne d'Arc: Her Life and Death* in 1896, and Francis Cabot Lowell's scholarly *Joan of Arc* of 1896. The dominant tone in this period was pity toward a childlike, adventurous Joan. This inclination followed the return to chivalric sources in children's books by the Grimm brothers, Andrew Lang, Howard Pyle, and others, which was initiated by Sidney Lanier's *The Boy's King Arthur.* In 1884 Dr. John Lord described Joan in Volume 4 of his *Beacon Lights of History* as a religious girl with the gift of common sense.

Emily Dickinson follows this regressive mode in the unpublished, untitled poem about Joan that begins "A mien to move a queen—." Dickinson describes Joan as tearful, wrenlike, slight:

> Too small to fear,
> Too distant to endear,—
> And so men compromise
> And just revere.

Yet amidst the physical description of Joan (which calls to mind the sixteenth-century Hôtel de Ville portrait), Dickinson concentrates on Joan's voice. She describes a

> voice that alters—low—
> And on the ear can go
> Like set of snow, [45]

which is both heard and spoken by this tiny Joan. Dickinson finds this interior voice compelling and profound in spite of the cultural trend to diminish Joan by making her childlike. Joan's far-reaching appeal is evident in the name chosen by the Knights of Labor in Toledo, Ohio, for their pioneering baked goods cooperative in the 1880s: the Joan of Arc Assembly.[46]

The plethora of Joan of Arc imagery was part of a larger resurrection of medievalism inspired to a great degree by the *Waverley* novels of Sir Walter Scott.[47] Although the Puritan mind-set considered Catholicism to be the realm of Satan and the pope to be the Antichrist, a romanticized view of the feudal agrarian past provided an appealing antidote to industrialism. As Brian Stock has written, "the Renaissance invented the Middle Ages in order to define itself; the Enlightenment perpetrated them in order to admire itself; and the Romantics revived them in order to escape from themselves."[48] Since the United States had no authentic Gothic ruins, the influential landscape architect Andrew Jackson Downing advocated the insertion of picturesque details wherever possible. James Gamble Rogers's Gothic buildings at Yale University and Ralph Adams Cram's chapel at Princeton further popularized the style, which was then widely adopted by Protestant churches. New York City's Cathedral of St. John the Divine, which was financed by urban industrialists, offers the most telling and monumental example of the return of the medieval and the motivations behind it.

The second half of the nineteenth century saw the influence of medievalism in literature and academia as well. Motivated by a new conception of the period, which had shifted from being an era of superstition to being the embodiment of the elevated pursuit of a kind of knowledge in which reason and intuition were in balance, Johns Hopkins and Harvard initiated the study of what had been called the "Dark Ages." At Harvard, Henry Wadsworth Longfellow and Charles Eliot Norton adapted medieval ballads and poetry for Americans and advocated a reexamination of the vital communal cultures of the late Middle Ages, so seemingly idyllic in comparison with the dehumanized industrial way of life that had taken root in the United States. At the end of the century Henry Adams wrote the influential *Mont-Saint-Michel and Chartres,* which cemented the new appreciation of the era in question by charting the connections between economics, social structure, and symbolic expression.

Finally, the position and representation of Joan of Arc just before the twentieth century could not be better exemplified than by Mark Twain's novel of 1896 titled *Personal Recollections of Joan of Arc by the Sieur Louis de Conte (Her Page and Secretary),* described as "Freely Translated out of the Ancient French into Modern English from the Original Unpublished Manuscript in the National Archives of France by Jean François Alden." Twain writes that he became obsessed with Joan at the age of fifteen when a page from a book about her blew across his path, leading him to read voraciously in medieval history, French, and Latin. The book that he finally wrote was published privately and has been largely ignored by Twain scholars, although Twain claimed it as his favorite work.

Twain's obsession with Joan is part of a general concern with protecting the "unfallen woman" that occupied American male writers in the mid–nineteenth century.[49] Henry James's *Portrait of a Lady* concentrates on women who use the tactics of confrontation and resistance, while Nathaniel Hawthorne's *Marble Faun* privileges the response of moral isolation. For Twain, Joan's unique devotion to her private ideals, her moral rebellion, and the risk these things entailed offered a unique model. The Victorian urge to examine the unfallen woman or her counterpart, the untainted child, reveals a fear of the accelerated pace of change faced by the modern world, particularly in the roles of women. Twain dealt with the issue in the mode of the Romantic Michelet, who idolized the virginal child Joan for being naturally noble and unsullied by corrupting institutions. In addition, Twain's Joan appears as the very prototype of the new democratic hero, particularly in regard to the 1492 date of the story's presumed telling.[50]

Twain's devotion to Joan can also be seen as part of the Romantic return to a time when the most troubling of questions could be answered through faith in the supernatural. The atheist Twain seemed to exhibit some of the blasphemy of the true believer in his love of Joan's transcendence. Joan can be seen as a safety valve for the historical determinist Twain, for whom salvation may be possible when it comes through a marvelous, independent, unsullied child rather than through the church. On a personal level, Twain used Joan of Arc to celebrate his beloved daughter, Suzy, who drowned at the age of twenty-four as the book was nearing completion. This intimate loss combined with Twain's frustration and disgust with religion's inability to deal with life's most profound issues to make Joan of Arc the very image of a saint in a godless world. The last line of the supposed Translator's Preface captures his agony: "And for all reward, the French King, whom she had crowned, stood supine and indifferent, while French priests took the noble child, the most innocent, the most lovely, the most adorable the ages have produced, and burned her alive at the stake."[51]

Joan of Arc exits the nineteenth century as a lovely but pitiful child, obscured by a haze of sentimental longing and anguish. Twain has subsumed Joan and all her potential glory and achievement in the person of his doomed daughter. Having fallen victim to the drive for strong dichotomies that separate male and female, innocence and experience, Joan had lost her connection to the causes of freedom and justice that had held for the early women's rights supporters. Instead, Joan rested firmly in the grip of the right, appearing either as a pious stalwart of any conservative cause or as the avenging angel of a patriarchal God.

Notes

Preface

1. The frequently used English word "Maid" does not carry all the complexity of the term used by Joan, *La Pucelle*. The French word, which was used in all levels of society, implies a state of transition and promise as well as virginity. The English "maiden" is a closer match, since it does not suggest servitude. See Warner, *Joan of Arc*, 41–43.

2. I frequently use the adjective "American" to refer to the United States of America for want of an equally fluid but more specific term.

3. Since this book is not a study of films about Joan of Arc per se, it is limited to films that were released or at least known in the United States. This criterion eliminates for the most part the two great films about Joan of Arc, Carl Theodor Dreyer's *La Passion de Jeanne d'Arc* of 1928 and Robert Bresson's *Le Procès de Jeanne d'Arc* of 1962. These films have been studied elsewhere, most notably in Bordwell, *Films of Carl Theodor Dreyer;* Carney, *Speaking the Language of Desire;* Schrader, *Transcendental Style in Film;* Hanlon, *Fragments;* and Quant, *Robert Bresson.*

4. My work is indebted to ideas about the ideological construction of history found in White, *Metahistory;* Jameson, *Political Unconscious;* Sorlin, *Film in History;* and, more generally, the work of Roland Barthes, Werner Berthoff, Robert Rosenstone, and Vivian Sobchack. I also note that studies similar to mine have been conducted in relation to other frequently revived historical and legendary figures. See, for example, Joan DeJean, *Fictions of Sappho, 1546–1937* (Chicago: University of Chicago Press, 1989), and Mary Hamer, *Signs of Cleopatra* (New York: Routledge, 1993).

5. Any study of the ways in which females are constructed in narrative film is indebted to the work of Laura Mulvey and the feminist film theorists who elaborated on her work. See Mulvey's "Visual Pleasure and Narrative Cinema" and other essays in Erens, *Issues in Feminist Film Criticism.* This investigation relies particularly on De Lauretis, *Alice Doesn't,* and Jardine's *Gynesis* for its formulation of the relation of Joan of Arc's story to the romance plot.

6. I relied on Banta, *Imaging American Women,* to relate images of Joan of Arc to more general female types in American culture through the First World War. Nochlin, *Women, Art, and Power,* and Wolff, *Feminine Sentences,* helped me understand the relation between commercial and artistic versions of Joan of Arc and the larger culture in which they were located.

7. Even political figures such as Corazon Aquino of the Philippines and Benazhir Bhutto of Pakistan were referred to as the Joan of Arcs of their countries in relation to their political struggles in the 1980s. Automatically calling a fighting woman Joan of Arc is simple cultural shorthand but also an indication that the woman is seen as an anomaly.

8. Stanley Kubrick's *Full Metal Jacket* of 1987 is a case in point. The culminating sequence of the film shows American soldiers trapped by a sniper who turns out to be a young girl in braids. The extended scene in which she is finally killed, surrounded ritualistically by a circle of men, suggests fear and horror of the iconoclastic female warrior.

9. In *Bring Me Men and Women* Judith Stiehm discusses the repercussions of the government's 1976 mandate that women be admitted to the service academies. In "'The Mother of All Battles'"Susan Linville notes that while women accounted for 2% of the armed services in 1972, by 1997 women made up 14% of the Army, 17% of the Air Force, 5% of the Marine Corps, and 13% of the Navy.

10. Brun, "Jeanne d'Arc," 1–8.

11. Although I used studies of the shifting roles of American women during and after the Second World War by Rupp, Honey, and others to contextualize films about Joan of Arc, it is beyond the scope of this book to analyze how Joan of Arc's image may have affected real women.

12. Friedan, *Feminine Mystique.*

13. Jeffords, *Remasculinization of America,* aided my understanding of why Joan of Arc the warrior was replaced in the 1960s and afterward by the naive peasant Joan of the nineteenth century.

Introduction

1. The complete records of Joan of Arc's trial exist in the Latin original at the Bibliothèque Nationale in Paris, in French translations such as P. Paul Doncoeur's *La Minute française des interrogatoires de Jeanne la Pucelle: D'après le Requisitoire de Jean d'Estivet et les manuscrits d'Urfe et d'Orléans* (Melun: Librairie d'Argences, 1952), published in English as *The Trial of Joan of Arc,* trans. W. P. Barrett (London: G. Routledge, 1931), and Pierre Duparc's edition for the Société de l'Histoire de France, *Procès*

en nullité de la condamnation de Jeanne d'Arc (Paris: Klincksieck, 1977), published in English as *The Trial of Joan of Arc*, trans. W. S. Scott (London, 1956). Régine Pernoud has edited and written several books based on both the original trial and the rehabilitation trials of 1455–56, particularly *Retrial of Joan of Arc*. While there are thousands of biographies of the heroine, I have relied principally on Warner, *Joan of Arc*.

2. The appendix to this book offers a compendium of visual and literary representations of Joan of Arc, from the first poem written about her in 1429 to Mark Twain's *Joan of Arc* of 1895. I have included this background material for interested readers and to suggest the broad parameters of this story before the twentieth century. This matter fully informs this study but is not necessary to the book's central concern with the relation of Joan of Arc to women's roles in the United States during wartime.

3. Jameson, *Political Unconscious*, 53.

4. My interpretation of Joan of Arc's life in terms of the romance plot is indebted to Frye, *Anatomy of Criticism*, and also to Propp, "Morphology of the Folktale"; Genette, *Narrative Discourse*; and Brooks, *Body Work*.

5. Jameson, *Political Unconscious*, 230.

6. Two inclusive bibliographies of Johannic material are Margolis, *Joan of Arc in History, Literature, and Film*, and Raknem, *Joan of Arc in History, Legend, and Literature*.

7. Most of the information about Joan of Arc's life and myth contained below is so well known and is present in so many references that footnotes are largely irrelevant. For most of this material I have depended on Marina Warner's account in the first half of her *Joan of Arc*. Divergences are noted.

8. Ibid., 43–45.

9. Joan of Arc's presence in the democratic United States may be attributed to the fact that she helped the French view their existence as a people as divine. By the end of the French Revolution, Joan's status as a daughter of the French soil had become superior to the status given by royal birth. As described by Auerbach, *Mimesis*, 48, Joan's life is figural in the biblical sense. Joan's existence is prefigured by the lives of Christ and the Virgin Mary and in turn prefigures the eternal fate of France in a providential plan.

10. Warner, *Joan of Arc*, 140–43.

11. Ibid., 70–78.

12. Ibid., 168–73, 233.

13. Ibid., 79–86.

14. See Sackville-West, *Saint Joan of Arc*, 288, for a description of the trial, conducted by a cardinal, 6 bishops, 32 doctors of theology, 16 bachelors of theology, 7 doctors of medicine, and 103 associates.

15. On 7 July 1456, Joan of Arc's sentence was annulled in a papal court after sixteen years of rehabilitation hearings. The issue was not Joan's innocence, which was not declared, but the relationship between the church and Charles VII of France. Since Joan's word had supported the king's claim to legitimacy in 1429, her name had to be vindicated. The English alone were blamed for destroying Joan. Warner, *Joan of Arc*, 194.

16. See Chesler, *Women and Madness*, 25–27.

17. Warner, *Joan of Arc*, 46–47.

18. My discussion of androgyny is indebted to Heilbrun, *Toward a Recognition of Androgyny*; Warner, *Monuments and Maidens*; Bell-Metereau, *Hollywood Androgyny*; and Garber, *Vested Interests*. For information about women in the Middle Ages, I have relied chiefly on Boulding, *Underside of History*; Davis, *Society and Culture*; Bynum, *Holy Feast*; and Barstow, *Joan of Arc*.

19. Boulding, *Underside of History*, 443, and Barstow, *Joan of Arc*, 21.

20. Davis, *Society and Culture*, 132.

21. McLaughlin, "Woman Warrior," 201.

22. Elshtain, *Women and War*, 139.

23. These martial maids were akin to the Amazons and to Diana on the battlefield but revealed their erotic core when their helmets were removed to reveal a cascade of hair. The models for this figure are Lodovico Ariosto's Bradamente in *Orlando Furioso* and Britomart and Radegunde in Edmund Spenser's *Faerie Queene*. See Warner, *Joan of Arc*, 213–17.

24. Barstow, *Joan of Arc*, 3.

25. My understanding of the importance of virginity to the female warrior comes in part from Mary Douglas, *Purity and Danger*; O'Brien, *Politics of Reproduction*; Rabuzzi, *Motherself*; and Huston, "Matrix of War."

26. Warner, *Joan of Arc*, 36.

27. Heilbrun, *Toward a Recognition of Androgyny*, 9.

28. Warner, *Alone of All Her Sex*, 41–48.

29. Bynum, *Holy Feast*, 20.

30. Barstow, *Joan of Arc*, 123.

31. See Warner, *Alone of All Her Sex*, 68–73, and Bynum, *Holy Feast*, 222–27.

32. See Huston, "Matrix of War," 161–65, for a detailed analysis of the virgin warrior, whose glorification is seen as part of the discourse that seeks to position war as equal to or greater than the spectacle of childbirth. Also, see Andrea Dworkin, *Intercourse* (New York: Free Press, 1987), 100, who reads Joan of Arc's male dress as a rhetorical signifier against men.

33. My understanding of Joan of Arc as a sacrificial victim is derived from Girard,

Violence and the Sacred, esp. 92–94. (I note that with very few exceptions, the French have celebrated every 7 May, the day of the liberation of Orléans, for close to 600 years. The holiday is marked by parades in which a young girl is dressed like Joan of Arc to reenact the events of 1429. In Orléans the event is generally attended by the highest secular and religious leaders of the country.)

1. Joan of Arc in America, 1911–1920

1. Eco, *Travels in Hyperreality,* 67.
2. Barker, *"Double-Armed Man,"* 101–4.
3. Banta, *Imaging American Women,* 192, 598.
4. Lears, *No Place of Grace,* 42, 33–35.
5. Mary Douglas, *Purity and Danger,* 76.
6. Lears, *No Place of Grace,* xvi.
7. Fussell, *Great War,* 115.
8. The title of John Patrick Finnegan's study of the entry of the United States into the First World War: *Against the Specter of a Dragon.*
9. Lears, *No Place of Grace,* 32–33, 50.
10. Ibid., 120.
11. Fraser, *America and the Patterns of Chivalry,* 33.
12. Lears, *No Place of Grace,* 12, 20.
13. Warner, *Joan of Arc,* 229.
14. Lears, *No Place of Grace,* 35–38, 4.
15. Ibid., 108.
16. Lupack, "Visions of Courageous Achievement," 50.
17. Lears, *No Place of Grace,* 110.
18. Lupack, "Visions of Courageous Achievement," 52, 125.
19. The employment of Joan of Arc during wartime is similar to the use of the female form to embody and obscure the contradictions between the world of traditional labor and craft and the technological environment that was replacing it. See Bathrick, "Female Colossus," 81–82.
20. See the large but uncatalogued collection of small bronze sculptures in the Joan of Arc Collection of the Boston Public Library, as well as the public sculptures that can be found in cities across the United States.
21. The tradition from which this representation derives is typified by the appearance and reception in 1875 of a painting of the dead Elaine, another medieval icon, as she lies at the bottom of a boat that floats down a river, posed in a white gown, with flowing hair and a lily in her hand. Wherever this painting was shown

in the United States it was greeted with phenomenal enthusiasm. See Pinder, "Reception of Toby E. Rosenthall's *Elaine*," 38

22. Dijkstra, *Idols of Perversity,* 54, 50.

23. Bathrick tells of a woman who won a prize at a fair for a sculpture made entirely of butter. In a mode reminiscent of Joan's dissolution in smoke, the manifestations of female labor are meant to disappear: "Female Colossus," 85.

24. Humphries, "Anna Vaughn Hyatt's Statue," XLVII.

25. The statue was restored and rededicated on 30 Oct. 1987. See the brochure published for the occasion by the Municipal Art Society of New York, which was edited by Phyllis Samitz Cohen.

26. Caffin, "Miss Hyatt's Statue of Joan of Arc," 309.

27. Ibid., 310.

28. Humphrey, "A New Statue of Jeanne d'Arc," 404.

29. Banta, *Imaging American Women,* xxviii, 545.

30. Warner, *Joan of Arc,* 38. See Bynum, *Holy Feast,* 222, for more speculation about the relationship between abstinence and unusual dress and the desire to avoid marriage in the Middle Ages.

31. It is notable that a book called *Our Country: Its Possible Future and Its Present Crisis,* written by Reverend Josiah Strong in 1891, could note that French Huguenots were considered to be acceptable candidates for eventual Americanization. See Banta, *Imaging American Women,* 117. The apparent American type did not involve nationality as much as the delicacy of features that differentiated the WASP from Eastern and Mediterranean types in this era of massive immigration.

32. Ferris, *Acting Women,* 133.

33. Dijkstra, *Idols of Perversity,* 115.

34. Banta, *Imaging American Women,* 208.

35. Ibid., 17, 64–65.

36. Ibid., 642, 238.

37. It was not until Joan Riviere's pivotal work of 1929, "Womanliness as Masquerade," *International Journal of Psychoanalysis* 10, that the issue of femininity as masquerade was discussed in relation to women's actual lives. The negative fate of Joan of Arc in representation in the decades after the First World War, culminating in the years after the Second World War, suggests that the potential effects of the cross-dressing heroine had been recognized.

38. Banta, *Imaging American Women,* 269–75.

39. For more information about the Delsarte method, particularly in relation to cinema, see Roberta E. Pearson, *Eloquent Gestures: The Transformation of Performance Style in the Griffith Biograph Films* (Berkeley: University of California Press, 1992).

40. Banta, *Imaging American Women*, 513.

41. Vorse, "Elizabeth Gurley Flynn," 81 (my italics). For more information about Flynn, see Elizabeth Gurley Flynn, *The Rebel Girl, an Autobiography: My First Life (1906–1926)* (New York: International Publishers, 1973).

42. Finnegan, *Against the Specter of a Dragon*, 4, 31. This invaluable book lays out the grid of events that led the United States from neutrality to war in the early years of the twentieth century. Finnegan says nothing, however, of how the campaign worked in culture or how discrete groups, such as women, were led to participate both emotionally and in actuality. The task remains to describe how thinking itself was changed.

43. Ferro, *Great War*, 124.

44. Lears, *No Place of Grace*, 175, and Brun, "Jeanne d'Arc," 5.

45. Fussell, *Great War*, 157, 22.

46. Van Dyke, "Come Back Again, Jeanne d'Arc," in Wagenknecht, *Joan of Arc*, 401.

47. "Jeanne d'Arc," *The Outlook* 3 (15 Dec. 1915): 886.

48. Newman, "Doughboy's Girl in France," 28, 106.

49. Vachel Lindsey, "Mark Twain and Joan of Arc," in *The Poetry of Vachel Lindsey*, ed. Dennis Camp (Granite Falls, Minn.: Spoon River Poetry Press, 1984). Used by permission of the publisher.

50. Powers, "Joan of Arc Vogue," 185.

51. See the Inventory of American Paintings at the National Museum of Art in Washington, D.C. The Inventory, begun in 1970, is an attempt to uncover paintings created before 1914 that are hidden in homes and institutions throughout the United States. There is also an Inventory of American Sculpture.

52. "Some Joan of Arc Medals," LIII.

53. Powers, "Joan of Arc Vogue," 180.

54. Stevens, *Wonderful Story of Joan of Arc*, introductory description.

55. Barstow, *Joan of Arc*, 26, 125. Jörg Nagler, in "Pandora's Box," 495, notes that the United States made more war posters than any other belligerent nation in an attempt to create national unity in a country of immigrants.

56. Scholars writing about propaganda, film, and popular culture in the early part of the century often note how little attention has been paid to the cinema as a shaping force during the war. In view of the fact that only the United States continued to produce films during the war, films that circulated around the world, the omission is odd. More than other art forms, film both shapes and reflects behavior because of the profit motive that drives the industry. Films must please people if they are to pay at the box office, while also satisfying the capitalist interests that support

them and the government that censors and uses them during war (Higashi, "Cinderella vs. Statistics," 107). The circular nature of this process provides a continual and automatic renegotiation between the producing and consuming branches of culture.

57. Uricchio and Pearson, *Reframing Culture*, 195.

58. Craig W. Campbell, *Reel America*, 3–7. See also Robert Sklar, *Movie-Made America: A Cultural History of American Movies* (New York: Vintage,1994).

59. Craig W. Campbell, *Reel America*, 16.

60. Ward, *Motion Picture Goes to War*, 10.

61. Hugo Munsterberg, *The Photoplay* (1916) (New York: Arno Press, 1970).

62. Ward, *Motion Picture Goes to War*, 46.

63. Craig W. Campbell, *Reel America*, 77, 82.

64. DeBauche, *Reel Patriotism*, 151.

65. Finnegan, *Against the Specter of a Dragon*, 3.

66. Craig W. Campbell, *Reel America*, 38.

2. "Joan of Arc Saved France, Women of America Save Your Country": Cecil B. DeMille's *Joan the Woman*, 1916

1. Johnston, "A Jeanne d'Arc Pilgrimage," 11.

2. Porterfield, "New Tellers of a Tale Outworn," 306.

3. The following resources were used to determine and locate films of this nature and descriptions of such films no longer extant: *The American Film Institute Catalog;* Ward, *Motion Picture Goes to War;* and Craig W. Campbell, *Reel America*.

4. Distribution document from the Eclectic Film Company about F. Wolff's *Joan of Arc/Jeanne*, Library of Congress no. LU2159, 17 Feb. 1914. (In a letter published in *L'Ecran*, 13 July 1948, 7, Georges Méliès claimed to have made his *Joan of Arc* in 1897.)

5. DeBauche, "Mary Pickford's Public," 157.

6. Ward, *Motion Picture Goes to War*, 103.

7. *Moving Picture World*, 29 July 1911, 223, and Huston, "Matrix of War," 161–65.

8. Custen, *Bio/Pics*, 150–90.

9. The Matinee Girl, "Quivering Heart of Womankind," *New York American*, in *Joan of Arc Journal*, 8.

10. Ward, *Motion Picture Goes to War*, 123.

11. "Coronation Scene Conducted," *New York Times*, 15 Dec. 1916, 7:1.

12. *New York Sun*, in *Joan of Arc Journal*, 7, 6.

13. "Young Theatrical Man," *New York American*, in *Joan of Arc Journal*, 6.

14. William J. Robinson to Jesse L. Lasky, in *Joan of Arc Journal*, 4.

15. Heywood Broun, "Play Has Rare Virtue in Story," *New York Tribune*, in *Joan of Arc Journal*, 4.

16. *Moving Picture World*, 30 Dec. 1916, 1941.

17. "Gorgeous as Pageant," *New York Morning Telegraph*, in *Joan of Arc Journal*, 2.

18. "Spectacular, Impressive," *New York World*, in *Joan of Arc Journal*, 8. DeMille was not the first to add a love story to the life of Joan of Arc. In 1801 Friedrich Schiller gave Joan an English lover named Lionel in *Die Jungfrau von Orleans*. Following Schiller's plot, Giuseppe Verdi's *Giovanna d'Arco* of 1845 and Peter Tchaikovsky's *Maid of Orleans* of 1878, as well as lesser known plays by N. J. C. de Hédouville (1829) and Jean-Joseph Olivier (1870), also include love stories. See Warner, *Joan of Arc*, 217–18.

19. *Exhibitor's Trade Review*, 23 Dec. 1916, 192.

20. Alexander Woollcott, "Joan the Prima Donna," *New York Times*, 25 Feb. 1917, 2:3.

21. Higashi, *DeMille*, 136.

22. Julian Johnson, review of *Joan the Woman*, *Photoplay*, March 1917, 113–16, in Slide, *Selected Film Criticism*, 141–43. (Hugo Munsterberg, a German-born professor of experimental psychology at Harvard University between 1892 and 1916, wrote the first book of film theory, *The Photoplay* [1916; New York: Arno Press, 1970].)

23. DeMille, *Autobiography*, 169.

24. Jane M'Lean, "Joan's Life Shaped," *New York Evening Journal*, in *Joan of Arc Journal*, 5.

25. The Matinee Girl, "Quivering Heart, *New York American*, in *Joan of Arc Journal*, 8.

26. Rev. Thomas B. Gregory, "Reveals Greatness of Woman," *New York American*, in *Joan of Arc Journal*, 3.

27. *Joan of Arc Journal*, 8.

28. Of the six images painted by Clifford F. Pember in the lobby of the theater, "after suggestions contained in the illustrations by Boutet de Monvel," five are replicas of the originals. Pember's only original painting is the striking *Joan's Body Lying in State* (ibid., 3).

29. Ibid., 5.

30. *New York Evening Journal*, in *Joan of Arc Journal*, 7, 2, 8.

31. Craig W. Campbell, *Reel America*, 54.

32. *Joan of Arc Journal*, 2, 6, 7.

33. Luc Moullet, review of *The Ten Commandments*, *Cahiers du cinéma* 80 (February 1958): 58.

34. Barthes, *Mythologies*, 26.

35. Williams, "Varieties of American Medievalism," 14.

36. Brill, *Hitchcock Romance*, 8.

37. MacPherson, script of *Joan the Woman*, 8, 11, in Library of Congress, Cecil B. DeMille file (italics in original).

38. With remarkable efficiency, the scenes in the original version containing the character named Trent are recut and retitled here to create this new, historically accurate character, John Talbot. The ease with which this reconstruction is effected speaks of the pervasiveness of the romance plot in even the most imaginative of Joan of Arc tales.

39. Higashi, *DeMille*, 118.

3. The Demise of Joan of Arc

1. Yancey, *Soldier Virgin of France*, 19, 32, 43.

2. Ibid., 4.

3. Ibid., 33.

4. Finnegan, *Against the Specter of a Dragon*, 63.

5. Ibid., 103. Finnegan makes light of the women's camp, noting that the women were said to have eaten twice what the men ate and that they worried about whether to wear skirts or not. Nothing in Finnegan's otherwise serious book indicates an awareness that women were half of the population of the country and an essential component of the national psyche.

6. Brun, "Jeanne d'Arc," 6.

7. *Exhibitor's Trade Review*, 13 Apr. 1918, 1533; 5 May 1918, 1845; 10 Nov. 1917, 1845.

8. Ibid., 11 May 1918, 1840.

9. "Mabel Normand Is Here in 'Joan of Plattsburg,'" 29 Apr. 1918, in Library of Congress, *Joan of Plattsburg* file.

10. *Variety*, 3 May 1918.

11. Quoted in Betty Harper Fussell, *Mabel*, 107.

12. Ibid., 107–9. Although this story may be apocryphal, Normand did perpetuate this irreverent persona.

13. Warner, *Monuments and Maidens*, 238.

14. Elshtain, *Women and War*, 92.

15. Quoted in DeBauche, "Mary Pickford's Public," 151.

16. Patterson, "On the Edge of the War Zone," 68–70.

17. Isenberg, *War on Film*, 200.

18. Quoted in Girouard, *Return to Camelot*, 285.

19. Isenberg, *War on Film*, 190.

20. Goldman, *Female Soldiers*, 7.

21. Review of *Susan Rocks the Boat* in *Moving Picture World*, 13 May 1916.

22. Review of *Susan Rocks the Boat* in *Variety*, 12 May 1916.

23. Quoted in Craig W. Campbell, *Reel America*, 56.

24. Ibid.

25. *American Film Institute Catalog*, F1:1053. *Woman* describes tales of "women's evil" in history and legend, such as Adam and Eve, Messalina and Claudius, and Héloïse and Abélard. A reviewer of the film notes the misogynist anachronism of an Adam who looks primitive and an Eve who is "an obviously modern young lady minus her clothes," which sounds remarkably similar to the representation of couples in the post–Second World War film *The Story of Mankind* (discussed in Chapter 7).

26. In a concise description of Western culture's mode of initiating boys into men, the poem "Before Action," written by the First World War soldier William Hodgson two days before his death, says: "Make me a soldier. . . . Make me a man. . . . Help me to die." See Higonnet, "Women in the Forbidden Zone," 193.

27. Quoted in Elshtain, *Women and War*, 194.

28. Quoted in Isenberg, *War on Film*, 106.

29. Amy Lowell, *The Complete Poetical Works of Amy Lowell* (Boston: Houghton Mifflin, 1955), 238–39.

30. Higonnet, "Women in the Forbidden Zone," 197–98.

31. Lears, *No Place of Grace*, 302.

32. *Literary Digest*, 5 June 1920, 47.

33. Katherine Brégy, "The Maid," and Anon., "The Maid of France," quoted in Wagenknecht, *Joan of Arc*, 409–10. Note the absence of Joan's actual name; inserted into patriarchal order via sanctification she becomes an abstract figure of goodness rather than an agent in history.

34. *The Mentor*, October 1924, 48.

35. *Living Age*, 14 June 1919, 674.

36. *Journal of the American Society for Psychical Research* 12 (1927).

37. Murray, *Witch Cult*.

38. Sheppard, "St. Jeanne d'Arc," 111–20.

39. Heilbrun, *Toward a Recognition of Androgyny*, 110.

40. Review of *Sheltered Daughters*, *Variety*, 20 May 1921.

41. Production document in *Sheltered Daughters* file, Library of Congress, no. 16416, 25 Apr. 1921, 2.

4. Joan of Arc between the Wars

1. Rupp, *Mobilizing Women for War,* 55.

2. Abbott, "Credo," 154. Rapp and Ross note in "The 1920s," 55, that the *Ladies Home Journal* called the 1920s the decade of the "cosmetics revolution," in which women's rights activists came to be seen as "stodgy and outmoded."

3. Quoted in Rupp, *Mobilizing Women for War,* 61. By 1932 the taboo against women's employment had become institutionalized by the National Economy Act, which permitted discrimination in the hiring and firing of married female government workers under the excuse that "double-earning" was unfair.

4. Ibid., 67.

5. Higashi, "Cinderella vs. Statistics," 110–14.

6. Quoted in Salls, "Joan of Arc," 176.

7. Hartmann, *Home Front and Beyond,* 125.

8. Baker, *Images of Women in Film,* 14.

9. Nathan, "The Theatre," 241.

10. Doherty, *Projections of War,* 87.

11. One of the few positive references to Joan of Arc in the late 1920s occurred in 1927, when the American ambassador to Paris, Myron T. Herrick, compared Charles Lindbergh to Joan of Arc. See Eksteins, *Rites of Spring,* 248.

12. See *L'Avant-scène* 100 (February 1970): 46–54, and Jean-José Frappa in *Chantecler,* 1 Jan. 1927.

13. Joseph Delteil, *Jeanne d'Arc* (Paris: B. Grasset, 1926).

14. Reviews of *La Passion de Jeanne d'Arc, Exhibitors Herald and Moving Picture World,* 25 Feb. 1928; *Atlanta Georgian,* 13 May 1929. I note that *Variety* found the film's close-ups and slow pace "deadly tiresome" (10 Apr. 1929).

15. H.D., "Joan of Arc," *Close Up,* July 1928, 15–23.

16. "Special to Exhibitors," *Exhibitors Herald and Moving Picture World,* 25 Feb. 1928. The article does not specify to which *Joan of Arc* it is referring.

17. *La Vie merveilleuse de Jeanne d'Arc,* which the film historian Kevin Brownlow has compared formally with the best of Eisenstein, has been restored at the British Film Institute. (Interview, London, May 1985.)

18. The plays are *St. Joan of the Stockyards* (1930), *The Visions of Simone Machard* (1940, for radio), and *The Trial of Joan of Arc in Rouen* (1952).

19. Brecht, *Plays,* 194.

20. Orliac, *Joan of Arc and Her Companions,* 5.

21. Shaw, *Collected Screenplays,* 35–55.

22. In *Civilian in War,* 2, Jeremy Noakes makes it clear that all the nations that

had been involved in the First World War had worked hard during the 1920s and 1930s to learn how to control popular support in time of war.

5. The War Years: *Between Us Girls, Joan of Paris,* and *Joan of Ozark*

1. Rupp, *Mobilizing Women for War,* 145.
2. Ibid., 88.
3. Koppes, *Hollywood Goes to War,* 1.
4. Ibid., vii.
5. Ibid., 143.
6. Holsinger and Schofield, *Visions of War,* 105. Unfortunately, this poster was not available for reproduction.
7. Gaines, "Showgirl and the Wolf," 64.
8. In William Wellman's *Wings* of 1927, for example, a locket with the girlfriend's picture plays an important role.
9. Rupp, *Mobilizing Women for War,* 5.
10. Honey, *Creating Rosie the Riveter,* 111.
11. Quoted in Polan, *Power and Paranoia,* 95.
12. Karen Anderson, *Wartime Women,* 92.
13. Hartmann, *Home Front and Beyond,* 168.
14. Rupp, *Mobilizing Women for War,* 146.
15. Hartmann, *Home Front and Beyond,* 199.
16. Doane, *Desire to Desire,* 26.
17. The film's original ending was to show the Cummings character arguing with the star backstage and in anger pulling her Joan of Arc helmet down over her face, where it would become stuck. When the curtain was accidentally raised on the battle, Cummings was to say to the audience, "Is there a can-opener in the house?" See the script provided for the OWI in the Library of Congress, no. LP11571.
18. Holsinger and Schofield, *Visions of War,* 127.
19. *New York Times,* 25 May 1942, 25:3.
20. Polan, *Power and Paranoia,* 204.
21. Quoted in Rupp, *Mobilizing Women for War,* 96.
22. In the first year of the war, the numbers of female workers in airplane factories rose from 143 to 65,000 and in ship construction from 36 to 160,000; and by the end of the war female government workers had doubled to account for 38% of the federal workforce. In addition, wages for women increased 40% over the course of the war as the nature of the work available to them changed. See Chafe, *World War II as a Pivotal Experience,* 23.

23. Honey, *Creating Rosie the Riveter,* 47–48.

24. Doherty, *Projections of War,* 153–54.

25. Renov, "From Fetish to Subject," 17.

26. *New York Times,* 26 Jan. 1942, 18:2.

27. Review of *Joan of Paris, PM,* 26 Jan. 1942.

28. Review of *Joan of Paris, Variety,* 26 Jan. 1942.

29. Review of *Joan of Paris, New York Post,* 26 Jan. 1942.

30. Renov, *Hollywood's Wartime Women,* 22.

31. A 16mm print of *Joan of Ozark* has recently surfaced at the Margaret Herrick Library at the American Academy of Motion Pictures in Los Angeles. Descriptions, photographs, and critical responses to the film are found at the Library of Congress.

32. Review of *Joan of Ozark* in *Hollywood Reporter,* n.d., located in the Museum of Modern Art film files. The casting of Canova as Joan of Arc is not unlike the earlier use of Mabel Normand in *Joan of Plattsburg.*

33. Koppes, *Hollywood Goes to War,* 12, 104.

34. Clarke, *New Treasury of War Poetry,* 37.

6. The Return of the Maid: *The Miracle of the Bells* and *Joan of Arc*

1. Bernstein, "Hollywood Martyrdoms," 91.

2. Carringer and Allen, *Annotated Catalog,* no. 235.

3. Elshtain, *Women and War,* 91.

4. Honey, *Creating Rosie the Riveter,* 122.

5. Rupp, *Mobilizing Women,* 163.

6. Karen Anderson, *Wartime Women,* 176.

7. For a full exploration of what is known as the "woman's film" of the 1940s, which addressed women's concerns in roundabout ways, see Doane, *Desire to Desire.*

8. Rupp, *Mobilizing Women,* 160.

9. In a negative review of *The Miracle of the Bells* in *Look,* 30 Mar. 1948, 93–95, several small production photographs from the film summarize the story. The one large photograph is of Valli enacting Joan of Arc in the audition scene.

10. See Blaetz, " 'La Femme Vacante,'" for an examination of the casting of Joan of Arc in the cinema in relation to notions of authenticity.

11. Review of *The Miracle of the Bells, Time,* 29 Mar. 1948.

12. Review of *The Miracle of the Bells, Variety,* 3 Mar. 1948.

13. File for *The Miracle of the Bells,* Library of Congress.

14. *New York Times,* 17 Mar. 1948, 30:1.

15. Maxwell Anderson, *Joan of Lorraine,* 85, 14.

16. Ibid., 21.

17. Ibid., 62, 128.

18. Brun, "Jeanne d'Arc," 7.

19. The first essay, "Saint Joan in Eight Moods," appeared on 19 Jan. 1947 (20–21); the second, "Seven Ideas of Joan," ran on 14 Oct. 1951 (17); and the third, "The Maid in Many Guises," appeared on 4 Dec. 1955 (28–29). The films represented, all of which show the historical Joan of Arc rather than Joan of Paris or Ozark, are Fleming's *Joan of Arc* and Irving Pichel's *Miracle of the Bells,* both of 1948, and Otto Preminger's *Saint Joan* and Irving Allen's *Story of Mankind,* both of 1957. Significant Broadway plays after Anderson's include the 1951 revival of Bernard Shaw's *Saint Joan* with Uta Hagen and the 1955 production of Jean Anouilh's *Lark* with Julie Harris.

20. Barthes, *Mythologies.*

21. Robo, *Saint Joan,* 9, 7.

22. Winwar, *Saint and the Devil,* 1.

23. Bernstein, "Hollywood Martyrdoms," 104.

24. The late date of *Ingrid Bergman—My Story* (co-authored with Alan Burgess and published in 1980) makes it a more reliable source than the reports by the film's adviser, Père Paul Doncoeur, that Bergman had become enchanted with Joan at the age of thirteen, just the age at which Joan started hearing voices; that she wore a ring like Joan's; and that she was a peasant like Joan ("Un Film américain"). However, Bergman's star persona of the earthy, pure domestic goddess had little in common with her actual life at the time.

25. The archives at the University of California at Los Angeles have a restored print of *Joan of Arc* that was completed in 1998 but was not available for viewing as of July of 2000.

26. Review of *Joan of Arc, Variety,* 20 Oct. 1948.

27. *New York Times,* 12 Nov. 1948, 30:5.

28. "Ingrid Bergman: A Picture Personality," *Look,* 20 July 1948, 34–42.

29. See McLean, "Cinderella Princess," for a discussion of Bergman's persona and career during the late 1940s. Bergman's reputation for personal integrity, which caused her to be considered as an ideal Joan of Arc, made her lack of regret over the affair and her willingness to profit from it truly shocking to the American public.

30. See Blaetz, " 'La Femme Vacante,' " for a consideration of the pervasive reports of actresses who "become Joan" rather than act the role.

31. The fragmented *Look* layout differs considerably from the more typical, cohesive layout of *Life's* coverage of the film the same year. The effect of the advertisements was so striking upon first view that the following analysis seemed essential. Unfortunately, no other Joan of Arcs of the time were covered as extensively in

popular magazines as Bergman was, so no comparisons with the discourses surrounding other films are possible.

32. In designing film and dance costumes, Karinska followed George Balanchine's advice that a dancer's tutu should no longer have the dropped yoke that accentuates narrow hips but a high waist to exaggerate the line of the leg. Her beautiful costumes were known to be precisely cut with luxurious details that were imperceptible to the audience but that made them worthy of a museum exhibit. See Brubach, "Confectioner's Art," 81.

33. The studio produced an extensive confidential booklet (in my possession) detailing how the Joan of Arc fashions were to be produced and marketed.

34. Bernstein, "Hollywood Martyrdoms," 108–9.

35. Ben Hecht's script for David Selznick of November 1946 is closer to the revised Fleming film from the start. This film would have opened with a young priest in the Vatican library researching material about Joan, with a voice-over narrating her life as scenes are shown, beginning with the capture. In the script, the narrator claims to be using Joan's own words as taken down by the priest and a notary. Starting with the trial, Joan is asked twice to change from her male dress so as not to anger the judges; two jokes about rape are made; one character is granted permission to "try to make love to Joan"; she is tortured; counseling angels are ever-present; and all is forgiven at the end. See Carringer and Allen, *Annotated Catalog*, no. 235.

36. Anderegg, *Inventing Vietnam*, 13.

37. Basinger, *World War II Combat Film*, 73–75.

38. Several of the almost uniformly negative French reviews of the film refer to yet another genre with which the film can be connected, the Western. One writer refers to "Joan of Arc the star of a rodeo" ("Tout New-York defile à Broadway pour applaudir Joan of Arc," *Vie nouvelle*, 11 Dec. 1948). Another review that refers to the film's multi-generic quality claims that bishops talk like gangsters, La Hire plays the good sheriff, and the cavalry act like football players (Bernard Gaston-Cherau, "Dans une apothéose de lumières est née la 'Joan of Arc' americaine," *Figaro*, 13 Nov. 1948).

7. Looking for Joan of Arc: Hedy Lamarr in *The Story of Mankind* and Jean Seberg in *Saint Joan*

1. Although most married women returned to the home, many continued working in less prestigious and challenging jobs where they did not compete with men. William Chafe indicates that the war had a lasting impact on female labor, since employment rates for women had doubled between 1940 and 1960; the percentage of married women in paid employment jumped from 15% to 30%; the percentage of

mothers with jobs increased by 400%; and the number of middle-class women who worked outside the home tripled in this period. See Chafe, "World War II as a Pivotal Experience," 28.

2. See Karen Anderson, *Wartime Women;* Chafe, "World War II as a Pivotal Experience"; Hartmann, *Home Front and Beyond;* and Honey, *Creating Rosie the Riveter.*

3. Honey, *Creating Rosie the Riveter,* 3. To highlight the regression of literary images of women in the 1940s, Maureen Honey compares the stories in popular magazines of the era with those of the 1930s. The latter feature adventurous, attractive, strong, smart heroines who make their way in a man's world. One story describes a character as a "natural member of that well-corseted, firm-jawed little band of determined females who have climbed from oblivion to well-publicized successes without the help of husband or children or other awkward connections" (71). A reader can almost envision these women wearing armor and recall the heroines of the cinema of the prewar years, such as Katharine Hepburn wearing her metallic gown in *Christopher Strong* of 1933 (Dorothy Arzner), as she chooses to crash her airplane rather than deal with the complexities of marriage, birth, and home.

4. "Seven Ideas of Joan," *New York Times,* 14 Oct. 1951, 17.

5. In discussing her performance in *Saint Joan* in 1951–52, Uta Hagan noted that the McCarthy hearings were the direct impetus for redoing Shaw and that she received letters from all over the country threatening to picket the play because of her liberal positions. See Hill, *Playing Joan,* 44. While Joan of Arc may have spoken to individuals in serious and complex ways, the popular discourse around Joan's appearances was narrowly focused on the proper role of women.

6. Attesting to the continued presence of Joan of Arc and to the influence of cinematic Joans is a book about Joan of Arc published in 1955 in Spain, which featured Ingrid Bergman on the cover and comic book–style illustrations based on the film. In addition, a 1957 juvenile biography published in the United States modeled all its line drawings on the Fleming film. See Brunetti, *Juana d'Arco,* and De Wohl, *St. Joan,* respectively.

7. See Helpern, "Technique of Martha Graham," 2. *The Triumph of St. Joan,* with music by Norman Dello Joio and sets by Frederick Kiesler, was also costumed by Graham. It was first performed in Louisville, Ky., on 5 Dec. 1951. *Seraphic Dialogue* premiered in New York on 8 May 1955, with a new set by Isamu Noguchi (and later with new costumes by Halston).

8. Milton Waldmar, "St. Joan of Arc," *The Month* 12 (6 Dec. 1954): 334–47.

9. Elizabeth Bartelme, "Maid of Honor," *Commonweal* 63, no. 13 (30 Dec. 1955): 336–37.

10. "Saint Revisited," *Time,* 14 Nov. 1955, 81–83.

11. John Steinbeck, "The Joan in All of Us," *Saturday Review of Literature*, 14 Jan. 1956, 17.

12. De Wohl, *St. Joan*, and Ross, *Joan of Arc*, respectively.

13. The mask and the dolls that are found in the Joan of Arc Collection in the Boston Public Library are impossible to date accurately. From the materials used, the facial type, and the styles, I speculate that they were made in the 1950s and perhaps the 1960s. Other objects in the collection, such as bookends and small toys featuring the childish Joan of Arc on horseback, in their size, style, and material are reminiscent of the widespread use of the image of Davy Crockett in the 1950s.

14. "The 10 Proofs of Joan of Arc," *Fate*, September 1952, 14–24.

15. Richard Gilman, "Joan of Arc," *Jubilee*, May 1956, 21–27.

16. Seymour Peck, "The Maid in Many Guises," *New York Times Magazine*, 4 Dec. 1955, 28–29.

17. D. B. Wyndham Lewis, "Joan of Arc," *Atlantic Monthly*, January 1954, 25, 30, 31.

18. Roberto Rossellini also made a filmed version of *Giovanna d'Arco al rogo* in 1954 starring his wife, Ingrid Bergman, based on Paul Claudel's libretto for Arthur Honegger's oratorio *Jeanne d'Arc au bûcher* (1939). There is no evidence that this film was distributed or discussed in the United States.

19. Review of *Destinées*, *Variety*, 10 Feb. 1954.

20. See Jean Delannoy to Jean Nile, 6 Feb. 1976, Delannoy file, Centre Jeanne d'Arc, Orléans. The only potentially complete copy of the film in existence is in the Prague Film Archive and was unavailable for viewing during the writing of this book. The Centre Jeanne d'Arc owns only the ten-minute section of *Destinées* that deals with Joan of Arc.

21. A case in point is the phenomenal success of the designer Christian Dior's New Look for women after the war as a rejection of what was described with distaste as Amazonian apparel. Dior replaced the efficient, economical suits that were popular during the war years with "clothes for flowerlike women, clothes with rounded shoulders, full feminine busts, and willowy waists above enormous spreading skirts." With the high heels and well-filled bras (padded if necessary) that the look demanded, women were quite ready to, as the *Ladies Home Journal* observed, "feel different, decorative" (Hartmann, *Home Front and Beyond*, 203).

22. Landon, "New Heroes," 20.

23. Kane, *Visions of War*, 145.

24. Review of *The Story of Mankind*, *New York Herald-Tribune*, 9 Nov. 1957.

25. Review of *The Story of Mankind*, *Variety*, 23 Oct. 1957; *Newsweek*, 18 Nov. 1957.

26. Review of *The Story of Mankind*, *Newsweek*, 6 May 1957.

27. Review of *The Story of Mankind*, *New Yorker*, 16 Nov. 1957.

28. Pratley, *Cinema of Otto Preminger,* 119.

29. See Cole and Chinoy, *Actors on Acting,* 3; Ferris, *Acting Women,* 76.

30. Quoted in Damico, "Ingrid from Lorraine to Stromboli," 250.

31. Quoted in Frischaur, *Behind the Scenes,* 151. There are other modes of film-making in which the actor is conceptualized and used in very different ways. The work of Robert Bresson, who made *Le Procès de Jeanne d'Arc* in 1961, is of particular interest in this regard. For example, Bresson cast only nonactors who had the moral outlook and physiognomy he desired because they were free from the preconditioning of other roles. His particular methods of rehearsing, photographing the world, and editing were all designed to facilitate a revelation of character. For further discussion of Bresson and more in-depth examination of the complexities involved in casting Joan of Arc in film over the course of the century, see Blaetz, " 'La Femme Vacante.' "

32. Press book for *Saint Joan,* Library of Congress, LP9011.

33. Also found in the "School Promotions" section of the publicity material are suggestions for museum exhibitions of medieval objects from the era of Joan of Arc, high school theater parties, and the distribution within schools of a photo-essay version of Preminger's film written by Marjorie Mattern with photographs by Bob Willoughby. In the back of the Mattern publication, intended to be used for class discussion, is a section headed "The Making of the Movie," which echoes the title of the short film about the production, "The Making of *St. Joan.*" The twelve-page section features two types of photographs, in which either Seberg is captured as the young girl that she is, whether acting frightened or silly, or Preminger is seen directing an awe-struck Seberg. The largest photograph shows Preminger sitting high on the boom with Seberg tied to the stake below.

34. Mourlet, "*Saint Joan,*" 79.

35. Review of *Saint Joan, New York Times,* 17 Feb. 1957.

36. Alan Nadel has suggested that the act of dismemberment characterizes many representations of Joan of Arc. The broken, partial body of Joan in the Bass poster follows the recutting of DeMille's *Joan the Woman* in 1916 and the array of ads that fragment both the story about Bergman and women's lives in the *Look* article of 1948.

37. There is a history in Hollywood filmmaking of making the most of lurid, risqué, or dangerous events as part of the publicity for a given film. Since one can never know of events that are *not* publicized, one can make sense of those that are only in the context of the entire film's production. See "St. Joan Really Burns," *Life,* 11 Mar. 1957, for more coverage of the event, including five photographs documenting the burning.

38. Shaw, *Saint Joan,* 45.

39. In fact, at least the cathedral scene from the play had been filmed on 27 July 1926 by the DeForest Film Company with Shaw's original British Joan of Arc, the forty-one-year-old actress Sybil Thorndike. See Shaw, *Collected Screenplays*, 12.

40. See, for example, *New York Times*, 17 Feb. 1957.

41. Brecht, *Brecht on Theatre*, 11.

42. See reviews of *Saint Joan* in *Time*, 1 July 1957, and *Newsweek*, 24 June 1957.

43. See the reviews of *Saint Joan* in *New Republic*, 12 Aug. 1957; *Saturday Review*, 29 June 1957; *The Nation*, 20 July 1957; and *Variety*, 8 May 1957.

44. Gilbert Millstein, "Evolution of a New Saint Joan," *New York Times Magazine*, 7 Apr. 1957.

8. Conclusions: The Vietnam War and Afterward

1. A 1999 film about Joan of Arc, *The Messenger: The Story of Joan of Arc*, was directed by Luc Besson in English and features primarily American actors although it was made in France. A second film made in 1999, *Joan of Arc*, was produced by the Canadian Broadcasting Company for American television by Christian Duguay. An experimental film about Joan called *Wired Angel* was made by Sam Wells in 2000. Several other feature films about Joan of Arc are in production or rumored to be, including *Joan of Arc: The Virgin Warrior* by Ronald F. Maxwell, which is a four-hour historical reconstruction, and two others supposedly to be directed by Steven Spielberg and Kathryn Bigelow. The latter film, called *The Company of Angels* in various press releases, has been rumored to star the Irish singer Sinead O'Connor.

2. *Boston Herald Traveler*, 20 Nov. 1968. See Hill, *Playing Joan*, for interviews with some of the women who played Joan in important productions in the United States in this era, including Ellen Geer (1964), Jane Alexander (1965), Lee Grant (1966), Joyce Ebert (1967), Sarah Miles (1973), Laurie Kennedy (1973, 1976), and Lynn Redgrave (1977).

3. Michelet, *Joan of Arc*, 236.

4. Daniel Rankin to Bishop Wright, 26 Feb. 1961, Joan of Arc Collection, Boston Public Library.

5. Paradoxically, Robert Bresson, one of international cinema's most respected directors, chose this moment to resurrect Joan's trial and death as the focus of his most condensed, rigorous, and formally challenging film about the nature of freedom, *Le Procès de Jeanne d'Arc* of 1961. Bresson's film would have been seen by very few Americans during its limited appearance in New York City, where it was shown on the art house circuit through the 1970s. In recent years, *Le Procès de Jeanne d'Arc* has been largely unavailable in any form in the United States.

6. Myla Jo Closser, "Buddha and St. Joan," *New York Times,* 6 Mar. 1957.

7. "The Trouble with Joan," *Time,* 17 Nov. 1958, 48.

8. St. Joan's International Alliance was founded in 1911 in England, with sections located in Ireland, France, Belgium, Australia, and the United States. The Alliance is a nongovernmental organization with consultative status to the Economic and Social Council of the United Nations. It works to improve the status of women in the Catholic Church and to combat sexism wherever it occurs, and has a particular interest in gaining approval of the Equal Rights Amendment.

9. David Allen Bliss, "Joan of Arc," Dare Music, 1964. See *Report,* January 1966, 15, for the lyrics.

10. Leonard Cohen, "Joan of Arc," in *Stranger Music: Selected Poems and Songs* (New York: Pantheon, 1993), 147–48.

11. Bates, "Men, Women, and Vietnam," 33.

12. Gies, *Joan of Arc,* 257.

13. Lightbody, *Judgements of Joan,* 39, 66, 30.

14. Salomon, "Escape from History," 108, 115.

15. Davidson, "France."

16. Eco, *Travels in Hyperreality,* 80.

17. Jack Anderson, "Entering a World Only Meredith Monk Can Map," *New York Times,* 16 June 1996, 8; Patti Smith, *Early Work,* 1970–79 (New York: Norton, 1994), 24–25.

18. Sarris, *Confessions of a Cultist,* 193.

19. Quoted in Jeffords, *Remasculinization of America,* 60.

20. Barstow, *Joan of Arc,* 110; Karen Hsiao, "Report: Joan of Arc May Have Had Epilepsy," *Boston Herald,* 25 May 1990.

21. I am grateful to Suzanne Sowinska (formerly of the Department of English at the University of Washington) for calling my attention to this film.

22. "The Politics of Virtue," *New York Times Magazine,* 23 May 1993, 22–25, 63–66; "Getting into Character," ibid., 29 Oct. 1995, 48.

23. *Better Homes and Gardens,* September 1992. I am grateful to Alan Nadel for pointing out the complexities of this advertisement.

24. As discussed earlier, conventionally only a virgin can take part in war because she has not participated in childbirth, which is the female equivalent of war. In addition, as Linville notes in "'Mother of All Battles,'" 114, the war film demands that men take responsibility for initiating young males into the symbolic order of war.

25. "Women without Hair: Lost or Found?" *New York Times,* 7 Aug. 1994.

26. Rayner, "Women in the Warrior Culture," 27, 29.

27. Films, books, scholarly studies, and art about Joan of Arc continue to appear,

and the number of Web sites about the heroine is astounding. A good place to begin exploring the current state of Johannic phenomena is the site of the International Joan of Arc Society at <http://dc.smu.edu/ijas/>.

Appendix: Visions of the Maid, 1492–1895

1. Warner, *Joan of Arc,* 221.
2. Bynum, *Holy Feast,* 240.
3. Ibid., 17.
4. Mary Douglas, *Purity and Danger,* 99.
5. Mayer, *Outsiders,* 30.
6. Quoted in Gies, *Joan of Arc,* 242, 248.
7. Christine de Pisan, *Ditié de Jehanne d'Arc,* 45.
8. Barstow, *Joan of Arc,* 77.
9. Gies, *Joan of Arc,* 241.
10. William Shakespeare, *King Henry the Sixth, Part I,* act 5, scene 4.
11. Barstow, *Joan of Arc,* 125.
12. Warner, *Monuments and Maidens,* 160.
13. Quoted ibid., 110.
14. Ibid., 242.
15. Warner, *Joan of Arc,* 201.
16. Ibid., 204–6.
17. Ribéra-Pervillé, "Jeanne d'Arc," 61.
18. Warner, *Joan of Arc,* 225.
19. Lightbody, *Judgements of Joan,* 155.
20. Mayer, *Outsiders,* 29.
21. Evans, *Born for Liberty,* 22.
22. Lang, *Prophetic Woman,* 7.
23. Kerber and De Hart, *Women's America,* 48–50.
24. Lang, *Prophetic Woman,* 9, 14, 64, 215.
25. Quoted in Patterson, "On the Edge of the War Zone," 125.
26. Evans, *Born for Liberty,* 2, 41.
27. Ibid., 47.
28. Warner, *Joan of Arc,* 241.
29. Brun, "Jeanne d'Arc," 1–2.
30. Warner, "Personification," 102.
31. Quoted in Warner, *Monuments and Maidens,* 21.
32. Warner, *Joan of Arc,* 218.

33. Ibid., 262.

34. Quoted in Lang, *Prophetic Woman*, 193.

35. Elshtain, *Women and War*, 143, 197.

36. Evans, *Born for Liberty*, 73.

37. Ibid., 74.

38. Warner, "Personification," 103.

39. Barstow, *Joan of Arc*, 130.

40. Brun, "Jeanne d'Arc," 3, 4.

41. Ibid., 4.

42. Barstow, *Joan of Arc*, 129.

43. Warner, "Personification," 108.

44. Quoted in Salls, "Joan of Arc," 182.

45. Dickinson, *Unpublished Poems*, 41.

46. Evans, *Born for Liberty*, 137.

47. Williams, "Varieties of American Medievalism."

48. Stock, *Listening for the Text*, 69.

49. Searle, *Saint and the Skeptics*, 50.

50. Warner, *Joan of Arc*, 248.

51. Twain, *Personal Recollections of Joan of Arc*, xiii.

Bibliography

Archival Sources

Boston Public Library. Joan of Arc Collection.
Centre Jeanne d'Arc, Orléans. Files containing assorted reviews, production notes, letters, manuscripts, interviews, photographs, and descriptions concerning films about Joan of Arc made by the following directors:

Bresson, Robert
Delannoy, Jean
Dreyer, Carl Theodor
Fleming, Victor
Gastyne, Marc de
Panfilov, Gleb
Preminger, Otto
Rossellini, Roberto

George Eastman House, Rochester, N.Y. Cecil B. DeMille file. *The Joan of Arc Journal*, press book, 15 Dec. 1916.
Library of Congress, Washington, D.C. Files containing assorted reviews, production notes, letters, manuscripts, interviews, photographs, and descriptions concerning the following films about Joan of Arc:

Between Us Girls, Henry Koster. LP11571
Joan of Arc, Victor Fleming. LP2050
Joan of Ozark, Joseph Santley. LP11508
Joan of Paris, Robert Stevenson. LP11058
Joan of Plattsburg, George Loan Tucker. LP12340
Joan the Woman, Cecil B. DeMille. LP9782
The Miracle of the Bells, Irving Pichel. LP1605
Saint Joan, Otto Preminger. LP9011

Sheltered Daughters, Realart Pictures. LP16416

The Story of Mankind, Irving Allen. LP12921

Cecil B. DeMille file. Jeannie MacPherson's script of *Joan the Woman* (22 pp., damaged).

Municipal Art Society, New York. Booklet commemorating the restoration of Anna Vaughn Hyatt's *Joan of Arc,* 30 Oct. 1987.

Museum of Modern Art, New York. Files containing assorted reviews, production notes, letters, manuscripts, interviews, and descriptions concerning films about Joan of Arc made by the following directors:

Allen, Irving

Delannoy, Jean

Dreyer, Carl Theodor

Fleming, Victor

Koster, Henry

Pichel, Irving

Rossellini, Roberto

Santley, Joseph

Stevenson, Robert

Tucker, George Loan

Secondary Works

Abbott, Harriet. "Credo of the Newest New Woman." *Ladies Home Journal,* August 1920, 154.

Abrams, Ann Uhry. "Frozen Goddess: The Image of Woman in Turn-of-the-Century American Art." In *Woman's Being, Woman's Place,* ed. Mary Kelley. Boston: G. K. Hall, 1979.

Agel, Henri. *Le Cinéma et le sacré.* Paris: Cerf, 1961.

Agulhon, Maurice. *Marianne au combat: L'Imagerie et la symbolique républicaines de 1789–1889.* Paris: Flammarion, 1979.

The American Film Institute Catalog of Motion Pictures Produced in the United States. Berkeley: University of California Press, 1971–.

Anderegg, Michael, ed. *Inventing Vietnam: The War in Film and Television.* Philadelphia: Temple University Press, 1991.

Anderson, Karen. *Wartime Women: Sex Roles, Family Relations, and the Status of Women during World War II.* Westport, Conn.: Greenwood, 1981.

Anderson, Maxwell. *Joan of Lorraine.* Washington, D.C.: Anderson House, 1947.

Armes, Roy. *French Cinema*. Vol. I. New York: A. S. Barnes, 1970.

Aronstein, Susan, and Nancy Coiner. "Twice Knightly: Democratizing the Middle Ages for Middle-Class America." In *Medievalism in North America*, ed. Kathleen Verduin. Cambridge: D. S. Brewer, 1994.

Auerbach, Erich. *Mimesis: The Representation of Reality in Western Literature*. Trans. Willard R. Trask. Princeton: Princeton University Press, 1953.

Auster, Albert, and Leonard Quart. *How the War was Remembered: Hollywood and Vietnam*. New York: Praeger, 1988.

Ayfre, Amadée. *Conversion aux images*. Paris: Cerf, 1964.

Baker, M. Joyce. *Images of Women in Film: The War Years, 1941–45*. Ann Arbor: UMI Research Press, 1980.

Bakhtin, Mikhail. *Rabelais and His World*. Trans. Helene Iswolsky. Cambridge: MIT Press, 1968.

Banta, Martha. *Imaging American Women: Idea and Ideals in Cultural History*. New York: Columbia University Press, 1987.

Barker, Simon. "*The Double-Armed Man*: Images of the Medieval in Early Modern Military Idealism." In *From Medieval to Medievalism*, ed. John Simons. London: Macmillan, 1992.

Barstow, Anne Llewellyn. *Joan of Arc: Heretic, Mystic, Shaman*. Lewiston, N.Y.: Edwin Mellen, 1986.

Barthes, Roland. "Historical Discourse." In *Introduction to Structuralism*, ed. Michael Lane. New York: Basic Books, 1970.

———. *Mythologies*. Trans. Annette Lavers. New York: Hill & Wang, 1972.

Basinger, Jeanine. *The World War II Combat Film: Anatomy of a Genre*. New York: Columbia University Press, 1986.

Bastaire, Jean. "De Christine de Pisan á Jean Anouilh: Jeanne d'Arc á travers la littérature." *Etudes cinématographiques* 18–19 (Autumn 1962): 11–31.

Bates, Milton J. "Men, Women, and Vietnam." In *America Rediscovered: Critical Essays on Literature and Film of the Vietnam War*, ed. Owen W. Gilman and Lorrie Smith. New York: Garland, 1990.

Bathrick, Serafina K. "The Female Colossus: The Body as Facade and Threshold." In *Fabrications: Costume and the Female Body*, ed. Jane Gaines. New York: Routledge, 1990.

Beevers, John. *St. Joan of Arc*. New York: Hanover House, 1959.

Bell-Metereau, Rebecca. *Hollywood Androgyny*. New York: Columbia University Press, 1985.

Benjamin, Walter. "Theses on the Philosophy of History." In Benjamin, *Illuminations*. New York: Schocken, 1969.

Berger, John. *Ways of Seeing*. London: Penguin, 1972.

Bergman, Ingrid, and Alan Burgess. *Ingrid Bergman—My Story.* New York: Delacorte, 1980.

Bernstein, Matthew. "Hollywood Martyrdoms: *Joan of Arc* and Independent Production in the Late 1940s." *Current Research in Film* 4 (1988): 89–113.

———. *Walter Wanger: Hollywood Independent.* Berkeley: University of California Press, 1994.

Berthoff, Warner. *Fictions and Events.* New York: Dutton, 1971.

Blaetz, Robin. "'La Femme Vacante,' or The Rendering of Joan of Arc in the Cinema." *Post Script* 12 (Winter 1993): 63–78.

Bloom, Harold, ed. *Joan of Arc.* New York: Chelsea House, 1992.

Bly, Robert, and David Ray, eds. *A Poetry Reading against the Vietnam War.* Madison, Minn.: Sixties Press, 1966.

Bondanella, Peter. *Italian Cinema: From Neo-Realism to the Present.* New York: Frederick Ungar, 1983.

Bordwell, David. *The Films of Carl Theodor Dreyer.* Berkeley: University of California Press, 1981.

Boulding, Elise. *The Underside of History: A View of Women through Time.* Boulder, Colo.: Westview, 1976.

Boutet de Monvel, Maurice. *Joan of Arc.* Trans. A. I. Du Pont. (1897.) New York: Pierpont Morgan Library/Viking Press, 1980.

Brecht, Bertolt. *Brecht on Theatre.* Trans. and ed. John Willett. New York: Hill & Wang, 1964.

———. *Plays.* Trans. Frank Jones. Vol. 2. London: Methuen, 1962.

Bresson, Robert. *Notes on Cinematography.* Trans. Jonathan Griffin. New York: Urizen Books, 1977.

———. *Le Procès de Jeanne d'Arc.* Paris: René Julliard, 1962.

Brill, Lesley. *The Hitchcock Romance: Love and Irony in Hitchcock's Films.* Princeton: Princeton University Press, 1988.

Brooks, Peter. *Body Work: Objects of Desire in Modern Narrative.* Cambridge: Harvard University Press, 1993.

Brooks, Polly Schoyer. *Beyond the Myth: The Story of Joan of Arc.* Philadelphia: Lippincott, 1990.

Brown, Robert McAfee. *Theology in a New Key.* Philadelphia: Westminster Press, 1978.

Brownlow, Kevin. *The Parade's Gone By.* Berkeley: University of California Press, 1968.

Broyles, William. "Why Men Love War." *Esquire,* November 1984, 55–65.

Brubach, Holly. "The Confectioner's Art." *New York Times Magazine,* 17 Dec. 1995, 81.

Brun, Marcelline. "Jeanne d'Arc des pays de Loire à ceux du Potomac." *Les Amis de Jeanne d'Arc* 137 (Winter 1989): 1–8.

Brunetti, Aldo. *Juana de Arco*. Barcelona: Bruguera, 1955.

Bryan, Alfred, Willie Weston, and Jack Wells. "Joan of Arc, They Are Calling You." New York: Waterson, Berlin & Snyder, 1917.

Butler, Ivan. *Religion in the Cinema*. New York: A. S. Barnes, 1969.

———. *The War Film*. New York: A. S. Barnes, 1974.

Butterfield, John, and Isobel-Ann Butterfield. "Joan of Arc: A Medical View." *History Today*, September 1958, 628–33.

Bynum, Caroline Walker. *Holy Feast, Holy Fast: The Religious Significance of Food to Medieval Women*. Berkeley: University of California Press, 1987.

Caffin, Charles H. "Miss Hyatt's Statue of Joan of Arc." *Century Magazine*, June 1916, 309–11.

Campbell, Craig W. *Reel America and World War I: A Comprehensive Filmography and History of Motion Pictures in the United States, 1914–1920*. Jefferson, N.C.: McFarland, 1985.

Campbell, D'Ann. *Women at War with America: Private Lives in a Patriotic Era*. Cambridge: Harvard University Press, 1984.

Carney, Raymond. *Speaking the Language of Desire: The Films of Carl Dreyer*. New York: Cambridge University Press, 1989.

Carringer, Robert, and Nancy Allen. *Annotated Catalog of Unpublished Film and Television Scripts*. Urbana: University of Illinois Press, 1983.

Carter, Susanne. *War and Peace through Women's Eyes: A Selective Bibliography of Twentieth-Century American Women's Fiction*. New York: Greenwood, 1992.

Chadwick, Whitney. "The Fine Art of Gentling: Horses, Women, and Rosa Bonheur in Victorian England." In *The Body Imaged: The Human Form and Visual Culture since the Renaissance*, ed. Kathleen Adler and Marcia Pointon. New York: Cambridge University Press, 1993.

Chafe, William H. "World War II as a Pivotal Experience for American Women." In *Women and War: The Changing Status of American Women from the 1930s to the 1950s*, ed. Maria Diedrich and Dorothea Fischer-Hornung. New York: St. Martin's Press, 1990.

Charney, Leo. "Historical Excess: *Johnny Guitar's* Containment." *Cinema Journal* 29 (Summer 1990).

Chesler, Phyllis. *Women and Madness*. New York: Avon, 1973.

Christine de Pisan. *Ditié de Jehanne d'Arc*. Ed. Angus J. Kennedy and Kenneth Varty. Oxford: Society for the Study of Mediaeval Languages and Literature, 1977.

Cixous, Hélène, and Catherine Clément. *The Newly Born Woman*. Trans. Betsy Wing. Minneapolis: University of Minnesota Press, 1986.

Clarke, George Herbert, ed. *The New Treasury of War Poetry: Poems of the Second World War*. Freeport, N.Y.: Books for Libraries Press, 1943.

Claudel, Paul. *Jeanne d'Arc au bûcher.* Trans. Dennis Arundell. Ed. Beatrice Baron. New York: Salabert Contemporary Music Publishers, n.d.

Cole, Toby, and Helen Krich Chinoy, eds. *Actors on Acting.* New York: Crown, 1970.

Comolli, Jean-Louis. "Historical Fiction: A Body Too Much." *Screen* 19 (Summer 1978): 41–53.

Cook, Frederick. *Young Girl of France and Other Stories.* Patterson, N.J.: St. Anthony Guild Press, 1956.

Cooper, Helen M., Adrienne Auslander Munich, and Susan Merrill Squier, eds. *Arms and the Woman: War, Gender, and Literary Representation.* Chapel Hill: University of North Carolina Press, 1989.

Crawford, Anthony R., ed. *Posters of World War I and World War II in the George C. Marshall Research Foundation.* Charlottesville: University Press of Virginia, 1979.

Custen, George F. *Bio/Pics: How Hollywood Constructed Public History.* New Brunswick: Rutgers University Press, 1992.

Damico, James. "Ingrid from Lorraine to Stromboli: Analyzing the Public's Perception of a Film Star." In *Star Texts: Image and Performance in Film and Television,* ed. Jeremy G. Butler, 240–53. Detroit: Wayne State University Press, 1991.

Davidson, Spencer. "France: Hot Time in an Old Town." *Washington Post,* 23 May 1971, B1.

Davis, Natalie Zemon. *Society and Culture in Early Modern France.* Stanford: Stanford University Press, 1975.

DeBauche, Leslie Midkiff. "Mary Pickford's Public on the Home Front and at the Movies." In *Film and the First World War,* ed. Karel Dibbets and Bert Hogenkamp. Amsterdam: Amsterdam University Press, 1995.

———. *Reel Patriotism: The Movies and World War I.* Madison: University of Wisconsin Press, 1997.

De Lauretis, Teresa. *Alice Doesn't: Feminism, Semiotics, Cinema.* Bloomington: Indiana University Press, 1984.

———. *Technologies of Gender: Essays on Theory, Film, and Fiction.* Bloomington: Indiana University Press, 1987.

DeMille, Cecil B. *The Autobiography of Cecil B. DeMille.* Ed. Donald Hayne. Englewood Cliffs, N.J.: Prentice-Hall, 1959.

Deutelbaum, Marshall, ed. *"Image" on the Art and Evolution of the Film.* New York: Dover, 1979.

De Wohl, Louis. *St. Joan, the Girl Soldier.* (1957.) New York: Guild Press, 1962.

Dickinson, Emily. *Unpublished Poems of Emily Dickinson.* Ed. Martha Dickinson Bianchi and Alfred Leete Hampson. Boston: Little, Brown, 1936.

Diedrich, Maria, and Dorothea Fischer-Hornung. *Women and War: The Changing Sta-*

tus of American Women from the 1930s to the 1950s. New York: St. Martin's Press, 1990.

Dijkstra, Bram. *Idols of Perversity: Fantasies of Feminine Evil in Fin-de-Siècle Culture.* New York: Oxford University Press, 1986.

Dillenberger, Jane. *Style and Content in Christian Art.* New York: Abington Press, 1965.

Dillenberger, John. *The Visual Arts and Christianity in America.* New York: Crossroads, 1989.

Diner, Helen. *Mothers and Amazons: The First Feminine History of Culture.* Trans. John Philip Lundin. New York: Julian Press, 1965.

Dinnerstein, Dorothy. *The Mermaid and the Minotaur.* New York: Harper & Row, 1977.

Dittmar, Linda, and Gene Michaud, eds. *From Hanoi to Hollywood: The Vietnam War in American Film.* New Brunswick: Rutgers University Press, 1990.

Doane, Mary Ann. *The Desire to Desire: The Woman's Film of the 1940s.* Bloomington: Indiana University Press, 1987.

Doherty, Thomas. *Projections of War: Hollywood, American Culture, and World War II.* New York: Columbia University Press, 1993.

Doncoeur, Père Paul. "Un Film américain sur Jeanne d'Arc." *Cahiers Ste Jeanne* (Paris), November 1947.

Douglas, Mary. *Purity and Danger: An Analysis of Concepts of Pollution and Taboo.* New York: Praeger, 1966.

Douglas, Roy. *The World War, 1939–1945: The Cartoonists' View.* New York: Routledge, 1990.

Dreyer, Carl Theodor. *Dreyer in Double Reflection: Translation of Carl Th. Dreyer's Writings about the Film.* Trans. and ed. Donald Skoller. New York: Dutton, 1973.

———. *Four Screenplays.* Trans. Oliver Stallybrass. Bloomington: Indiana University Press, 1970.

Dyer, Richard. *Stars.* London: BFI Publishing, 1979.

Eco, Umberto. *Travels in Hyperreality.* Trans. William Weaver. New York: Harcourt Brace Jovanovich, 1986.

Eksteins, Modris. *Rites of Spring: The Great War and the Birth of the Modern Age.* New York: Bantam, 1989.

Elshtain, Jean Bethke. *Women and War.* New York: Basic Books, 1987.

Emery, Anne. *Joan of Arc.* Evanston, Ill.: Row, Peterson, 1951.

Erens, Patricia, ed. *Issues in Feminist Film Criticism.* Bloomington: Indiana University Press, 1990.

Ernest, Brother. *Flames against the Sky: A Story of St. Joan of Arc.* Notre Dame, Ind.: Dujarie Press, 1951.

Estève, Michel, ed. "Jeanne d'Arc à l'écran." *Etudes cinématographiques* 18–19 (Autumn 1962).

———. *Robert Bresson.* Paris: Seghers, 1974.

Evans, Sara M. *Born for Liberty: A History of Women in America.* New York: Free Press, 1989.

Fabré, Lucien. *Joan of Arc.* Trans. Gerald Hopkins. New York: McGraw-Hill, 1954.

Ferguson, George. *Signs and Symbols in Christian Art.* New York: Oxford University Press, 1964.

Ferris, Lesley. *Acting Women: Images of Women in Theatre.* New York: New York University Press,1989.

Ferro, Marc. *The Great War, 1914–1918.* Trans. Nicole Stone. London: Routledge & Kegan Paul, 1973.

Finnegan, John Patrick. *Against the Specter of a Dragon.* Westport, Conn.: Greenwood, 1974.

Ford, Charles. *Le Cinéma au service de la foi.* Paris: Plon, 1953.

Fraioli, Deborah. "The Literary Image of Joan of Arc: Prior Influences." *Speculum* 56 (1981): 811–30.

Fraser, John. *America and the Patterns of Chivalry.* New York: Cambridge University Press, 1982.

Freud, Sigmund. "The Taboo of Virginity." (1918.) In *Sexuality and the Psychology of Love.* New York: Collier, 1963.

Friedan, Betty. *The Feminine Mystique.* New York: Norton, 1964.

Frischaur, Willi. *Behind the Scenes of Otto Preminger: An Unauthorized Biography.* New York: Morrow, 1974.

Frye, Northrop. *Anatomy of Criticism.* Princeton: Princeton University Press, 1975.

Fuchs, Cynthia J. "Vietnam and Sexual Violence: The Movie." In *America Rediscovered: Critical Essays on Literature and Film of the Vietnam War,* ed. Owen W. Gilman and Lorrie Smith. New York: Garland, 1990.

Fussell, Betty Harper. *Mabel.* New York: Ticknor & Fields, 1982.

Fussell, Paul. *The Great War and Modern Memory.* New York: Oxford University Press, 1975.

Gaboriau, Marc. "Structural Anthropology and History." In *Introduction to Structuralism,* ed. Michael Lane. New York: Basic Books, 1970.

Gaines, Jane. "The Showgirl and the Wolf." *Cinema Journal* 20 (Fall 1980): 53–67.

———, ed. *Fabrications: Costume and the Female Body.* New York: Routledge, 1990.

Galloway, Stan. "The Greystoke Connection: Medievalism in Two Edgar Rice Burroughs Novels." In *Medievalism in North America,* ed. Kathleen Verduin. Cambridge: D. S. Brewer, 1994.

Garber, Marjorie. *Vested Interests: Cross-Dressing and Cultural Anxiety.* New York: Routledge, 1992.

Genette, Gérard. *Narrative Discourse: An Essay in Method.* Trans. Jane E. Lewin. Ithaca: Cornell University Press, 1980.

Gies, Frances. *Joan of Arc: The Legend and the Reality.* New York: Harper & Row, 1981.

Gilder, Rosamond. "New Year, New Plays: Broadway in Review." *Theatre Arts* 31 (January 1947): 12, 15–16.

Gilman, Owen W., Jr., and Lorrie Smith, eds. *America Rediscovered: Critical Essays on Literature and Film of the Vietnam War.* New York: Garland, 1990.

Girard, René. *Violence and the Sacred.* Trans. Patrick Gregory. Baltimore: Johns Hopkins University Press, 1977.

Girouard, Mark. *The Return to Camelot: Chivalry and the English Gentleman.* New Haven: Yale University Press, 1981.

Gitter, Elizabeth. "The Power of Women's Hair in the Victorian Imagination." *PMLA* 99 (October 1984): 936–54.

Goldman, Nancy Loring, ed. *Female Soldiers—Combatants or Noncombatants?: Historical and Contemporary Perspectives.* Westport, Conn.: Greenwood, 1982.

Gotera, Vince. *Radical Visions: Poetry by Vietnam Veterans.* Athens: University of Georgia Press, 1994.

Gray, Agnes Kendrick. "Jeanne d'Arc after Five Hundred Years." *American Magazine of Art* 22 (1931): 369–74.

Greene, Graham. *Graham Greene on Film, 1935–1940.* Ed. John Russell Taylor. New York: Simon & Schuster, 1972.

Griffin, Susan. *Woman and Nature: The Roaring Inside Her.* New York: Harper & Row, 1978.

Guérin, André, and Jack Palmer White. *Operation Shepherdess.* London: Heinemann, 1961.

Gutierrez, Nancy A. "Gender and Value in *I Henry VI:* The Role of Joan de Pucelle." *Theatre Journal* 42 (May 1990).

Hanlon, Lindley. *Fragments: Bresson's Film Style.* Rutherford, N.J.: Fairleigh-Dickinson University Press, 1986.

Hanna, Martha. "Iconology and Ideology: Images of Joan of Arc in the Idiom of the Action Française, 1908–31." *French Historical Studies* 14 (1985): 215–39.

Hartmann, Susan M. *The Home Front and Beyond: American Women in the 1940s.* Boston: Twayne, 1982.

Harty, Kevin J. *Cinema Arthuriana.* New York: Garland, 1991.

Hawkes, Terence. *Structuralism and Semiotics.* Berkeley: University of California Press, 1977.

Heilbrun, Carolyn. *Toward a Recognition of Androgyny.* New York: Norton, 1964.

Helpern, Alice. "The Technique of Martha Graham." *Studies in Dance History* 2, no. 2 (1991).

Herlihy, David. "Am I a Camera? Other Reflections on Films and History." *American Historical Review* 93 (December 1988): 1186–92.

Higashi, Sumiko. *Cecil B. DeMille and American Culture: The Silent Era.* Berkeley: University of California Press, 1994.

———. "Cinderella vs. Statistics: The Silent Movie Heroine as a Jazz-Age Working Girl." In *Woman's Being, Woman's Place,* ed. Mary Kelley. Boston: G. K. Hall, 1979.

Higham, Charles. *Cecil B. DeMille.* New York: Scribner, 1973.

Higonnet, Margaret R. "Women in the Forbidden Zone: War, Women, and Death." In *Death and Representation,* ed. Sarah Webster Goodwin and Elisabeth Bronfen. Baltimore: Johns Hopkins University Press, 1993.

Higson, Andrew. "The Victorious Recycling of National History." In *Film and the First World War,* ed. Karel Dibbets and Bert Hogenkamp. Amsterdam: Amsterdam University Press, 1995.

Hill, Holly. *Playing Joan: Actresses on the Challenge of Shaw's Joan of Arc.* New York: Theatre Communications Group, 1987.

Holsinger, M. Paul, and Mary Anne Schofield. *Visions of War: World War II in Popular Literature and Culture.* Bowling Green, Ohio: Bowling Green State University Press, 1992.

Honey, Maureen. *Creating Rosie the Riveter: Class, Gender, and Propaganda during World War II.* Amherst: University of Massachusetts Press, 1984.

Houghton, Leighton. *In the Steps of Joan of Arc.* New York: Rich & Cowan, 1951.

Hugo, Jean. *Le Regard de la mémoire.* Paris: Actes Sud, 1983.

Huizinga, Johan. *The Waning of the Middle Ages.* New York: St. Martin's Press, 1924.

Humphrey, Grace. "A New Statue of Jeanne d'Arc." *St. Nicholas,* March 1916, 402–6.

Humphries, Grace. "Anna Vaughn Hyatt's Statue." *International Studio* 57 (December 1915): XLVII–L.

Huston, Nancy. "The Matrix of War: Mothers and Heroes." *Poetics Today* 6, nos. 1–2 (1985): 152–70.

"Ingrid Bergman: A Picture Personality." *Look,* 20 July 1948, 34–42.

Isenberg, Michael T. *War on Film: The American Cinema and World War I, 1914–1941.* Rutherford, N.J.: Fairleigh Dickinson University Press, 1981.

Jameson, Fredric. *The Political Unconscious: Narrative as a Socially Symbolic Act.* Ithaca: Cornell University Press, 1982.

Jardine, Alice A. *Gynesis: Configurations of Woman and Modernity.* Ithaca: Cornell University Press, 1985.

Jauss, Hans Robert. *Toward an Aesthetic of Reception.* Trans. Timothy Bahti. Minneapolis: University of Minnesota Press, 1982.

"Jeanne d'Arc." *Outlook* 3 (15 Dec. 1915): 885–86.

Jeffords, Susan. "Friendly Civilians: Images of Women and the Feminization of the Audience in Vietnam Films." In *Film Genre Reader II,* ed. Barry Keith Grant, 428–40. Austin: University of Texas Press, 1995.

————. *The Remasculinization of America: Gender and the Vietnam War.* Bloomington: Indiana University Press, 1989.

Jeffords, Susan, and Lauren Rabinovitz. *Seeing through the Media: The Persian Gulf War.* New Brunswick: Rutgers University Press, 1994.

Johnston, Charles. "A Jeanne d'Arc Pilgrimage by Automobile." *Harper's Weekly,* 4 Nov. 1911, 11.

Kane, Kathryn. *Visions of War: Hollywood Combat Films of World War II.* Ann Arbor: UMI Research Press, 1976.

Kawain, Bruce. *Telling It Again and Again: Repetition in Literature and Film.* Ithaca: Cornell University Press, 1972.

Keegan, John. *The Battle for History: Re-fighting World War II.* New York: Random House, 1995.

Kerber, Linda K., and Jane Sherron De Hart, eds. *Women's America: Refocusing the Past.* New York: Oxford University Press, 1991.

Kinney, Judy Lee. "The Mythical Method: Fictionalizing the Vietnam War." *Wide Angle* 7, no. 4 (1985): 35–40.

Koppes, Clayton. *Hollywood Goes to War: How Politics, Profits, and Propaganda Shaped World War II Movies.* New York: Free Press, 1987.

Kurzweil, Edith. *The Age of Structuralism: Lévi-Strauss to Foucault.* New York: Columbia University Press, 1980.

La Bretèque, François de, ed. "Le Moyen Age au cinéma." *Cahiers de la cinémathèque* 42/43 (Summer 1985).

Lallou, William J. "Saint Joan of the Screen." *American Ecclesiastical Review* 119 (December 1948): 405.

Landon, Philip J. "New Heroes: Post-War Hollywood's Image of World War II." In *Visions of War: World War II in Popular Literature and Culture,* ed. Paul M. Holsinger and Mary Anne Schofield, 18–26. Bowling Green, Ohio: Bowling Green State University Press, 1992.

Lang, Amy Schrager. *Prophetic Woman: Anne Hutchinson and the Problem of Dissent in the Literature of New England.* Berkeley: University of California Press, 1987.

Langman, Larry, and Ed Borg. *Encyclopedia of American War Films.* New York: Garland, 1989.

Lant, Antonia. *Blackout: Reinventing Women for Wartime British Cinema.* Princeton: Princeton University Press, 1991.

Lears, T. J. Jackson. *No Place of Grace: Antimodernism and the Transformation of American Culture, 1880–1920.* New York: Pantheon, 1981.

Leprohon, Pierre. *Cinquante ans de cinéma français.* Paris: Cerf, 1954.

———. *The Italian Cinema.* Trans. Roger Greaves and Oliver Stallybrass. New York: Praeger, 1972.

Lightbody, Charles Wayland. *The Judgements of Joan: Joan of Arc, a Study in Cultural History.* Cambridge: Harvard University Press, 1961.

Linville, Susan E. "'The Mother of All Battles': *Courage under Fire* and the Gender-Integrated Military." *Cinema Journal* 39, no. 2 (2000): 100–120.

Lippard, Lucy R. *From the Center: Feminist Essays on Women's Art.* New York: Dutton, 1976.

Lourcelles, Jacques. *Otto Preminger.* Paris: Seghers, 1965.

Lupack, Alan. "Visions of Courageous Achievement: Arthurian Youth Groups in America." In *Medievalism in North America,* ed. Kathleen Verduin. Cambridge: D. S. Brewer, 1994.

Lyons, Timothy. "Hollywood and World War I, 1914–1918." *Journal of Popular Film* 1 (Winter 1972): 15–30.

Macheret, Alexander. "Beginning." *Soviet Film* 4 (1971): 26–30.

Margolis, Nadia. *Joan of Arc in History, Literature, and Film.* New York: Garland, 1990.

Mark, Elaine, and Isabelle de Courtivron. *New French Feminisms.* New York: Schocken, 1981.

Martin, Susan, ed. *Decade of Protest.* Santa Monica, Calif.: Smart Art Press, 1996.

Masson, Gustave. *Mediaeval France.* New York: Putnam, 1901.

Mattern, Marjorie, and Bob Willoughby. *Saint Joan.* New York: Feature Publications, 1957.

May, Elaine Tyler. *Homeward Bound: American Families in the Cold War Era.* New York: Basic Books, 1988

Mayer, Hans. *Outsiders: A Study in Life and Letters.* Trans. Denis M. Sweet. Cambridge: MIT Press, 1982.

McLaughlin, Megan. "The Woman Warrior: Gender, Warfare, and Society in Medieval Europe." *Woman's Studies* 17, nos.3–4 (1990).

McLean, Adrienne. "The Cinderella Princess and the Instrument of Evil." *Cinema Journal* 34 (Spring 1995): 36–56.

Michelet, Jules. *Joan of Arc.* Trans. Albert Guerard. Ann Arbor: University of Michigan Press, 1957.

Miller, Jean Baker. *Toward a New Psychology of Women.* 2nd ed. Boston: Beacon, 1986.

Mithers, Carol Lynn. "Missing in Action: Women Warriors in Vietnam." *Cultural Critique* 3 (Spring 1986): 79–90.

Morgan, Pamela S. "'One Brief Shining Moment': Camelot in Washington, D.C." In *Medievalism in North America*, ed. Kathleen Verduin. Cambridge: D. S. Brewer, 1994.

Mourlet, Michel. *Cecil B. DeMille*. Paris: Seghers, 1968.

———. "Jeanne d'Arc et le cinéma." *Spectacle du monde* 197 (August 1978): 75–80.

———. "*Saint Joan* d'Otto Preminger." *Etudes cinématographiques* 18–19 (Autumn 1962).

Murray, Leo. "*Le Procès de Jeanne d'Arc*." In *The Films of Robert Bresson*, ed. Ian Cameron, 90–105. New York: Praeger, 1970.

Murray, Margaret. *The Witch Cult in Western Europe*. (1921.) London: Oxford University Press, 1962.

Muse, Eben J. *The Land of Nam: The Vietnam War in American Film*. Lanham, Md.: Scarecrow Press, 1995.

Nagler, Jörg. "Pandora's Box: Propaganda and War Hysteria in the United Sates during World War I." In *Great War, Total War: Combat and Mobilization on the Western Front*, ed. Roger Chickering and Stig Förster. New York: Cambridge University Press, 2000.

Naish, Camille. *Death Comes to the Maiden: Sex and Execution, 1431–1933*. New York: Routledge, 1991.

Nathan, George Jean. "The Theatre." *American Mercury*, February 1924, 241–42.

Nead, Lynda. *The Female Nude: Art, Obscenity, and Sexuality*. New York: Routledge, 1992.

Newman, A. Evelyn. "The Doughboys' Girl in France." *Ladies Home Journal*, January 1920, 28–29, 104–6.

Newman, Carol. "Joan of Arc in English Literature." *Sewanee Review* 34 (October–December 1926): 431–39.

Nichols, Stephen G. "The New Medievalism: Tradition and Discontinuity in Medieval Culture." In *The New Medievalism*, ed. Marina S. Brownlee, Kevin Brownlee, and Stephen G. Nichols. Baltimore: Johns Hopkins University Press, 1991.

Noakes, Jeremy, ed. *The Civilian in War: The Home Front in Europe, Japan, and the USA in World War II*. Exeter: University of Exeter Press, 1992.

Nochlin, Linda. *Women, Art, and Power and Other Essays*. New York: Harper & Row, 1988.

O'Brien, Mary. *The Politics of Reproduction*. Boston: Routledge & Kegan Paul, 1981.

O'Connor, John. "History in Images/Images in History: Reflections on the Importance of Film and Television Study for an Understanding of the Past." *American Historical Review* 93 (December 1988): 1200–1209.

Orliac, Jehanne. *Joan of Arc and Her Companions.* Trans. Elizabeth Abbott. Philadelphia: Lippincott, 1934.

Panofsky, Dora, and Erwin Panofsky. *Pandora's Box: The Changing Aspects of a Mythical Symbol.* New York: Pantheon, 1956.

Paris, Michael, ed. *The First World War and Popular Culture: 1914 to the Present.* New Brunswick: Rutgers University Press, 2000.

Patterson, Celia Ann. "On the Edge of the War Zone: American Women's Fiction and World War I." Ph.D. dissertation, University of Tulsa, 1990.

Pernoud, Régine, ed. *Jeanne d'Arc.* Paris: Seuil, 1981.

———. *Joan of Arc.* Trans. Jeanne Unger Duell. New York: Grove Press, 1961.

———. *Joan of Arc by Herself and Her Witnesses.* (1964.) Trans. Edward Hyams. New York: Stein & Day, 1982.

———. *The Retrial of Joan of Arc: The Evidence at the Trial for Her Rehabilitation, 1450–1456.* Trans. J. M. Cohen. New York: Harcourt, Brace, 1955.

Pernoud, Régine, and Marie-Véronique Clin. *Jeanne d'Arc.* Paris: Fayard, 1986.

Pinder, Kymberly. "The Reception of Toby E. Rosenthall's *Elaine:* Medievalism in San Francisco." In *Medievalism in North America,* ed. Kathleen Verduin. Cambridge: D. S. Brewer, 1994.

Pipolo, Anthony T. "Carl Dreyer's *La Passion de Jeanne d'Arc:* A Comparison of Prints and Formal Analysis." Ph.D. dissertation, New York University, 1981.

Polan, Dana. *Power and Paranoia: History, Narrative, and the American Cinema, 1940–1950.* New York: Columbia University Press, 1986.

Pollock, Griselda. *Vision and Difference: Femininity, Feminism, and the Histories of Art.* New York: Routledge, 1988.

Porterfield, Allen Wilson. "New Tellers of a Tale Outworn." *Dial,* 16 Apr. 1911, 306–8.

Powers, Anne Bleigh. "The Joan of Arc Vogue in America, 1894–1929." *American Society of the Legion of Honor Magazine* 49 (1978):177–92.

———. "Three Images of Jeanne d'Arc in Seventeenth-Century French Literature." In French Literature Conference, *Historical Figures in French Literature.* Columbia: University of South Carolina, College of Humanities and Social Sciences, Department of Foreign Languages and Literature, 1981.

Pratley, Gerald. *The Cinema of Otto Preminger.* New York: A. S. Barnes, 1971.

Propp, Vladimir. "Morphology of the Folktale." Ed. Svatava Pirdova-Jacobson. Trans. Laurence Scott. *International Journal of American Linguistics* 24 (October 1958).

Purcell, Mary. *The Halo on the Sword: St. Joan of Arc.* Westminster, Md.: Newman Press, 1952.

Quant, James, ed. *Robert Bresson.* Toronto: Cinémathèque Ontario, 1998.

Quintal, Claire, and Daniel Rankin. *The First Biography of Joan of Arc*. Pittsburgh: Pittsburgh Diocesan Council of Catholic Women, 1964.

———, eds. *Letters of Joan of Arc*. Pittsburgh: Pittsburgh Diocesan Council of Catholic Women, 1969.

Rabine, Leslie W. *Reading the Romance Heroine: Text, History, Ideology*. Ann Arbor: University of Michigan Press, 1985.

Rabuzzi, Kathryn Allen. *Motherself: A Mythic Analysis of Motherhood*. Bloomington: Indiana University Press, 1988.

Raknem, Ingvald. *Joan of Arc in History, Legend, and Literature*. Oslo: Universitetsforlaget, 1971.

Rapp, Rayna, and Ellen Ross. "The 1920s: Feminism, Consumerism, and Political Backlash in the United States." In *Women in Culture and Politics: A Century of Change*, ed. Judith Friedlander et al. Bloomington: Indiana University Press, 1986.

Rayner, Richard. "Women in the Warrior Culture." *New York Times Magazine*, 19 Oct. 1997, 24–29, 40, 49, 53–56.

Renov, Michael. "From Fetish to Subject: The Containment of Sexual Difference in Hollywood's Wartime Cinema." *Wide Angle* 5, no. 1 (1982): 16–27.

———. *Hollywood's Wartime Woman: Representation and Ideology*. Ann Arbor: UMI Research Press, 1988.

Reynolds, Quentin. "It Isn't in the Book: How Joan of Arc Got into *The Miracle of the Bells*." *48 Magazine*, April 1948.

Ribéra-Pervillé, Claude. "Jeanne d'Arc illustrée." *L'Histoire* 15 (September 1979): 60–67.

Rider, Jeff. "Roger Sherman Loomis: Medievalism as Antimodernism." In *Medievalism in North America*, ed. Kathleen Verduin. Cambridge: D. S. Brewer, 1994.

Robinson, Hilary. *Visibly Female: Feminism and Art: An Anthology*. New York: Universe Books, 1988.

Robo, Etienne. *Saint Joan: The Woman and the Saint*. New York: Spiritual Books Associates, 1948.

Rollins, Peter C., ed. *Hollywood as Historian*. Lexington: University Press of Kentucky, 1983.

Rosenstone, Robert A. "History in Images/History in Words: Reflections on the Possibility of Really Putting History onto Film." *American Historical Review* 93 (December 1988): 1173–85.

———. *Visions of the Past: The Challenge of Film to Our Idea of History*. Cambridge: Harvard University Press, 1995.

Ross, Nancy Wilson. *Joan of Arc*. New York: Random House, 1953.

Rupp, Leila J. *Mobilizing Women for War: German and American Propaganda, 1939–1945*. Princeton: Princeton University Press, 1978.

Rupprecht, Carol Schreier. "The Martial Maid and the Challenge of Androgyny." *Spring: An Annual of Archetypal Psychology and Jungian Thought*, 1974, 269–93.

Sackville-West, Vita. *Saint Joan of Arc*. Garden City, N.Y.: Country Life Press, 1936.

Sadoul, Georges. *French Film*. New York: Arno Press, 1972.

Salls, Helen Harriet. "Joan of Arc in English and American Literature." *South Atlantic Quarterly* 35 (1936): 167–84.

Salomon, Roger B. "Escape from History: Mark Twain's Joan of Arc." In *Joan of Arc*, ed. Harold Bloom. New York: Chelsea House, 1992.

Sarris, Andrew. *Confessions of a Cultist*. New York: Simon & Schuster, 1970.

Schrader, Paul. *Transcendental Style in Film: Ozu, Bresson, Dreyer*. Berkeley: University of California Press, 1972.

Searle, William. *The Saint and the Skeptics*. Detroit: Wayne State University Press, 1976.

Shain, Russell Earl. *An Analysis of Motion Pictures about War Released by the American Film Industry, 1930–1970*. New York: Arno Press, 1976.

Sharpe, Lesley. *Schiller and the Historical Character*. New York: Oxford University Press, 1982.

Shaw, Bernard. *The Collected Screenplays of Bernard Shaw*. Ed. Bernard F. Dukore. Athens: University of Georgia Press, 1980.

———. *Saint Joan: A Chronicle Play in Six Scenes and an Epilogue*. (1924.) New York: Penguin, 1946.

Sheppard, E. W. "St. Jeanne d'Arc as a Soldier." *National Review* 9 (October 1920): 111–20.

Showalter, Elaine. *Sexual Anarchy: Gender and Culture at the Fin de Siècle*. New York: Viking, 1990.

Simons, John, ed. *From Medieval to Medievalism*. London: Macmillan, 1992.

Slide, Anthony. *Selected Film Criticism*. Vol. 2, *1912–1920*. Metuchen, N.J.: Scarecrow Press, 1982.

Slide, Anthony, and Edward Wagenknecht. *Fifty Great American Silent Films, 1912–1920: A Pictorial Survey*. New York: Dover, 1980.

Sobchack, Vivian, ed. *The Persistence of History: Cinema, Television, and the Modern Event*. New York: Routledge, 1996.

"Some Joan of Arc Medals." *International Studio* 69 (November 1919): LIII.

Sontag, Susan. "Spiritual Style in the Films of Robert Bresson." In *Against Interpretation*. New York: Dell, 1964.

Sorlin, Pierre. *The Film in History: Restaging the Past*. Totawa, N.J.: Barnes & Noble, 1980.

Stevens, Charles McClellan. *The Wonderful Story of Joan of Arc and the Meaning of Her Life for Americans.* New York: Cupples & Leon, 1918.

Stiehm, Judith Hicks. *Bring Me Men and Women: Mandated Change at the U.S. Air Force Academy.* Berkeley: University of California Press, 1981.

Stock, Brian. *Listening for the Text: On the Uses of the Past.* Baltimore: Johns Hopkins University Press, 1990.

Stolpe, Sven. *The Maid of Orléans.* Trans. Eric Lewenhaupt. New York: Pantheon, 1956.

Theweleit, Klaus. *Male Fantasies.* Trans. Stephen Conway. Minneapolis: University of Minnesota Press, 1987.

Todorov, Tzvetan. *The Fantastic: A Structural Approach to a Literary Genre.* Trans. Richard Howard. Ithaca: Cornell University Press, 1975.

Twain, Mark. *Personal Recollections of Joan of Arc by the Sieur Louis de Comte (Her Page and Secretary).* (1896.) New York: Grammercy Books, 1995.

Uricchio, William, and Roberta E. Pearson. *Reframing Culture: The Case of the Vitagraph Quality Films.* Princeton: Princeton University Press, 1993.

Van Loon, Hendrik. *The Story of Mankind.* New York: Boni & Liveright, 1921.

Vorse, Mary Heaton. "Elizabeth Gurley Flynn." In *The Female Experience,* ed. Gerda Lerner. Indianapolis: Bobbs-Merrill, 1977.

Wagenknecht, Edward, ed. *Joan of Arc: An Anthology of History and Literature.* New York: Creative Age Press, 1948.

———. *Movies in the Age of Innocence.* Norman: University of Oklahoma Press, 1962.

Walsh, Jeffrey, and James Aulich, eds. *Vietnam Images: War and Representation.* New York: St. Martin's Press, 1989.

Ward, Larry Wayne. *The Motion Picture Goes to War: The U.S. Government Film Effort during World War I.* Ann Arbor: UMI Research Press, 1985.

Warner, Marina. *Alone of All Her Sex: The Myth and Cult of the Virgin Mary.* New York: Knopf, 1976.

———. *From the Beast to the Blonde: On Fairy Tales and Their Tellers.* London: Chatto & Windus, 1994.

———. *Joan of Arc: The Image of Female Heroism.* New York: Vintage, 1982.

———. *Monuments and Maidens: The Allegory of the Female Form.* London: Weidenfeld & Nicolson, 1985.

———. "Personification and the Idealization of the Feminine." In *Medievalism in American Culture,* ed. Bernard Rosenthal and Paul E. Szarmach. Binghamton, N.Y.: Medieval and Renaissance Texts and Studies, 1989.

Wheeler, Bonnie, and Charles T. Wood, eds. *Fresh Verdicts on Joan of Arc.* New York: Garland, 1996.

White, Hayden V. "Historiography and Historiophoty." *American Historical Review* 93 (December 1988): 1193–99.

———. *Metahistory: The Historical Imagination in Nineteenth-Century Europe.* Baltimore: Johns Hopkins University Press, 1973.

Williams, Peter W. "The Varieties of American Medievalism." *Studies in Medievalism* 1 (Spring 1982): 7–20.

Wilson, James C. *Vietnam in Prose and Film.* Jefferson, N.C.: McFarland, 1982.

Windeatt, Mary Fabyan. *St. Joan of Arc Coloring Book.* St. Meinrad, Ind.: Grail, 1955.

Winwar, Frances. *The Saint and The Devil: Joan of Arc and Gilles de Rais.* New York: Harper, 1948.

Wolff, Janet. *Feminine Sentences: Essays on Women and Culture.* Berkeley: University of California Press, 1990.

Workman, Leslie J. Editorial. *Studies in Medievalism* 1 (Spring 1982): 1–3.

Wuthnow, Robert, James Davison Hunter, Albert Bergesen, and Edith Kurzweil. *Cultural Analysis.* Boston: Routledge & Kegan Paul, 1984.

Yancey, William Paul. *The Soldier Virgin of France: A Message of World Peace.* Gainesville, Fla., 1926.

Zipes, Jack. *The Trials and Tribulations of Little Red Riding Hood: Versions of the Tale in Sociocultural Context.* South Hadley, Mass.: Bergin & Garvey, 1983.

Filmography

An asterisk (*) indicates a film discussed in the text. Since many of the early films are either lost or available only in fragments, parts of this filmography are speculative.

Films on the Life of Joan of Arc

Joan of Arc/The Burning of Joan of Arc (1895)

Production company   Edison

Fragment found at Centre Jeanne d'Arc, Orléans, France, at the end of a reel entitled "Orléans glorifié la Pucelle" (1929) and at the National Archives of Canada in Ottawa.

Jeanne d'Arc (1900)

Production company	Star-Film (France)
Director	Georges Méliès
Cinematography	Leclerc
Art direction	Claudel

Cast: Mlle Calvière (Joan of Arc), Georges Méliès, Jeanne d'Arcy/Mme Méliès.

Hand-tinted copy without titles available for viewing at Centre Jeanne d'Arc, Orléans.

La Béatification de Jeanne d'Arc (1900)

Production company	? (Italy)
Director	Mario Caserini

Lost.

Jeanne d'Arc au bûcher (Joan of Arc at the Stake) (1905)

Production company   Gaumont (France)

Cast: Boissieu (Joan of Arc).

Lost.

Jeanne d'Arc (1908)

Production company   Pathé (France)
Director   Albert Capellani

Lost.

Vie de Jeanne d'Arc (Life of Joan of Arc) (1909)

Production company   Cinès (Italy)
Director   Mario Caserini
Script   Guido Gozzano, after Friedrich Schiller, *Die Jungfrau
                       von Orleans*

Cast: Maria Gasperini (Joan of Arc), Amleto Palermi, Ubaldo del Colle, Mario Caserini.

Lost.

Giovanna d'Arco (1913)

Production company   Pasquali (Italy)
Director   Nino Oxilia

Cast: Maria Jacobini (Joan of Arc).

Lost.

Jeanne (1914)

Production company   ? (Italy/Austria)
Director   Nollif/Wolff

Lost.

*Joan the Woman (1916)

Production company   Paramount (USA)
Director   Cecil B. DeMille
Script   Jeannie MacPherson

Cinematography	Alvin Wyckoff
Editor	Cecil B. DeMille
Music	William Furst

Cast: Geraldine Farrar (Joan of Arc), Wallace Reid (English soldier/Trent), Raymond Hatton (Charles VII), Theodore Roberts (Cauchon), Charles Clary (La Trémouille), Hobart Bosworth (La Hire), Tully Marshall, James Neill.

Original version: black and white, hand-tinted; silent with English titles. Available for viewing at George Eastman House, Rochester, N.Y.; available on videotape.

French version: black and white; silent with French titles. Available for viewing at Centre Jeanne d'Arc, Orléans.

La Passion de Jeanne d'Arc (1928)

Production company	Société Générale de Films (France)
Director	Carl Theodor Dreyer
Script	Carl Dreyer and Joseph Delteil, based on original records of the trial
Cinematography	Rudolf Maté
Art direction	Hermann Warm, Jean Hugo
Music	Victor Alix, Léo Pouget
Costumes	Valentine Hugo
Historical adviser	Pierre Champion

Cast: Renée Falconetti (Joan of Arc), Eugène Sylvain (Cauchon), Maurice Schutz (Loyseleur), Antonin Artaud (Massieu), Michel Simon (Lemaître), Ravet (Beaupère), André Berley (Estivet), Jean d'Yd (Erard).

Black and white; silent with French titles.

Widely available.

La Vie merveilleuse de Jeanne d'Arc (The Marvelous Life of Joan of Arc) (1928)

Production company	Aubert-Natan (France)
Director	Marc de Gastyne
Script	Jean-José Frappa

Cast: Simone Genevoix (Joan of Arc), Philippe Hériat (Giles de Rais), Jean Toulout (La Trémouille), Jean Debucourt (Charles VII), Pierre Douvan (Cauchon), Georges Paulais (Loyseleur), Louis Allibert (Rémy Loiseau), Gaston Modot (Glasdall), Nasthasio (Warwick), François Viguier (Pasquerel), Daniel Mendaille (Talbot), Fernand Mailly (La Hire), Jean Manou (Metz), Choura Milena (Isabeau), Dorah

Starny (Gilda), J. P. Stock (Poitou), Jean Lemaistre (Florus).

Black and white; silent with French titles.

Available for viewing at Centre Jeanne d'Arc, Orléans, and on videotape.

Das Mädchen Johanna (The Maid of Orléans) (1935)

Production company	UFA (Germany)
Producer	Bruno Duday
Director	Gustav Ucicky
Script	Gerhard Menzel
Cinematography	Günther Krampf
Editor	Eduard von Borsody
Art direction	Robert Herlth, Walter Röhrig
Music	Peter Kreuder
Costumes	Robert Herlth
Sound	Hermann Fritzsching

Cast: Angela Salloker (Joan of Arc), Gustaf Gründgens (Charles VII), Heinrich George (Duke of Burgundy), René Deltgen (Maillezais), Erich Ponto (Talbot), Willy Birgel (La Trémouille), Theodor Loos (Dunois), Aribert Wäscher (Alençon), Veit Harlan (Pierre), Paul Bildt, Albert Florath, Fritz Genschow, Maria Koppenhöfer, Bernhard Minetti, Franz Nicklisch, Elsa Wagner.

Black and white; German with English subtitles.

Available for viewing at Library of Congress, Washington, D.C.

Joan of Arc (1948)

Production company	RKO (USA)
Producer	Walter Wanger
Director	Victor Fleming
Assistant director	Richard Day
Script	Maxwell Anderson, Andrew Solt, from Anderson's play *Joan of Lorraine*
Cinematography	Joseph Valentine
Editor	Frank Sullivan
Art direction	Richard Day
Music	Hugo Friedhofer
Musical direction	Emil Newman
Costumes	Herschel, Karinska, Dorothy Jeakins

Set decoration	Edwin Roberts, Joseph Kish
Sound	William Randall, Gene Garvin
Religious adviser	Paul Doncoeur

Cast: Ingrid Bergman (Joan of Arc), José Ferrer (Charles VII), Francis L. Sullivan (Cauchon), Gene Lockhart (La Trémouille), Leif Erickson (Dunois), Alan Napier (Warwick), J. Carroll Naish (John of Luxembourg), Ward Bond (La Hire), Sheppard Strudwick (Massieu), John Ireland (La Boussac),William Conrad (Erard), Cecil Kellaway (Le Maistre), John Emery (Duke of Alençon).

Color; in English.

Shortened version widely available. Full version in restoration at UCLA Archives.

Giovanna d'Arco al rogo (Joan of Arc at the Stake) (1954)

Production company	Franco-London-Film /PCA (France/Italy)
Director	Roberto Rossellini
Script	Based on Paul Claudel's libretto for Arthur Honegger's oratorio *Jeanne d'Arc au bûcher*
Music	Arthur Honegger
Cinematography	G. Pogany
Editor	Robert Audenet
Art direction	C. M. Cristini
Sound	W. Robert Sivel

Cast: Ingrid Bergman (Joan of Arc), Tullio Carminati (Dominique), Giacinto Prandelli, Marcella Pobbe, Miriam Pirazzini, Mario Prandelli, Saturno Meletti.

Color; in French.

Black-and-white version available for viewing at Cinémathèque Suisse, Lausanne.

*"Jeanne" (one of three segments of *Destinées*) (1954)

Production company	Franco-London-Film/Continental-Produzione (France/Italy)
Producer	Henri Baum
Director	Jean Delannoy
Script	Pierre Bost, Jean Aurenche
Cinematography	Robert Le Febvre
Editor	Laure Casseau
Set decoration	Serge Pimenoff

Cast: Michèle Morgan (Joan of Arc), Andrée Clément, Daniel Ivernel, Robert Dalban, Dora Doll, Jacques Fabres, Gérard Buhr, Michel Piccoli.

Other segments include "Elizabeth" by Marcello Pagliero and "Lysistrata" by Christian-Jacque, with Claudette Colbert, Eleanora Rossi-Drago, Martine Carol, Raf Vallone, Paola Stoppa.

Black and white; in French.

Available for viewing at Centre Jeanne d'Arc, Orléans.

*Saint Joan (1957)

Production company	United Artists (USA)
Producer	Otto Preminger
Director	Otto Preminger
Script	Graham Greene, after Bernard Shaw's play *Saint Joan*
Cinematography	Georges Périnal
Editor	Helga Cranston
Art direction	Roger Furse
Music	Misha Spoliansky
Historical adviser	Charles Beard
French subtitles	Jean Anouilh

Cast: Jean Seberg (Joan of Arc), Richard Widmark (Charles VII), Richard Todd (Dunois), Anton Walbrook (Cauchon), John Gielgud (Warwick), Felix Aylmer (Inquisitor), Harry Andrews (Stogumber), Barry Jones (Courcelles), Finlay Currie (Archbishop of Rheims), Bernard Miles (Executioner), Patrick Barr (La Hire), Kenneth Haigh (Ladvenu), Archie Duncan (Beaudricourt), Margot Grahame (Duchesse de La Trémouille), Francis de Wolff (La Trémouille), Victor Maddern (English Soldier), David Oxley (Giles de Rais).

Black and white; in English.

Available for viewing at Library of Congress, Washington, D.C., and on videotape.

*The Story of Mankind (1957)

Production company	Warner Bros. (USA)
Producer	Irwin Allen
Director	Irwin Allen
Script	Irwin Allen, Charles Bennett
Story	Hendrik Van Loon, based on his book
Cinematography	Nicholas Musuraca

| Editors | Roland Gross, Gene Palmer |
| Music | Paul Sawtell |

Cast: Hedy Lamarr (Joan of Arc), Ronald Colman, Vincent Price, Henry Daniell.

Segment of an omnibus film depicting multiple historical characters, with the Marx Brothers, Virginia Mayo, Agnes Moorehead, Peter Lorre, Charles Coburn, Sir Cedric Hardwicke, Cesar Romero, John Carradine, Dennis Hopper, Marie Wilson, Helmut Dantine, Edward Everett Horton, Reginald Gardiner, Marie Windsor, George E. Stone, Cathy O'Donnell, Melville Cooper, Henry Daniell, Francis X. Bushman.

Color; in English.

Available for viewing at Library of Congress, Washington, D.C.

Le Procès de Jeanne d'Arc (The Trial of Joan of Arc) (1962)

Production company	Agnès Delahaie (France)
Director	Robert Bresson
Assistant director	Serge Roullet
Script	Robert Bresson, based on the minutes of the trial and rehabilitation
Cinematography	Léonce-Henry Burel
Editor	Germaine Artus
Art direction	Pierre Charbonnier
Music	Francis Seyrig
Costumes	Lucilla Mussini
Sound	Antoine Archimbaud

Cast: Florence Carrez (Joan of Arc), Jean-Claude Fourneau (Cauchon), Roger Honorat (Beaupère), Marc Jacquier (Lemaître), Richard Pratt (Warwick), Jean Gillibert (Chatillon), Michel Herubel (La Pierre), André Regnier (Estivet), Marcel Darbaud (Houppeville), Philippe Dreux (Ladvenu), Paul-Robert Mimet (Erard), Gérard Zingg (Lohier), André Brunet (Massieu), André Maurice (Morice), Michael Williams (Englishman), Harry Sommers (Bishop of Winchester), Donald O'Brian (English Priest).

Black and white; in French.

Occasionally available through commercial distribution.

Joan of Arc (1966)

Production company	Independent (USA)
Director	Piero Heliczer

Cast: Andy Warhol, Gerard Malanga.

Occasionally screened.

St. Joan (1977)

Production company	Triple Action Films/East Midlands Arts Association (England)
Director	Steven Rumbelow
Script	Steven Rumbelow
Cinematography	Michael Zimbrich
Editor	Steven Rumbelow, Michael Zimbrich
Music	John Barry
Sound	Roy Huckerby, Steve Thomas, Mick Audsley

Cast: Monica Buferd (Joan of Arc).

Black and white; in English.

Filmmaker's possession, unavailable for viewing.

Joan of Arc (1983)

Production company	British Film Institute
Producer	Jeremy Newson
Director	Gina Newson
Cinematography	Chris Morphet, Richard Gibb, Ken Morse
Editor	Christopher Spencer
Sound	Ray Beckett, Derek McColm
Commentator	Marina Warner

Black and white; in English.

Distributed through British Film Institute.

Jeanne La Pucelle. Part I, Les Batailles; Part II, Les Prisons (1994)

Production company	France 3 Cinéma/La Sept Cinéma/Pierre Grisé (France)
Producers	Martine Marignac, Maurice Tinchant
Director	Jacques Rivette
Script	Jacques Rivette, Pascal Bonitzer, Christine Laurent

Cinematography	William Lubtchansky
Editor	Nicole Lubtchansky
Production design	Emmanuel de Chauvigny
Music	Guillaume Dufay, Jordi Savall
Costumes	Christine Laurent

Cast: Sandrine Bonnaire (Joan of Arc), Olivier Cruveiller, Jean-Pierre Lorit, André Marcon, Jean-Louis Richard, Jean-Pierre Becker, Marcel Bozonnet, Yann Colette.

Color; in French.

Theatrical release and available on videotape.

Joan of Arc (1999)

Production company	Canadian Broadcasting Company
Producer	Peter Bray
Director	Christian Duguay
Script	Michael Alexander Miller, Ronald Parker
Cinematography	Pierre Gill
Editor	Ralph Brunjes
Production design	Michael Joy
Music	Asher Ettinger, Tony Kosinec
Costumes	John Hay

Cast: Leelee Sobieski (Joan of Arc), Jacqueline Bisset (Isabelle d'Arc), Powers Boothe (Jacques d'Arc), Neil Patrick Harris (King Charles), Maury Chaykin, Olympia Dukakis, Jonathan Hyde, Robert Loggia, Shirley MacLaine, Peter O'Toole, Maximilian Schell, Peter Strauss, Chad Willett, Ron White, Jaimz Woolvett.

Color; in English.

Television release and available on videotape.

The Messenger: The Story of Joan of Arc (1999)

Production company	Leeloo Productions/Gaumont (France)
Producers	Bernard Grenet, Patrice Ledoux
Director	Luc Besson
Script	Luc Besson, Andrew Birkin
Production designer	Hugues Tissandier
Cinematography	Thierry Arbogast
Editor	Sylvie Landra
Art direction	Alain Paroutand

Music	Eric Serra
Costumes	Catherine Leterrier

Cast: Milla Jovovich (Joan of Arc), John Malkovich (Charles VII), Faye Dunaway (Yolande d'Aragon), Dustin Hoffman (The Conscience), Pascal Greggory, Vincent Cassel, Tchéky Karyo, Richard Ridings, Desmond Harrington, Timothy West.

Color; in English.

Theatrical release and available on videotape.

Wired Angel (2000)

Producer	Sam Wells
Director	Sam Wells
Script	Sam Wells
Cinematography	Sam Wells
Production design	Stefan Avalos, Pamela O'Neil
Sound	Fred Szymanski
Music	Joe Renzetti
Costumes	Claudia Reeves, Yvonne Skaggs, Juliette Jansen

Cast: Caroline Ruttle (Joan of Arc), Ed Stout, Claudia Reeves, Yuri Delaney, Marc Masino, Casey Reslier-Wells, Jay McDonald.

Black and white; in English.

Joan of Arc: The Virgin Warrior (in postproduction)

Producer	Ronald F. Maxwell
Director	Ronald F. Maxwell
Script	Ronald F. Maxwell
Cinematography	Kees Van Oostrum
Production design	Emile Ghigo
Art direction	Denis Seiglan
Sound	Steve Albert
Costumes	Yvonne Blake

Cast: Mira Sorvino (Joan of Arc), Albert Finney, Derek Jacobi, Kevin Conway, Carey Elwes, Steven Lang.

Color; in English.

Films Partially Dealing with Joan of Arc

Joan of Plattsburg (1918)

Production company	Goldwyn (USA)
Director	George Loan Tucker
Script	Porter Emerson Browne
Cinematography	Oliver T. Marsh

Cast: Mabel Normand (Joan), Robert Elliot, William Fredericks, Joe Smiley, Edward Elkas, John Webb Dillon.

Lost.

Between Us Girls (1942)

Production company	Universal (USA)
Producer	Henry Koster
Director	Henry Koster
Script	Myles Connolly, True Boardman
Story	Regis Gignoux, Jacques Thiery (*Le Fruit vert*)
Adaptation	John Jacoby
Cinematography	Joseph Valentine
Editor	Frank Gross
Music	Charles Previn

Cast: Diana Barrymore (Caroline/Joan of Arc), Kay Francis, Robert Cummings, John Boles, Andy Devine, Ethel Griffies, Walter Catlett, Guinn Williams, Scotty Beckett, Andrew Tombes.

Black and white; in English.

Available for viewing at Library of Congress, Washington, D.C.

Joan of Paris (1942)

Production company	RKO (USA)
Producer	David Hempstead
Director	Robert Stevenson
Script	Charles Bennett, Ellis St. John
Story	Jacques Thiery, Georges Kessels
Cinematography	Russell Metty
Editor	Sherman Todd
Art direction	Albert S. D'Agostino, Carroll Clark

Music	Roy Webb
Musical direction	Constantin Bakaleinikoff
Costumes	Edward Stevenson

Cast: Michèle Morgan (Joan), Paul Henreid, Thomas Mitchell, Laird Cregar, May Robson, Alan Ladd, James Monks, Jack Briggs, Richard Fraser, Alexander Granach.

Black and white; in English.

In Library of Congress, Washington, D.C. (unavailable for viewing). In television release.

Joan of Ozark (1942)

Production company	Republic (USA)
Associate producer	Harriet Parsons
Director	Joseph Santley
Script	Robert Harari, Eve Green, Jack Townley
Cinematography	Ernest Miller
Editor	Charles Craft
Art direction	Russell Kimball

Cast: Judy Canova (Joan), Joe E. Brown, Eddie Foy Jr., Jerome Cowan, Alexander Granach, Wolfgang Zilzer, Otto Reichow, Hans Heinrich von Twardowski, Anne Jeffrys, Donald Curtis, George Eldredge, Paul Fung.

Black and white; in English.

Available for viewing at Academy of Motion Picture Arts and Sciences, Los Angeles.

The Miracle of the Bells (1948)

Production company	? (USA)
Producers	Jesse L. Lasky, Walter MacEwen
Director	Irving Pichel
Assistant director	Harry D'Arcy
Script	Ben Hecht, Quentin Reynolds
Story	Pierre Norman, Russell Janney
Cinematography	Robert De Grasse
Editor	Elmo Williams
Art direction	Albert S. D'Agostino, Ralph Berger
Music	Leigh Harline
Musical direction	Constantin Bakaleinikoff

| Costumes | Renié |
| Sound | Philip Mitchell, Clem Portman |

Cast: Alida Valli (Olga/Joan of Arc), Fred MacMurray, Frank Sinatra, Lee J. Cobb, Harold Vermilyea, Charles Meredith, Jim Nolan, Veronica Pataky, Philip Ahn, Frank Ferguson, Frank Wilcox.

Black and white; in English.

Available for viewing at British Film Institute and on videotape.

Nachalo (The Beginning) (1970)

Production company	Lenfilm (USSR)
Director	Gleb Panfilov
Script	Gleb Panfilov, Yevgeni Gabrilovich
Cinematography	Dmitri Dolinin
Editor	Mariya Amosova
Production design	Marksen Gaukhman-Sverdlov
Sound	Galina Gavrilova

Cast: Inna Tchourikova (Actress/Joan of Arc), Leonid Kuravlyov, Valentina Telichkina, Tatyana Stepanova, Mikhail Konanov.

Black and white; in Russian with French subtitles.

Available for viewing at Centre Jeanne d'Arc, Orléans.

Johanna d'Arc of Mongolia (1988)

Producer	Renée Gundelach
Director	Ulrike Ottinger
Script	Ulrike Ottinger
Cinematography	Ulrike Ottinger
Music	Wilhelm Dieter Siebert

Cast: Inés Sastre (Giovanna), Delphine Seyrig, Irm Hermann, Gillian Scalici, Xu Re Huar, Peter Kern, Nouzgar Sharia, Christoph Eichhorn.

Color; in German with English subtitles.

Available on videotape.

Index of Films

Italicized page numbers refer to illustrations

Index of Subjects and Names

Italicized page numbers refer to illustrations

Joan of Arc (as icon): as Amazon, 2, 31, 104, 111, 188–89, 190, 193, 197–98; as child, 15, 20, 23, 25, 147, 170, 176, 198, 200–204; as Christ figure, 144, 201; as cover girl, 152; as femme fatale, 146–47; as girl/daughter, 49, 78–79; as legend, 42, 52, 75–76, 126, 146; as Mata Hari figure, 50; as maternal figure, 63, 89, 137, 144, 149, 151, 172, 176, 201; as occult figure, 17, 77, 146, 148, 197; as sacrificial victim, 10–11, 17, 18–20, 176; as shepherdess, xiv, 2, 11; as Virgin Mary figure, 66, 185; as warrior, xiv, 9–10, 42, 45, 49–50, 61, 73–74, 76, 80, 85, 106, 111, 146, 151–52, 176, 181; in advertising, 75, 170, 180; in books, magazines and newspapers, 15, 23, 24–25, 37, 39, 41–42, 47–48, 65–66, 67, 71, 76, 84, 90, 124–26, 126–28, 141–49, 170–71, 175–76, 178, 183, 185–86, 189, 191, 197–98, 200–201, 202; in cartoons and comics, 31, 32, 99, 100, 141, 172, 175, 179; in ephemera, xiii, 41, 146; in medals, engravings, and stamps, 41; in music and dance, xii, 37, 39, 78, 104, 117, 143, 170, 172–73, 176–78, 197, 215 n. 18, 224 n. 18; in paintings, lithographs and drawings, xiii, 19, 21, 40, 40–41, 54, 76, 77, 152, 184–87, 189, 196; in plays and theatrical productions, 41, 78, 85, 89–90, 123–25, 147, 170, 174, 177–78, 185–86, 190, 195–97, 215 n. 18; in poetry, xi, 37, 39, 66, 116–17, 171, 176, 190–91, 195, 203; in posters, xii, 15, 16, 33, 35, 78; in television shows, 170, 172; androgyny of, 2, 7–9, 185; biblical/classical heroines and, 186–88; clothes fashions and, 131–34, 180, 182; democratization of, 17, 197–98; dismemberment in representations of, 225 n. 36; dressing in costume as, 33, 146, 179; femininity and, 200–201; filmography of, 249–61; hairstyle of, 160, 179, 181, 196; inspirational value of, xiv, 167; nationalism and, 7, 11, 64, 89, 186, 193, 196, 202, 209 n. 9; propaganda value of, 36, 39, 42, 46, 52, 95, 118, 170; rape of, potential, 10; romance plot and, 2–3, 17, 56, 58–59, 61–63, 86, 216 n. 38; self-sacrifice and, 93–94, 117, 182; statues of, 15, 24–26, 27, 28, 29, 37, 40–41, 76, 88, 95–96, 189, 196–97; virginity of, 9–10, 111, 176; and war deaths, 71–72; women's rights activists and, 11, 200. *See also* Index of Films

Joan of Arc (books), 143–44, 147, 177, 202

"Joan of Arc" (magazine article), 148–49

Joan of Arc (painting), xiii

Joan of Arc (poem), 195

"Joan of Arc" (song), 172–73

"Joan of Arc: A Medical View" (essay), 171

Joan of Arc: An Anthology of History and Literature (book), 126

Joan of Arc: An Opinion of Her Life and Character, Derived from Ancient Chronicles (pamphlet), 200

Joan of Arc and Her Companions (Orliac), 90

Joan of Arc Assembly (Toledo, Ohio), 203

Joan of Arc Journal, The, 51–55

Joan of Arc Statue Committee, 41

Joan of Arc, "The Maid" (book), 202

Van Loon, Hendrik, 153
Van Pelt, John, 26
vaudeville, 33–34
Venerable Bede, 3
Verdi, Giuseppe, 178, 197, 215 n. 18
Verhoeven, Paul, 178
Vessels (dance), 176
Vidor, King, 119
Vietnam War, xiv, 173, 176–77, 182
virginity, xii, 9–10, 111, 191, 197
Virgin Mary, 199
virgin warrior, 29; beauty queen and, 154; and eroticism of pain, 20; flapper as, 29; Girl archetype and, 30, 71; in film, 52; Joan of Arc as, 9–10, 94, 111, 155; romantic heroines and, 189. *See also* warriors, female
visionaries, women, 184
Visions of Light (oratorio), 178
Voltaire, 190–91, 195, 196, 197, 202
voyeurism, 25, 33

Wagenknecht, Edward, 126
Waldmar, Milton, 144
Wallon, Henri, 198
Wanger, Walter, 127
War Advertising Council, 96
war documentaries, 49
war films, 68, 135, 152
war literature, European, 14, 36
War Manpower Commission, 106
Warner, Marina, 20, 198
war posters: of Spanish-American War, 31; of Vietnam War, 173; of World War I, xii, 15, 33, *35, 38,* 70, 71, 78, 82, *83,* 173, 213 n. 55; of World War II, 97, *98, 107*
warriors, female, xiv; active woman inspired by, 76, 80, 82; decline of, as icons, 126–27, 151–52; gender roles in war and, 59, 61, 73–74, 146, 169, 177, 181; integrity of, 72, 135; Joan of Arc as, 9–10, 73, 85, 106, 176; martial maids and, 8; sexuality of, 49–50; unnaturalness of, 8. *See also* virgin warrior
Wars of Religion, 190
Washington Post (newspaper), 175–76
Wayne, John, 152, 169
Wellman, William, 79, 219 n. 8
Wells, Sam, 226 n. 1
Westerns (film genre), 61, 222 n. 38
Wheeler, Bonnie, 177
White, Jack, 173–74
White, Pearl, 48
Widmark, Richard, 162, 167
Wiethaus, Ulrike, 181
Wilder, Billy, 108
Williams, Peter, 56
Wilson, Woodrow, 36, 43–44, 67, 73
Winn, Janet, 167
Winwar, Frances, 126
witches, 8, 62, 179, 181, 184, 192
Witte, Michael, 175
Wolff, F., 48
womanhood, cult of true, 30
women, 2, 14–15; as homemakers, 81–84, 98, 140; as household angel, 20, 100, 194; as invalids, 20, 22; as mothers, 30, 82, 101, 119; as pacifists, 69, 99; as sculptors, 26; as sex objects, 99, 155; as symbol of evil, 153–54; as the stake worth fighting for in war, 31, 45, 68–69, 72, 74, 99, 169, 176; as victims of violence, 169; as visionaries, 184; as warriors, xiv,

Cultural Frames, Framing Culture

Books in this series examine both the way our culture frames our narratives and the way our narratives produce the culture that frames them. Attempting to bridge the gap between previously disparate disciplines, and combining theoretical issues with practical applications, this series invites a broad audience to read contemporary culture in a fresh and provocative way.